Being a Historian
An Introduction to the Professional World of History

Based on the author's more than fifty years of experience as a professional historian in academic and other capacities, *Being a Historian* addresses both aspiring and mature historians. It offers an overview of the state of the discipline of history today and the problems that confront it and its practitioners in many professions. James M. Banner, Jr., argues that historians remain inadequately prepared for their rapidly changing professional world and that the discipline as a whole has yet to confront many of its deficiencies. He also argues that, no longer needing to conform automatically to the academic ideal, historians can now more safely and productively than ever before adapt to their own visions, temperaments, and goals as they take up their responsibilities as scholars, teachers, and public practitioners. Critical while also optimistic, this work suggests many topics for further scholarly and professional exploration, research, and debate.

James M. Banner, Jr., holds a B.A. from Yale and a Ph.D. from Columbia, where he studied with Richard Hofstadter. From 1966 to 1980, he was a member of the history department at Princeton University, which he left to found the American Association for the Advancement of the Humanities. He has also been a book publisher and foundation officer. A former Guggenheim Fellow, Fellow of the Charles Warren Center for Studies in American History at Harvard, member of the board of directors of the American Council of Learned Societies, and Fulbright Visiting Professor of American History at Charles University in Prague, he is the author of many books and essays on American history, education, and public affairs. He has written for the *New York Times*, the *Wall Street Journal*, and other newspapers. His most recent works include *The Elements of Teaching* and *The Elements of Learning*, both with Harold C. Cannon, and *Becoming Historians*, edited with John R. Gillis. He is also the editor of *A Century of American Historiography*. Banner is a co-founder of the History News Service and of the National History Center.

Being a Historian

An Introduction to the Professional World of History

JAMES M. BANNER, JR.

CAMBRIDGE
UNIVERSITY PRESS

CAMBRIDGE UNIVERSITY PRESS
Cambridge, New York, Melbourne, Madrid, Cape Town,
Singapore, São Paulo, Delhi, Mexico City

Cambridge University Press
32 Avenue of the Americas, New York, NY 10013-2473, USA

www.cambridge.org
Information on this title: www.cambridge.org/9781107697287

© James M. Banner, Jr. 2012

First published 2012
Reprinted 2013

A catalog record for this publication is available from the British Library.

Library of Congress Cataloging in Publication Data
Banner, James M., 1935–
Being a historian : an introduction to the professional world of history /
James M. Banner, Jr.
    p.   cm.
Includes bibliographical references and index.
ISBN 978-1-107-02159-4 (hardback) – ISBN 978-1-107-69728-7 (paperback)
  1. History – Philosophy.   2. Historiography.   3. Historians.   4. History – Methodology.
I. Title.
D16.8.B3134   2012
902.3–dc23   2011037173

ISBN 978-1-107-02159-4 Hardback
ISBN 978-1-107-69728-7 Paperback

To my historian colleagues, in the hope of making even stronger the professional world we share

Contents

Preface

If I intended this book to introduce readers to the nature of historical knowledge, I would entitle it, after Peter L. Berger's *Invitation to Sociology*, "An Invitation to History" or, after G. H. Hardy's *Mathematician's Apology*, "A Historian's Apology." If I sought to counsel aspiring historians about how to pursue their work, I would follow P. B. Medawar's *Advice to a Young Scientist* with my own "Advice to a Young Historian." If my purpose were to reflect on how historians create and present historical knowledge, I would follow the path blazed more than seventy years ago by Allan Nevins's *Gateway to History* and try to capture again what Nevins so bracingly and infectiously termed history's "free and joyous pursuit." Or if I wished to examine historical scholarship today, I would adopt the approach of John Higham's essential study, *History: Professional Scholarship in America*, and appraise the internal growth, intellectual development, and overall intellectual condition of the discipline of history. But I have written this book for other purposes and for other kinds of audiences than those to whom those authors directed their wise and enduring works.

Instead of being a welcome to readers who might like to learn something about the house of history from the outside, these pages are meant for people who wish to learn of history's dwelling place from within. I have two groups of readers especially, although not exclusively, in mind. The first are those, principally graduate students, who have already stepped through Clio's front door and now have need of guidance within her residence – guidance on many matters too seldom offered to them. The second are more experienced historians – and, as readers will see, I define that term broadly – who might find that what I write affects the ways in which they view our shared discipline, its condition, and our work as professionals.

The book is thus more than an introduction to history. It is instead a kind of companion to the world that historians have made and now inhabit, at least in the United States. It looks to the discipline's past so as to locate its present condition in relation to its origins, and it emphasizes its present condition in an effort to identify its strengths and weaknesses. But at the risk of disappointing those who would have me offer detailed proposals for the discipline's improvement, I offer only general suggestions in that regard. The work is rather a set of reflections on a choice of subjects, some of them frequently discussed, others less so, that I believe warrant consideration that is greater than or different from what they receive. Thus the book is less prescriptive than suggestive and is purposefully anchored concretely in the present when it does not survey parts of the past; it looks to the future only in general ways. Nor is this an advice manual, a what-to-do and what-to-avoid guide for graduate students. Other works of that sort already exist. Instead, it is a call for more attentiveness to matters usually overlooked in historians' preparation, in their work, and in their professional world. I have not designed it, for instance, to help students learn their crafts of research, teaching, writing, and the many other historians' arts, all of which they can learn elsewhere. Because I am less acquainted with historians' work outside the United States than within it, readers will find that I confine myself to American professional practices. They will also find that I have little to say about metaprofessional matters, such as the state of universities and the universalization of communications, or about research methods and historiographical issues – knowledge already conveyed superbly in the graduate programs of research universities and already the subject of authoritative works of scholarship and thought. By contrast with those studies, I examine here what practicing historians do, where they carry out their work, how the changing world of historical practices affects the choices they make, and what aspiring historians especially might consider as they prepare to make those choices – matters that are rarely encountered formally in graduate schools.

In fact, it is a sobering and disconcerting fact, freighted with ethical significance, that very few departments of history that award doctoral degrees bother to prepare their graduate students, as other kinds of professional schools prepare their students, for the full realities and conditions of employment in even the academic sector and instead leave the occupational dimension of professional life to on-the-job experience. Even those departments that make some gesture toward offering this kind of employment preparation consider their responsibilities largely discharged by helping doctoral candidates prepare for college and university hiring interviews, providing opportunities for students to gain some experience in teaching, and encouraging students to attain more knowledge of general world and comparative history in anticipation of having to teach survey courses in these subjects. No department to my knowledge offers courses, analogous to those in law and medical schools, in what might be called "clinical history" – experiences in the actual practices that historians perform.

While even modest departures from older, conventional norms of graduate training are all to the good, no one should lose sight of the fact that, at least at the leading, most powerful, and most prestigious research universities that often set the standards for professional preparation, most of these happy exceptions among preparatory programs are all focused on training for academic employment, not for the many other kinds of history work outside the academy in which an ever-larger proportion of young historians find themselves engaged. Furthermore, one may safely assume that the few departments preparing their students for the full range of historical practices, both academic and extra-academic, that historians pursue today do so principally through distinct programs in public history, programs usually designed for those who wish to pursue work in careers gathered under that general rubric and not designed for all graduate students whom the departments enroll. Thus, very few graduate students in history doctoral programs in the United States are exposed to knowledge of the entire universe of historical practices among which they may (and an increasing number of them will have to) choose. Accordingly, such are aspiring historians' attitudes in entering graduate school that, as surveys show, many graduate students complain less about being ill-prepared for the full range of work pursued by faculty members than about their ill preparation for being employed as historians outside higher education – in governments, archives, museums, businesses, and other professional settings where they may undertake research, write, teach, or otherwise use history but not make their livings as faculty members. That is to say, few are prepared to be historians in the full, possible, and contemporary connotations of that term. And yet perhaps more than one-half of them, as indicated repeatedly by annual employment surveys, will not, for whatever reason, enter the academy at all.

I have tried to compensate for these discipline-wide failures in the preparation of historians with this book. It can justifiably be read as an extended critique, albeit a sympathetic and optimistic one, of historians' preparation and their understanding of key dimensions of their discipline's history, as well as a set of suggestions as to what historians ought to be better aware of, even if not all of them will enter all of the professional worlds in which they can now practice. Therefore, *Being a Historian* principally concerns the professions, institutions, and practices of the discipline of history. For reasons that I am at pains to make clear throughout the book, however widespread may be the use of the word "profession" to indicate the intellectual and institutional landscape within which all practicing historians work, the term is usually incorrectly used when referring to what is carried out in Clio's name. What really constitutes work in "the history profession," as we usually term it, belongs instead to many practices and activities linked to the single discipline of history that are spread among many distinct professions and occupations, among them school, college, and university teaching; museum work; government employment; and independent consulting and writing. Each of these professions and occupations requires different forms and presentations of knowledge, and each is governed by particular conventions and rules of its own. Historians work within the same discipline through the use of many accepted practices in a growing variety of professions and occupations. This book concerns those practices and, by extension, all those kinds of work.

Neglecting the distinction between discipline and profession is more than an innocent terminological error that, once corrected, allows us to speak and write of history as before. Instead, the error strikes deep into the heart of the discipline of history and creates more than mere intellectual confusion. It fatefully affects the development of the discipline's structure and hierarchies, the training and employment of historians, the honors and compensation extended to individuals, and the aspirations and sense of self-worth of those who contribute in their many ways to history's welfare. The error also helps determine the mistelling of the history of historical studies and practices in the United States. To correct the error ought to allow us to keep faith with one of history's enduring purposes: to honor what in the past warrants honor and to free ourselves from those conditions that no longer serve us or our fellow citizens well.

To argue that we must learn to distinguish clearly between the discipline of which all historians are members and the distinct occupations in which historians pursue their work is not to deny that most practicing historians are "professional historians" in the sense that they pursue their work as people whose professional labors – be they on school, college, and university faculties or in museums, corporations, and national parks – are consecrated to the creation, transmission, evaluation, and preservation of historical knowledge and subject to roughly the same normative scrutiny in every case. Nor is it to deny that most practicing historians perform their work, as we say, "professionally" – that is, knowledgeably, skillfully, and ethically. Most have received their doctoral degrees from the history departments of research universities, and their work is evaluated against widely shared, universalistic standards of evidence, citation, argumentation, interpretation, presentation, and conduct. Nothing that I write is meant to suggest that I do not believe these historians to be professional historians or historians who act professionally.

Yet even many of those who practice history without having been formally trained to do so or who may not be compensated for the historical work they produce can be, and I believe ought to be, considered professional historians in the way I use that term. After all, in the role of historian – whether as writers of history, schoolteachers of history, or docents in museums of history – they know deeply (or at least should know deeply) one or more of the same bodies of knowledge that academic scholars have mastered. They are judged (or at least should be judged) by the same governing norms of historical research and presentation. Surely they are affected by the same institutional structures and realities of historical pursuits as are more conventionally defined historians, and they are expected to conduct themselves by the same ethical standards that govern the historical work of those to whom the term "professional" is customarily applied. Are we to consider them lesser historians and their endeavors lesser historical practices by virtue of their not possessing a doctorate in history or not devoting themselves full time on a college or university faculty to Clio's discipline?

In answering that question in the negative, I indicate my conviction that people like schoolteachers of history who choose to consider themselves members of the world of learning – and who does not wish that there were many more of them? – must be embraced as professional historians, as must be those writers and journalists who diffuse historical knowledge without holding professorial appointments or having secured their doctoral degrees. They must also be held to generally accepted standards in their work. Yet, as long as many of us confine our definition of professional historian to academic teachers and scholars of history, we shall both exclude such teachers, writers, and others from historians' ranks and from the critical scrutiny their work warrants and, perhaps worse, we shall fail to help aspiring doctoral candidates list secondary school teaching or independent writing among those many worthy occupations from which they may make reasoned choices while remaining practicing historians.

It is also essential to distinguish, as Christopher Jencks and David Riesman some years ago insisted we must, between the terms "intellectual" and "academic," as well as between the communities they denote. While most academic historians are intellectuals, not all intellectuals who practice history are found on school, college, and university faculties. Those who seek to create and diffuse historical knowledge in museums or through films have every right to expect to be accepted as intellectuals whose efforts aspire to the same *gravitas* and play of ideas and to the same influence on understanding as do the labors of academic historians. The burden of demonstrating that this is not so falls upon those who would level the charge.

Therefore, emphatically and purposefully so, this book is for all those who wish to carry out work toward understanding the past and helping others understand it in whatever ways they choose to do so. It is not a book just for those who serve in an academic capacity or just for those who are paid by some institution, be it a government, historical society, or museum, for some extra-academic pursuit of professional historical work. It is for everyone who practices history in any of its many forms. I thus hope that experienced practitioners of the historian's craft, especially those who educate graduate students for today's multifarious world of history, as well as those who plan to become professional historians, may learn something from what I have to say. For it has been my discouraging experience from both inside and outside university walls to observe that a still-too-large proportion of academic historians remains skeptical of the growing number of activities carried on professionally in history's name and, consequently, is unable, with knowledge and experience, to help students adjust to the changing realities of their professional world. Others, while deeply knowledgeable about the many dimensions of their world of work, simply fail to pass on that knowledge to their students when preparing them for a career within history's precincts. Perhaps, therefore, this book will help those who read it to enter with clearer understanding and expectations into the increasingly diverse world of historical practice. For while there are many portals into Clio's house and many rooms inside it, all those chambers are guarded by the same tutelary muse and, though inhabited by people of many professions and pursuits, are organized toward the same ends: the creation and diffusion of historical knowledge.

Because I have written this book for all historians, I have written it out of a firm conviction that all historians must adopt the broadest conception of the discipline of history and confer full recognition on all pursuits undertaken legitimately in history's service if the practices of history are to remain engaging and robust. This will no doubt displease some – even though, if my observations are accurate, a declining number – who think that what is presently carried out as history work is already too broad and often self-defeating and that history must remain centered on its academic core and on scholarly research principally. I believe that they are wrong. Although there was a time when written scholarship was almost the sole means of making a lasting contribution to historical knowledge, that is no longer the case. Of course, the creation of new knowledge and understanding through original scholarship remains one of the great glories of Clio's world, and nothing that I have written here is meant to suggest otherwise. Yet, while other historical practices besides scholarship now make signally important contributions to historical understanding, we still lack agreed-on professional guidelines for preparing our students for their lives as practicing historians, the shared terms of discourse for conveying much of what we do and ought to do, and consensus about the weighty professional issues, in addition to research and writing, for which all young students of history should be prepared. More important, due in large part to lapses in the preparation of young historians, in many respects we lack strong and adaptive professionalism. Many historians are fine scholars, filmmakers, and private consultants without engaging themselves fully and actively in the lives of their professions and without being citizens of their discipline. Therefore, much of what follows is also an effort to bring into the open many topics neglected in the professional lives, as well as in the education, of practicing historians.

While this work is not a memoir, in many respects it reflects my own experiences and beliefs; it certainly betrays many of the views formed by my more than half century as a historian who has practiced both inside and outside the academy. Like most professional historians, I was prepared in a demanding academic setting to be an academic historian. Throughout my graduate education, however, and unlike so many of today's aspiring historians who receive handsome fellowship funding, I had to support myself while in graduate school by teaching history to high schoolers, community college students, and collegians enrolled in general studies and part-time baccalaureate programs, and thus I inaugurated my career in a diversity of educational settings. Subsequently, I joined a research university faculty, where I taught undergraduate and graduate students, produced published historical scholarship, and came to think of myself as an academic – which I was. On being convinced that the humanities in the United States needed additional institutional and other resources, I resigned my university professorship and founded a nonprofit organization devoted to strengthening the humanities. When that effort failed, I was left to improvise a career as historian outside college and university walls. I did so as the book publisher of a research institute, then as a foundation officer, all the while working to maintain my bona fides as a historian. Not surprisingly, as I shifted from an academic to a more public setting in my work, my angle of vision similarly shifted and was enlarged. So was my understanding of what it means to be a historian.

Yet, while I never intended to become a public historian or, in fact, thought of myself as one, my somewhat inadvertent career trajectory has led most of my colleagues to consider me a public historian. They do so because I have not retained an academic berth but instead have functioned for three decades as a historian elsewhere. I do not, however, hold myself out either as an academic historian or as a public historian. I do not do so because I do not believe that my own or other historians' professional locations adequately convey how they can or ought to define themselves as historians. I have long felt that assuming the mantle of public or academic historian misrepresents the overlapping professional orbits in which I have worked and in which so many others find themselves working. For while not holding a formal academic position, I have continued to teach undergraduate and graduate students, for years directed an unaffiliated seminar for experienced historians, have kept abreast of and written historical scholarship, and still participate fully in the larger intellectual, as well as professional, life of the discipline of history. So what then am I, an academic or public historian?

I believe that I am both, a hybrid of sorts, and thus simply a historian. When I left the academy, in many respects I brought the academy along with me, just as those who enter academic historians' academic ranks from outside carry with them the experiences and ethos that they gained elsewhere. The simple designation of historian thus strikes me as fitting, honorable, factual, and clear. And so this book, drawn from all my experiences as well as from extensive reflection about the entire discipline, is about being a historian in the many dimensions of that term. I hope that the book conveys my conviction that, while different kinds and locales of history work must be distinguished for purposes of analysis, for the long-term health of history we would all serve ourselves best by using a single, unmodified noun – historian – to designate ourselves professionally. Our aim should be to incorporate into the ancient company of historians any and all who follow history's muse.

Some other historians might compose elegies to history's yesteryears and see in my account of its circumstances substantiation of the decline in the quality of history, the degradation of its pursuit, and the fallen ways of its practitioners. I would not. There were wonderful qualities, some of them no doubt lost forever, in history's prelapsarian days; but the price of their retention was too high – uniformity of view, insularity of interpretation, and, worst of all, an exclusiveness of approach and subject that resulted in ignorance of large parts of the past. Never should there be such innocence again.

History is a moral discipline. It leads us to conceive of the possible in human terms and to gain the courage to pursue our own aspirations guided by the exemplary achievements of those who have gone before us. By learning, writing about, and conveying historical knowledge, we create meaning and diffuse values. Not that we shall ever come to unanimous agreement about those meanings and values, or about the many options of emphasis and method we face in doing history. Powerful works of theory and epistemology in the past half century have made manifestly clear the insoluble complexity of problems of language, knowledge, memory, reality, presentation, and fact to allow complacency on that score. Yet this is all the more reason to wrestle unceasingly, each one of us, with meaning and value as we go about our work and, through the history we produce, to assist our readers, viewers, and listeners, our fellow citizens and fellow humans to understand their lives and the lives of others in historical terms.

Others would write a book with different emphases and contents about the nature and pursuit of history work in our time, and many will disagree with at least some of what I write and the convictions with which I write it. Others would also write a book that offered prescriptions for what should be done to ease history's difficulties and to move the discipline smartly forward. I happily leave that task to them – or to another time. Instead, I have tried in the pages that follow to consider most of the situations in which I believe both fledgling and experienced practicing historians today are likely to find themselves in future years. Although, as this account ought to make abundantly clear, I regret that the world of history still contains many shortcomings, I also believe that it is much better poised than it was more than five decades ago, when I began to become a professional historian, to reduce their number. I hope that this book makes a contribution toward that end and that it may help bring into being new elements in the preparation of historians and broader, more frequent, and more intense discussions about the professional roads historians have yet to travel.

James M. Banner, Jr.
Washington, D.C.
December 2011

Acknowledgments

Because this book grows from a half-century career, it owes itself to countless people, many no doubt beyond my own recall, who introduced me to the study of history; contributed to my historical and professional knowledge; made known to me their views of our discipline, its practitioners, institutions, and ways; and made me think clearly about what I was trying to achieve, whether that made sense to them or (as surely was often the case) it did not. In fact, I have accumulated debts that go back to a time before I had decided to become a historian – debts owed to teachers, some of them not historians, whom neither I nor they knew would serve later as examples to me. Were I to name them here, the roster of their names would be long, but I have paid tribute to the most important of them already elsewhere.

In preparing this book, I have taken on new debts to many people who have provided assistance along the way. Some read an entire draft of the book's manuscript before its publication; some took hold of single chapters and, shaking them hard, rid them of errors, imbalance, and infelicities; others gave me specific assistance on request. Among them, some of whom may not even recall the help they extended or were unaware that they were in fact giving me assistance, were the participants, especially Michael Kammen, in a jointly sponsored Salzburg Seminar–Smithsonian Institution conference on Public History and National Identity in Salzburg, Austria, in 1999; Otis L. Graham, Jr., friend of my college days, colleague for more than fifty years, and distinctive, as in so many other ways, in his understanding of public history; Victoria A. Harden, who, more than most historians, has thought deeply and to great effect about the ethical issues that confront historians but that too often they fail to confront;

Peyton McCrary and David Rosner, who provided help and reassurance in what I write about expert testimony; John R. Gillis, longtime friend and colleague to whose balanced, deeply considered, and critical views of our discipline I have long listened; Arnita A. Jones, former executive director of both the American Historical Association and the Organization of American Historians, whose knowledge of the entire discipline is unsurpassed and probably unequaled and who saved me from numerous errors; Richard S. Kirkendall, who generously allowed me to read the manuscript of a set of essays on the history of the Organization of American Historians, which he has gathered and edited and which have since been published; Robert B. Townsend, deputy director of the American Historical Association, an unsung student of the discipline, whose circumstances he regularly measures, who allowed me to read his own recent scholarship and who read this work in manuscript with characteristic penetration and thus assisted me in refining it; John R. Dichtl, executive director of the National Council on Public History, who helped me improve my treatment of public history; Eric Arnesen and Anthony Grafton, who took their sharp eyes to the text and greatly helped me strengthen it in both general terms and specific details; and Olivia P. Banner, scholar, writer, and experienced editor in her own right, who offered invaluable requested advice and, more important for her father, gave me a green editorial light to proceed ahead. Christina M. Gillis, Howard P. Segal, Jack R. Censer, Pillarisetti Sudhir, William Palmer, Richard H. Kohn, James B. Gardner, Zachary M. Schrag, Donald A. Ritchie, Julian E. Zelizer, Joel D. Kitchens, William Weber, Ralph E. Luker, and Albert L. Hurtado have offered collegial guidance and responded to my requests for assistance along the way. Lewis Bateman, of Cambridge University Press, a friend, neighbor, and colleague of long standing, has shepherded this work through his great publishing house, at every step assisted by Anne Lovering Rounds. I am particularly indebted there to Brian MacDonald for his superb editing, as well as to Shari Chappell and Mark Fox for managing the book's production. In gratitude to them all, I have tried to respond to their suggestions for improvement and the assistance that all have offered; when I have not done so, it has been in no derogation of what they have urged upon me. Only I, and not they, am responsible for what follows.

The subject of this book being what it is, I dedicate it to my colleagues. Were love, spirit, laughter, and wisdom its subject, I would dedicate it to Phyllis Kramer.

The Discipline and Professions of History

History is a single discipline practiced in many professions – in many places, in many ways, and through many means. Historians share the same discipline but not the same profession. In fact, they never have, unless an unwarrantedly limited definition of the term "discipline" is used. Throughout history's American history, even some of the most illustrious and ostensibly "academic" of academic historians have ventured to practice history, however episodically, in other occupations. This fact, until recently omitted from the taught history of history, lies at the heart of almost everything that touches the organized practices of the discipline today – just as it characterized those same practices more than a century ago, before historical study had become a clearly demarcated subject of inquiry and instruction. A full history of the efflorescence of history into many professions, one that goes beyond the elementary distinction between academic and public history, is yet to be written or yet to be incorporated into the way we normally speak of history and prepare students for careers in it. What follows is a sketch of how that history might be told.

Before the emergence of recognizably modern professions in the nineteenth century, historical knowledge was deeply implicated in the learning and arguments of lawyers, doctors, and clerics whose learned callings and occupations would be the first to form themselves into professions. No less significantly, argumentation from history was the stock-in-trade of statesmen and politicians. But from the late nineteenth century on, when the norm that governed a career in service to history came increasingly to be the creation, transmission, and evaluation of historical learning by specially trained people working full time as historians on college and university faculties, professional history became roughly coterminous with academic history. Yet it is now becoming clear that, rather than being a terminal point in the history of the discipline of history, history's main residence in the academy, although a century long, ought to be considered provisional and, while still the center of gravity in a larger constellation of professional locations, only one among many places from which history has begun to reemerge into the larger society. The consequences of ignoring the implications of these historical facts – of thinking that the history of the discipline in the United States is solely a correlative of the history of research universities – haunt historians' bearing, work, and thought and make difficult their adaptation to rapidly changing professional realities.

The collapse of the terms "discipline" and "profession" into each other mirrors the realities of a passing era in which a professional historian could with some accuracy be assumed to be an academic. Although that is no longer the case, almost all scholarly works and professional commentaries about history still refer to the "history profession" or the "historical profession" as if there were a single one. In such instances, those who employ the term are alluding either to the academic profession in which the largest single group of historians continues to work or to the body of knowledge that composes the entire discipline of history. They have confused profession with discipline.[1]

---

[1] Two illustrative examples chosen at random: the subtitle of Peter Novick, *That Noble Dream: The "Objectivity Question" and the American Historical Profession* (Cambridge: Cambridge University Press, 1988); and the comment, "It is difficult to discuss the historical profession, or American life, for very long nowadays without encountering references to 'diversity' – its history, current status, and future prospects," in Eric Foner, "On Diversity in History," *Perspectives* 38 (April 2000): 2. A more recent confusion of the terms is found in Barbara D. Metcalf, "Gender across the Generations," *Perspectives on History* 47 (October 2010): 5–7. The confusion is especially consequential for public history. Yet the *Public Historian* now advertises itself appropriately as "the definitive voice of the public history profession." A precise, and rare, use of the term "profession" in reference to the academic profession only is to be found throughout Anthony Grafton and Robert B. Townsend, "Historians' Rocky Job Market," *Chronicle Review*, July 11, 2008, B10–11. But see the title of Townsend, "A Profile of the History Profession, 2010," *Perspectives in History* 48 (October 2010): 36–39, which concerns only academic historians. For another rare example of the use of the term "academic profession" that by implication distinguishes "profession" from "discipline," see the fall 1997 issue of *Daedalus*, entitled "The American Academic Profession in Transition." Burton R. Clark, wise student of academics and their world, denominates that world "the academic profession" without any suggestion that the term is problematic. See Clark (ed.), *The Academic Profession: National, Disciplinary, and Institutional Settings* (Berkeley:

Were the distinction not central to understanding the state of history today, it might be passed over in silence, especially because, like so many concepts and terms, these two words are richly complex and because their definitions, especially that of profession, are widely contested. An effort at clarification is nevertheless warranted. A discipline is a domain of knowledge, a capacious province of inquiry (*science* in French, *Wissensgebiet* in German) with generally agreed-on, if not firm or impermeable, boundaries. It is a universe of thought, not, like a profession, an arena of action. As a field of intellectual endeavor, a discipline possesses distinctive, if neither unique nor unchanging, methods for pursuing its particular kind of knowledge and understanding, evaluating the evidence that creates that knowledge, and ascertaining the validity of assertions built on that evidence. Yet a discipline is constituted by much more than its subjects and methods. A particular broad subject matter and particular methods used to create it roughly mark off one discipline from others and create reasonably distinct domains of discourse. A particular institution, the university, becomes the normal, often idealized, location of preparation for pursuit of the discipline's subjects. A discipline is also a framework within which certain approaches are legitimated, certain kinds of language and argumentation accepted, certain outlets for the dissemination of knowledge favored, and certain kinds of standards of peer evaluation accepted as conventional – and within which others are not. A person occupies a place in that discipline by becoming immersed in its subject matter, its vocabulary, its methods, and its traditions. One joins a discipline but, unlike a profession, does not have to be admitted to it, and in this sense a historian is a historian by command of historical knowledge, not by skill in any particular activity.

Historians are defined as historians not by the kind or location of their work or by the audiences they address but rather by holding themselves out as people who seek to know what happened in the past and why

University of California Press, 1987); and Clark, *The Academic Life: Small Worlds, Different Worlds* (Princeton: Carnegie Foundation for the Advancement of Teaching, 1987). Some argue that use of the term "profession" to denominate the lofty work of history reduces it from an intellectual enterprise to a means of livelihood. I see no merit in this argument. For a different approach to the matter, which calls for fuller exploration than it has yet received, see the brief discussion, which in part I provoked, in Thomas Bender et al., *The Education of Historians for the Twenty-First Century* (Urbana: University of Illinois Press, 2004), 4–5. For a superb history of the disaggregation of discipline into professions, see Robert B. Townsend, "Making History: Scholarship and Professionalization in the Discipline, 1880–1940" (Ph.D. dissertation, George Mason University, 2009).

it did so and then to present that knowledge to others in the formats –
whether articles, books, films, radio transmissions, Web sites, or museum
exhibits – of their choice. Historical knowledge is the coinage of their
authority. Thus people with little proven competence as researchers or
teachers but great love and knowledge of history – amateur historians
who dedicate their labors to uncovering and teaching about the past
without professional training or even compensation for their work – are
historians, even if not trained to be or serving as professional historians. They participate in the same community of thought, in the same
parent discipline, as academic and public historians do. Because they
dedicate their labors to the same ends, they are entitled to bear the title of
historian.[2]

These amateurs are not, however, professional historians unless they
are working as writers, teachers, or filmmakers of history. A profession –
and here one enters a world of robust debate, extensive historical and
sociological literature, and considerable disagreement – is like a discipline in that it constitutes a community of people; but that profession
is a distinct kind of community, one composed of people who share the
same occupation without necessarily being members of the same discipline. Thus one can pursue the profession of museum curator as historian,
philosopher, paleographer, biologist, or linguist. A profession, as distinct
from a discipline, is a field defined by endeavor, not by a body of thought;
it concerns the direction and manner of use of a body of knowledge, not
that body of knowledge itself. More than that, a profession is an occupation for which roughly uniform education in a body of knowledge
and protocols of practice at a research university – sometimes said to be a
"learned" education for a "learned" calling, such as the law, medicine, or
teaching – is necessary. It is an occupation to which access is deeply influenced, if not totally controlled, by this training; and the training is itself
constituted of generally accepted curricula and requirements at research
universities (courses, oral and written examinations, and final rites of
passage such as moot court debates and dissertations leading to doctoral
degrees). In fact, a profession controls the training and admittance of its
successor generations in its own image, and for that privilege – in return

---

[2] For a fuller discussion of public history, see Chapter 5. Some historians view history
as both discipline and discourse, each distinct. It seems to me that efforts to make and
maintain that distinction only muddy the matter and lead to endless tangles of language
and philosophy. Be that as it may, this book is concerned with history as a discipline –
an arena of thought, endeavor, and institution – not as a universe of theory, discourse,
and philosophy.

for performing certain social functions considered necessary – it receives sanction from the community. Moreover, the knowledge and skills of a profession's members are ideally supposed to be employed altruistically, even when compensated, within a kind of compact with society, for which the professionals are granted by society the liberty to police themselves. An additional consequence of that liberty is that professionals are expected to adhere to the particular norms of their professions.

Increasingly, training as a historian and adherence to particular norms do not point to a single profession. Indeed, professional historians – people who make their living in the discipline of history – can today be and are academics, book publishers and editors, consultants, filmmakers, independent writers, or archivists, to name only a few endeavors in which historians serve as historians. Because there are many academic disciplines but only one academic profession, academic historians are professional historians, but professional historians are not all academics.[3] We can see the difference when we consider that, while the American Historical Association (AHA) admits all those who associate themselves with the discipline of history, academic faculties, like archives or museums, are more discriminating. One does not join a faculty by approaching its doors and paying a fee, as one does a scholarly or professional association; instead, an applicant to an academic faculty has to meet its entrance requirements. One is admitted to an academic history faculty by historian peers who, in evaluating applicants, are concerned as much with the quality of those applicants' training, their promise as teachers and scholars, their collegiality, and even their ability or willingness to administer departments as with their command of knowledge.

A profession, as distinct from a discipline, also maintains, because it can maintain, different roles for members and nonmembers, for insiders and outsiders. Academic and public historians, for instance, are historians together, but each group has a distinct sense of its own professional identity and distinct professional values, also to some degree distinct professional languages. Therefore, one can be an archivist or an editor of

---

[3] I use the noun "academic" rather than "academician" to designate a member of a college or university faculty throughout this book because the former seems more appropriate in denoting someone who holds appointment at a college or university, whereas the latter, more European in connotation, implies someone who holds appointment in an academy – an institution generally without instructional functions. Also, contrary to conventional usage, I use the word "faculty" as a collective noun meaning the people who constitute the faculty of any school, college, or university and the term "faculty member" to refer to an individual member of such a faculty.

scholarly books without being a member of a discipline, just as one can be a historian without holding membership in a profession. To speak of "the history profession" is to speak of no profession at all.[4]

To further complicate matters, none of these distinctions have anything to do with professional conduct or bearing. One can of course be consummately "professional" in any endeavor, not just a clearly professional one. People are "professional" carpenters and "professional" police officers without, strictly speaking, being members of a profession or working within a discipline. In this sense, professionalism has to do with competence, bearing, and ethics, not with occupation; and in this sense most historians are professionals. If, as Thomas L. Haskell writes, professionalization must be understood "to be a measure not of quality, but of community," then the universe in which all historians reside is their discipline, and they practice this discipline within distinct professional communities, each with its own collective activities and traditions, as academics, museum curators, consultants, and the like. What links these historians is that they share intellectual bonds and commitments within the same community of thought and are historians by virtue of that fact.[5]

---

[4] The difficulties of defining a profession are legion. A concise and cautionary review of them is to be found in Lawrence Veysey, "The Plural Organized Worlds of the Humanities," in Alexandra Oleson and John Voss (eds.), *The Organization of Knowledge in Modern America, 1860–1920* (Baltimore: Johns Hopkins University Press, 1979), 31–106, esp. 57–62. Veysey here points to the problems inherent in trying to make fast distinctions between professions and other kinds of occupational work, not between professions and disciplines. A brief, solid introduction to a large sociological literature on professions is Howard S. Becker, "The Nature of a Profession," in Nelson B. Henry (ed.), *Education for the Professions* (Chicago: National Society for the Study of Education, 1962), 27–46, and an introduction to some of the problems of the concept is Harold Wilensky, "The Professionalization of Everyone," *American Journal of Sociology* 70 (1964): 137–158. Historical works on specific professions, works that confront many of the difficulties with the concept, include Daniel H. Calhoun, *The American Civil Engineer: Origins and Conflict* (Cambridge, MA: Harvard University Press, 1960); Anton-Hermann Chroust, *The Rise of the Legal Profession in America* (Norman: University of Oklahoma Press, 1965); Mary O. Furner, *Advocacy and Objectivity: A Crisis in the Professionalization of American Social Science, 1865–1905* (Lexington: University of Kentucky Press, 1975); Thomas L. Haskell, *The Emergence of Professional Social Science: The American Social Science Association and the Nineteenth-Century Crisis of Authority* (Urbana: University of Illinois Press, 1977); Joseph F. Kett, *The Formation of the American Medical Profession: The Role of Institutions, 1780–1860* (New Haven: Yale University Press, 1968); and Raymond H. Merritt, *Engineering in American Society, 1850–1875* (Lexington: University of Kentucky Press, 1969).

[5] Haskell, *Emergence of Professional Social Science*, 18.

Any useful history of history – any history that is to be an applicable, as well as an accurate, guide for historians – must take into account the long process by which history became a discipline and then one practiced, as it is now and long has been, in many professions. And that history must today reckon with the rust of past decades, which obscures the underlying record on which a contemporary, relevant, and serviceable history, one that better guides us than the one that has long been told, must be based. While that history must start from a time beyond accurate knowledge, when history was oral chronicle, history of a kind more familiar to us – a means of securely recording and formally trying to understand the results of human agency in the past free from myth and fiction – originated in the era of Herodotus and Thucydides. But as a discipline – a distinct branch of knowledge possessing an agreed-on general subject matter, particular methods of inquiry and presentation, and specific canons of evaluation – history's beginnings belong to the nineteenth century. A few people – David Hume, William Robertson, and Edward Gibbon chief among them – were pursuing historical inquiry in a manner recognizably like our own, with its now established practices of empirical research in original materials and of argument based on cited sources, before 1800. But it was not until the early nineteenth century, principally although not exclusively in Germany, that those who wrote history began to develop the self-conscious methods and standards by which history would gradually distinguish itself from other intellectual pursuits as a separate domain of inquiry, one possessing its own more or less clearly defined range of questions and the conventions of competence that mark off its practitioners as composing a discrete community distinct from other intellectuals and professionals. And it was not until the late nineteenth century that the discipline, having gained its general intellectual and methodological definition, took up enduring residence in the academy.[6]

---

[6] Probably the best general histories of historical thought are now Donald R. Kelley's three volumes: *Faces of History: Historical Inquiry from Herodotus to Herder* (New Haven: Yale University Press, 1998), *Fortunes of History: Historical Thought from Herder to Huizinga* (New Haven: Yale University Press, 2003), and the capstone *Frontiers of History: Historical Inquiry in the Twentieth Century* (New Haven: Yale University Press, 2006). Kelley's approach is a rejoinder to Hayden V. White, *Metahistory* (Baltimore: Johns Hopkins University Press, 1973). Two other general surveys of historiography, each distinctively different from the other, are Ernst Breisach, *Historiography: Ancient, Medieval and Modern*, 2nd ed. (Chicago: University of Chicago Press, 1994), and John Burrow, *A History of Histories: Epics, Chronicles and Inquiries from Herodotus and Thucydides to the Twentieth Century* (New York: Alfred A. Knopf, 2008). A corrective to the hard-held view that post-Enlightenment historiographical thought was born in

Until the final third of that century in the United States, historical study
and reflection were part of the larger world of humane letters, including
literature, philology, theology, philosophy, and political economy. Pursued by patrician Anglo-American men and women of independent means
(themselves following the colonial founders of American historiography),
often taught at American colleges and universities by those who came by
their knowledge informally, and commonly presented within a nationalistic and religious framework, historical knowledge in the United States
long remained bound to its origins in moral and political philosophy and
the classics. As such, it was offered as a set of lessons, either gratifying
or cautionary, about human affairs and the advance of civilization over
barbarism and irreligion.

It was the German historian Leopold von Ranke and his successors
who, with avowed purpose, liberated history from philosophy and theology and firmly bound it to the dispassionate, empirical study of documents and other evidence. They did so by yoking historical study to
the emergence of nation-states and by lowering history from the celestial
realms of universality to the more confined ground of particular times and
places. What most distinguished humans from one another, these historians believed, was their distinct national cultures, each forged out of
Volkswanderungen, politics, and wars – subjects that, befitting the nineteenth century's romantic nationalism, became the grand themes of that
century's historiography. With that historiography every history produced since then has had to come to terms either by accepting its fundamental grounds or by endeavoring to escape from them. Our own time
constitutes the era in which history has broken farthest away from the
nationalistic and patriotic soil in which its nineteenth-century founders set
its roots, and the consequences of that escape constitute what is arguably
the most profound challenge facing historical understanding since its
emergence 2,500 years ago.[7]

Germany and nurtured only by academics is Jonathan Dewald, "'A la Table de Magny':
Nineteenth-Century French Men of Letters and Sources of Modern Historical Thought,"
American Historical Review 108 (October 2003): 1009–1033.

[7] The most powerful statement of this challenge is now Thomas Bender, *A Nation Among
Nations: America's Place in World History* (New York: Hill and Wang, 2006). An earlier
statement of Bender's position, plus other reflections on the entire range of intellectual
challenges posed by the effort to transcend national historiographies, is to be found in the
essays in Thomas Bender (ed.), *Rethinking American History in a Global Age* (Berkeley:
University of California Press, 2002). While both books' subject is ostensibly the history
of the United States, their contents and implications actually extend far more widely.
A summary of the role of the historical imagination in forming a sense of the American

In addition to setting the agenda for historical research and practice for a century, Ranke and his successors, spurred by the emergence of the modern physical and natural sciences, adopted an Enlightenment ideal of scientific, objective history arrived at through the application of evidence-based reasoning. Our current debates about the very nature of historical knowledge, debates more fundamental, widespread, and consequential than at any other time in the discipline's history since Ranke's era, are inconceivable without their emergence from the particulars of nineteenth-century national and cultural history and that history's claims to objectivity. Nineteenth-century historians bequeathed to every succeeding generation until our own the conviction that it was possible to approach, if not fully to achieve, full and agreed-on knowledge of every human act, creation, institution, and idea about which evidence remained. While the incompleteness of that evidence and limitations on human intelligence might put boundaries around historical understanding, these historians believed that some asymptotic proximity to knowledge of what had actually happened might be gained and a kind of detached, unbiased understanding achieved.[8]

Finally, and by no means any less significant than creating historical study as a separate discipline and binding it to norms of objectivity, the early professional historians of Germany made historical work a vocation. By establishing the standards and process by which historians would be trained and by creating the recognized, compensated occupation of "historian," however the definition of that occupation might change, they enabled future historians to chart their paths of professional work. Whether for those summoned by some mysterious inclination to history as a calling or for those with a more purely intellectual, even careerist interest in study of the past, the founders of vocational history made possible the pursuit of lifelong careers within the discipline.

---

nation is Joyce Appleby, Lynn Hunt, and Margaret Jacob, *Telling the Truth about History* (New York: W. W. Norton, 1994), chap. 3.

[8] The classic work on the history of the objectivity ideal in American historiography is Novick, *That Noble Dream*. Cf. E. H. Carr's characteristically witty comments on Ranke and his epigone in his enduring *What Is History?* (New York: Alfred A. Knopf, 1962), 5, in which Carr calls Ranke's celebrated statement that historians should present the past *wie es eigentlich gewesen* "not very profound" and writes that "three generations of German, British, and even French historians marched into battle intoning the magic words, '*wie es eigentlich gewesen*' like an incantation – designed, like most incantations, to save them from the tiresome obligation to think for themselves."

The transition from history produced by gentlemanly amateurs (the adjective being appropriate because men greatly outnumbered women among them) to that produced by academic historians, from historical study undertaken for the edification of readers and the creation of national states to history directed to the discovery and understanding of what actually took place in the past, required decades to accomplish and has never been fully completed.[9] In the United States as elsewhere, islands of creative amateurism – of history produced by men and women without formal graduate training who support themselves by writing, not actively teaching, history – have always remained to offer inspiration and reassurance to those who do not choose to become academic or other salaried historians. History with a philosophical, teleological, inspirational, and admonitory bent has continued to attract audiences, even though historians, some of whom used to think of themselves as moral philosophers, have now ceded much of that role to novelists, poets, and dramatists. And the status of no single historian, whether a university professor or a journalist undertaking historical research and writing, is left uncontested by people who challenge that historian's values, intentions, and competence. Yet by the early decades of the twentieth century, academic history

---

[9] The story of the capture of historiography by men, how the possibility of feminine historiography was dashed in the revolutionary era of the late eighteenth century, and how the professionalization of history in the nineteenth century was carried out on thoroughly masculine ground, see Bonnie G. Smith, *The Gender of History: Men, Women, and Historical Practice* (Cambridge, MA: Harvard University Press, 1998). Smith shows how white-male-dominated historiography linked itself to the nation-state and its central attributes – government, institutions, war, and politics – while female historiography was left with biography, travel, and culture and made to seem amateur thereby. A related study is Julie Des Jardins, *Women and the Historical Enterprise in America: Gender, Race, and the Politics of Memory, 1880–1945* (Chapel Hill: University of North Carolina Press, 2003), whose value lies in its excavation of the careers and struggles of particular women historians, many of whose works and contributions have been lost to the central narrative of the history of history in the United States. Also apposite is Ellen Fitzpatrick, *History's Memory: Writing America's Past, 1880–1980* (Cambridge, MA: Harvard University Press, 2002), which regains much of the American historiographical past and shows how a good proportion of what was taken to be new history starting in the 1960s was rooted in many older histories, whose authors are forgotten at our peril. Her chapter on the historiography of Native Americans is alone a revelation. A large gap in these studies is filled by Stephen G. Hall's *A Faithful Account of the Race: African-American Historical Writing in Nineteenth-Century America* (Chapel Hill: University of North Carolina Press, 2009). Hall exhumes the works of amateur as well as serious intellectual and professional African American historians all but forgotten now in the shadows of W. E. B. Du Bois and Carter G. Woodson and reveals how they, like long-overlooked women and Native American scholars and writers, greatly enriched the nation's historical understanding of itself.

had gained the upper hand, if not among the public, then within the intellectual circles that would from that time forward largely determine the direction and nature of historical research and thought. Even those given to writing and teaching moral history or, like Arnold Toynbee, offering grand schemes of historical change gradually became influenced by the empirical norms and expanding subjects of academic practice. Surely their work fell under academics' critical scrutiny and often accordingly suffered by comparison. More significantly, by the early twentieth century the pursuit of historical knowledge had become identified with the professoriate. To be a historian and not to be an academic effectively became, with few exceptions, for well over half a century a contradiction in terms.

The consequences of this transformation of history from belletristic art to empirical "science," from branch of moral philosophy to independent discipline, from largely clerical to overwhelmingly secular worldview, from scattered to academic locations, and from amateur practice to professional pursuit were as profound as the history of this transformation has been long and complex. Much of that history, in the United States as elsewhere, had to do with the transformation of higher education. As the elective system in American universities took hold, for example, courses in history assumed their place at the core of the collegiate arts and sciences curriculum, and the subjects taught by academic historians expanded beyond counting. The number of students of history – undergraduate and graduate – as well as of historians on academic faculties exploded. As it did so, the amount of historical knowledge fissioned too, and in most respects the accuracy of that knowledge improved and its weight increased as new methods for analyzing evidence and new approaches to criticism came into being. Also, with the creation and growth of great research libraries, it was no longer possible for historians to avoid immersion in original sources or to escape the acid test of historical work: evaluation by intellectual peers of the relation between evidence and the historical claims built upon it.[10]

These unchallengeable gains in the practices of history and this expansion in historical knowledge were not, however, without serious and enduring costs. We cannot say with certainty whether the

---

[10] The standard account of the American university's rise is Laurence R. Veysey, *The Emergence of the American University* (Chicago: University of Chicago Press, 1965). See also Roger L. Geiger, *To Advance Knowledge: The Growth of American Research Universities, 1900–1940* (New York: Oxford University Press, 1986).

professionalization of history could have occurred without the discipline's near monopoly by the academy. Suffice it to say at least that professionalization and effective monopolization by the academy were coincident. Moreover, those twinned and interrelated developments occurred, as such so often do, in negative reference to what had preceded them. The current predicaments of history cannot be understood without taking into account the way in which this particular negative stance in regard to history's own past – academic history emerging in reaction to belletristic, amateur history – became embodied within the discipline and especially within its academic practice. Nor can that predicament be understood and escaped without an effort to rearrange the way in which we view that history.

That the late nineteenth century was the birth time of modern research universities, the modern intellectual disciplines, and the related modern structure of learned and professional associations owes most to changes sweeping through the United States in a pivotal moment in American culture. The last two decades of the nineteenth century in particular, as Thomas Haskell has argued, experienced "a general crisis of authority" for the American intelligentsia and a "profound reorientation of social thought and culture" in general. In response to this transformation, universities, intellectual disciplines, and professional associations, while developing along separate trajectories, grew in close parallel with each other and for roughly the same reasons. All were responses to the growth in scientific and other knowledge and the gathering need to bring order – intellectual, methodological, and professional – to an intellectual culture spinning increasingly beyond the capacity of the existing organization of thought and practice to influence. In what Robert H. Wiebe famously termed this "search for order," domains of intellectual inquiry marked themselves off from each other and distinguished their practitioners from those (some skilled and knowledgeable amateurs, others simply dabbling gentlemen and gentlewomen) no longer considered to have the competence to direct the progress of thought. These developments occurred despite the extraordinary achievements of historical thought and writing during the preceding 250 years, long before the birth of modern research universities, by the likes of Cotton Mather, Thomas Hutchinson, George Bancroft, Francis Parkman, Edward Channing, William H. Prescott, and Henry Charles Lea – to name only a few major ones, all of them American and all male. Although some of their successors proved capable of moving into the emerging world of disciplines, universities, and scholarly societies, none could hold back the gathering forces of change.

One aspect of that change that seems especially noteworthy now was the energy expended and the time required to remove amateurs and dilettantes, as well as nonscholar teachers in schools and colleges, out of the new intellectual world eventually epitomized by modern research universities and many baccalaureate colleges. For while men like Moses Coit Tyler, Henry Charles Lea, and John Bach McMaster, some of whom ventured into the academy, lost the larger war over the center of gravity of the discipline, they fought with style and gusto to retain their influence and, more important, their audiences. Moreover, even if later overshadowed by more committed academics, many of these men, in ways too little appreciated, absorbed the norms of academic research and were as concerned as their academic colleagues to improve and effectively convey historical knowledge. Yet when the task of professionalizing the discipline had been accomplished, as it was by roughly 1915, it still required some decades for the historians who steered their bark by the German research model to overwhelm professionally, sometimes intellectually, the other historians, both independent amateurs and faculty historians in old-time collegiate institutions, whose role remained far longer the diffusion of cultural values and of religious and elite traditions to undergraduates. Theodore Roosevelt, himself president of the AHA in 1912, dismissively spoke for many of those left aside by the drive for professionalization against "the conscientious, industrious painstaking little pedants, who would have been useful in a rather small way if they had understood their own limitations" but who now had become "because of their conceit distinctly noxious." An attitude that was never to die, Roosevelt's biting, if adolescent, criticism flamed high from time to time and, in the final third of the twentieth century, paradoxically contributed to the reinvigoration of history outside the academy and to its spread into other professions and occupations.[11]

---

[11] Haskell, *Emergence of Professional Social Science*, vi–vii; Robert H. Wiebe, *The Search for Order, 1877–1920* (New York: Hill and Wang, 1967); John Higham, *History: Professional Scholarship in America* (Princeton: Princeton University Press, 1965; rev. ed., 1989), 7–8; and Higham, "The Reorientation of American Culture in the 1890s," in Higham, *Writing American History: Essays on Modern Scholarship* (Bloomington: Indiana University Press, 1970), 73–102. For cautions about applying the concept of professional development to any of the humanities disciplines, see Veysey's important "The Plural Organized World of the Humanities." The historical and social science literature on professions and professionalization is huge. On the social sciences, see Furner, *Advocacy and Objectivity*; Dorothy Ross, *The Origins of American Social Science*

The centering of history in the academy was not at first intended. In fact, what can be seen now to have laid the groundwork for the triumph of academic disciplines, subject specialization, and intellectual skepticism was an effort, growing out of the world of genteel reformers, to bring together like-minded men of culture – amateurs, public servants, and academics alike – to address social and cultural issues under the banner of the nascent social sciences. Their vehicle was the American Social Science Association (ASSA), founded in 1865; their hope, the application of cultured, genteel, and what they thought of as disinterested and dispassionate intelligences like their own to the day's pressing public problems. They acted not as people occupying distinct social roles or performing distinct functions but as a social class. Yet the mordants of a new intellectual culture, augmented by the growing aspirations of academic scholars being trained up at Johns Hopkins, Harvard, Columbia, and other universities rather quickly ate away at the association's broad ambitions and rendered academics' particular aims uncontainable within it. By the 1880s, the formation of what we now know as the modern disciplines and their distinct organizations out of gatherings of many of the same men (and the same class of men) who were originally its members left the ASSA bereft of active members, and it died. So did the hope of bringing all the social sciences, as well as their practitioners, together for the same ends. Social scientists were actuated by the search for general laws discovered through observation and experiment, whereas historians were becoming more firmly attached to an evolutionary, progressive model of the past. In addition, the pursuit of reform proved increasingly irreconcilable with the pursuit of new knowledge, which had already emerged as the distinguishing characteristic of the individual academic disciplines and their practitioners.[12] From then on, academics might be reformers, but reform would not be the central concern of the academic disciplines.

(Cambridge: Cambridge University Press, 1991); and Ross, "The Development of the Social Sciences," in Oleson and Voss, *Organization of Knowledge in Modern America*, 107–138. The indispensable foundation for the history of the discipline of history in the United States is Higham's *History*. Despite its assumption that professional history – as Higham significantly calls it "the profession" of history – is more or less coterminous with the academy, I have relied on it extensively in this chapter. For additional historical perspectives, see also Theodore S. Hamerow's often-rueful *Reflections on History and Historians* (Madison: University of Wisconsin Press, 1987), chaps. 2, 5, and 6.

12   The scholarly associations representing the social sciences eventually banded together as the Social Science Research Council in 1923 to pursue various programs of research of interest to them all. A fine history of these developments is Haskell, *Emergence of Professional Social Science*. The disciplines and organizations of the natural and

That historians had been members of the American Social Science Association did not mean that historians thought of themselves as social scientists. It did mean that some of them shared the hope for a general, historically informed approach to public issues, a hope that has never died out among academic and other historians. Yet those same historians could not long resist the intellectual and professional impulses that were leading to disciplinary particularity, and in 1884 some of them came together under the leadership of Herbert Baxter Adams of Johns Hopkins to form the American Historical Association.[13] While it ought to go without saying that had the modern discipline of history and the AHA come into being in our time they would ineluctably mirror the circumstances of our age, it bears emphasis that the characteristics of the particular birth era of the discipline and its senior organization stamped both with characteristics that continue decisively to affect the practices of history today.

At first, only roughly a third of the members of the AHA were academics, a figure markedly lower than that for the Modern Language Association, in which academics rose to 80 percent of the organization's membership. These professors would have felt comfortable in a room full of other cultured (and, one should add, almost without exception Protestant Anglo-Saxon) gentlemen self-assuredly confident in their membership in the social and cultural gentry whose larger social role was to uphold the verities of "civilization," join in the uplift of government and society, and apply their patriciate conviction that the people and government of the raw American nation needed their wise and authoritative guidance as it emerged to world power. It was such social and policy aspirations that moved the AHA, under Adams's firm hand, to seek and gain, uniquely among scholarly associations, a federal charter in 1889.[14] But whatever

physical sciences had a similar but earlier birth out of the American Association for the Advancement of Science, founded in 1848.

[13] The origins of the AHA are ably presented by David D. Van Tassel, "From Learned Society to Professional Organization: The American Historical Association, 1884–1900," *American Historical Review* 89 (October 1984): 929–956. A perceptive more recent work, one that shows the influence of developments and thinking since Van Tassel wrote and that covers a longer period, is Townsend, "Making History: Scholarship and Professionalization in the Discipline, 1880–1940," which is supplemented in Townsend, "The Social Shape of the AHA, 1884–1945," *Perspectives on History* 47 (December 2009), 36–40. Haskell, *Emergence of Professional Social Science*, chap. 8, relates how the AHA grew out of the American Social Science Association.

[14] Although the AHA has never figured out, perhaps because the complexities and obstacles are so great, how fully to exploit that charter for the good of public affairs, the claims that that charter implies have surely eventuated in some notable institutional gains to the

their shared social location and cultural pretensions, it was not long before the desires of the genteel amateurs and the academics among the AHA membership diverged, and gradually the two groups drifted apart. As a result, those who were trying to create a discipline out of the old congeries of subjects and a profession out of amateur practices were able to seize the initiative and fuel the creation of history's original American disciplinary norms and the discipline's initial American professional structures and practices – both heavily reliant on standards established earlier in German universities, standards that eventually became global. It was they who created those elements of the discipline that today we take as natural and immutable – the *American Historical Review* (founded in 1895) and other history journals, history departments within universities, periodic gatherings of scholars, graduate programs and their emblematic graduate seminars that culminate in the Ph.D., research fellowships and leaves, peer review by fellow historians of published and other historical work, university and other scholarly presses, and the emphasis on research proven first in a doctoral dissertation and then followed up in career-long pursuit of research scholarship.

Of these, none was more fateful in stamping academic norms and expectations on the entire discipline and laying the groundwork for the eventual triumph of professionalism over social status than Ph.D.-level graduate training. Yet all these institutions, practices, and norms, domesticated from their German origins, served the growing ranks of historian professors at American research universities now occupying the highest point in the educational system. Ever since then, most historians have taken research professors to stand in for professional historians, even though, increasingly, the identification of the one with the other has become anachronistic. Not surprisingly, of course, it is those professors who have written the discipline's history, just as their perspective has triumphed in the telling of that history. And while that history seems partial today, it has long served as a useful and powerful force. Indeed, that history has undergirded all the triumphs of academic history in the United States for well over a century.

national state and to history. Perhaps the greatest of these has been the creation of the National Archives. Even in its early years, as hoped-for benefits from the federal charter did not emerge, the AHA independently addressed such critical issues as the teaching of history in the schools and the condition of the public records of the states and in such instances achieved major gains for historical knowledge and the public good. It remains an open question whether the AHA might more effectively take advantage of its congressional charter for the benefit of history and nation.

But that result – the triumph of the academic – was not foreordained. The convivial Herbert Baxter Adams, not only the moving force behind the founding of the AHA but its secretary during the organization's initial sixteen years, strove from the start to maintain history's ties to the general public, however limited to cultured gentlemen his "public" seems to us now. Even while harboring a superior attitude toward local historical societies and their members' amateur practices, he promoted their work and labored to protect the interests and thus to ensure the involvement of amateurs among the AHA's initially small rank and file. In fact, amateurs were in the majority and academics in the minority of participants at the AHA's founding meeting in Saratoga Springs, New York, and professors similarly composed a minority of AHA presidents into the early years of the twentieth century. Yet it was not just the role of nonacademics in the early AHA that caused what more than one historian has characterized as the intellectual blandness of AHA meetings in its early decades. While we take universities to be the sites of new thinking and robust intellectual debate, late nineteenth-century universities had not yet taken on those qualities, however successful graduate training was in producing some superb historical talent. Historical and patriotic societies, museums, and such institutions as the Library of Congress also were, until the turn of the century, sleepy, largely antiquarian institutions trailing behind equally conformist university departments in serious intellectual work. History was still located within genteel culture, and it would remain there for some decades more.

In many respects, that was a good thing. Because of the similar social status of professional and amateur historians, academic and professorial norms were not anathema to the amateurs, who with zeal as well as support from the AHA and many professional historians achieved some notable successes. Among these, the many new state historical societies were the most significant, especially outside the East, where older antiquarian and genealogical societies had already taken firm root and served more to sustain an older social order than to advance an emerging discipline. In fact, many amateur historians were amateurs only by virtue of their lack of graduate training, not in their historical knowledge or organizational skills. They showed great ability not just in setting up state archives and historical programs but in successfully associating themselves and these institutions with universities and university-based historians and in adapting themselves to the increasingly demanding norms of academic history. Their greatest contribution to the advance of history in the United States was the collection and preservation of archives and the publication of historical documents. It is difficult to imagine that their successes, let alone their willingness to work with academic historians, would have been possible without their having felt themselves to be of the same social and professional group as the growing number of professional historians. The fact that institutions so closely tied to serious academic research were founded and managed largely by nonacademic historians meant that academic and public history were closely associated professionally from the start.

Secondary schools and their teachers also absorbed, if not quite so readily and for different reasons, some of the standards of professional history. By early in the twentieth century, school history curricula, textbooks, and instruction all felt the influence of the work of the AHA's Committee of Seven, organized in 1896, whose members brought about a significant strengthening of history programs and curricula in the schools after the issuance of their report in 1899. In addition to urging on high schools a sequence of courses beginning with ancient history and culminating in American history and government, these reformers advocated many of the attributes of historic instruction that we take as normative, if too rarely practiced in the schools, today: the accumulation of knowledge, the use of original source materials, the application of critical analysis to these sources as well as to secondary writings, and the stimulation of students' imagination in place of the memorization of disconnected facts. Until the faux-Deweyites and "educationists," marching behind the heralds of vocationalism and "democracy" and attacking this AHA-backed reformed way of teaching history as elitist, academic, and bookish, gained control of the schools by the 1930s, professional historians could take satisfaction in having ushered in a period, although all too brief, in which academic historians and schoolteachers shared a capacious vision and created an effective program for history in the schools.[15]

While all of these developments can be read as elements in the professionalization of history in general, which surely they were, they should

---

[15] A useful brief history of these developments is Diane Ravitch, "History's Struggle to Survive in the Schools," *OAH Magazine of History* 21 (April 2007): 28–32. For a sketch of the OAH's similar history of wavering involvement in the schools, see Ron Briley, "The MVHA and Teaching: A Strained Relationship," in Richard S. Kirkendall (ed.), *The Organization of American Historians and the Writing and Teaching of American History* (New York: Oxford University Press, 2011), 267–274. On history education itself and historians' halting engagement with it, see Robert Orrill and Linn Shapiro, "From Bold Beginnings to an Uncertain Future: The Discipline of History and History Education," *American Historical Review* 110 (June 2005): 727–751.

also be seen as evidence of the kindred aims of people both inside and outside the academy and of their ability to work together in the interests of the same discipline and of the students, teachers, and citizens who wished to learn and teach history. Of course, the joint efforts of professional and amateur historians also depended on their agreement that history serve a cultural and social role in promoting civic and moral norms. Only gradually would the discipline shed the heavy weight of these expectations until by the mid-twentieth century it had become more fully an enterprise of intellectual discovery and understanding largely free of civic purpose, with all the attendant costs, as well as benefits, of that transformation.[16]

Two dates stand out as moments when the discipline was set unalterably on its modern professional course into the academy. The first was 1895, when J. Franklin Jameson and other academic historians founded the *American Historical Review* independent of the AHA, succeeded in establishing a Historical Manuscripts Commission within the AHA (with Jameson as its chairman), and successfully engineered a vote to have AHA annual meetings rotate between Washington and other cities. This "revolt" (as it has come to be known) signified the emergence to leadership in the discipline of a new generation of largely, though not wholly, academically trained historians. The second date was 1907, when Jameson became president of the AHA and when the Mississippi Valley Historical Association (MVHA) (now known as the Organization of American Historians [OAH]) came into being. Although the full significance of this date was not recognized until later, Jameson's presidency made clear that from then on, while excluding neither amateur nor nonacademic historians, the AHA would be firmly under the control of professional academic historians, of whom Jameson was himself one of the earliest exemplars in the United States and already the leading statesman – even though he spent decades outside academic walls.[17] The founding of the MVHA gave professional historians in the United States their first institution devoted exclusively to the nation's history. Equally significant, the association's founding was largely the doing of midwestern state historical society directors, not of academic professors, and the association retained close associations with nonacademic historians considerably longer than did the AHA. If the MVHA's founders quickly indicated their desire to associate their organization with the AHA's professors, they also served notice

---

[16] As with so many other dimensions of the discipline, the relationships between amateur and professional historians deserve more study than they have received.

[17] See Chapter 5 for more on the significance of Jameson's fateful career.

that they would not sit idly by and surrender all institutional influence over history's development either to eastern professors or to academics alone.[18]

One can of course make too much of these developments. Without question, Jameson and the others involved in creating greater professional focus for the AHA were trying to give additional content to the AHA's charter mission of "promoting historical studies." Social gatherings masquerading as professional meetings, an insipid annual report taking the place of scholarly articles, and casual talks offering themselves as research scholarship – the leftovers from the AHA's origins – were the targets of the "revolt." And if a scholarly society is defined as being a "disciplined community of inquiry" whose members are driven by agreed-on aims, subjects, and methods, then the reformist leaders of the AHA had surely embarked on the next stage of the discipline's creation by forcing the issue of intellectual authority – the issue of who was to define the qualifications of those who, by training, occupation, and achievement, could assure the public that what they offered as historical knowledge was credible, dependable, and authoritative. Yet the programs of AHA meetings did not soon become noticeably less bland. Nor did historical thought change sharply. Historians, most of them disinclined to take up modernist ways, remained academically and culturally conservative. And the AHA's leaders could try to nationalize only their academic norms, not history's institutions. Although academic professionals now largely directed, or at least gave definition to, the discipline's affairs through its senior organizations and although the definition of "professional historian" increasingly came to mean "academic historian," the creation, organization, and support of historical knowledge remained, as it always

---

[18] Jameson's life and his activities in behalf of history can be followed in Morey Rothberg et al. (eds.), *John Franklin Jameson and the Development of Humanistic Scholarship in America*, 3 vols. (Athens: University of Georgia Press, 1993–2001). Rothberg's introductory essays to the volumes' contents and sections constitute a study of sorts of Jameson. A full biography of the man is sorely needed. But see also Rothberg, "Servant to History: A Study of John Franklin Jameson, 1859–1937" (Ph.D. dissertation, Brown University, 1982), and the biographical sketches and other articles cited in the bibliography in Rothberg et al., *Jameson and the Development of Humanistic Scholarship*, 3:355–377. A study of a contemporary of Jameson, who pursued analogous institution-building ventures, is Louis Leonard Tucker, *Worthington Chauncey Ford: Scholar and Adventurer* (Boston: Northeastern University Press, 2001). On the MVHA, see Ian Tyrrell, "Public at the Creation: Place, Memory, and Historical Practice in the Mississippi Valley Historical Association, 1907–1950," *Journal of American History* 94 (June 2007): 19–46, which offers an introduction to the association's history. A full history of the MVHA/OAH is needed.

has been, decentralized. Furthermore, the professional practitioners of history remained located in many kinds of institutions and involved in many kinds of work, their labors, however, unlike those of their European counterparts, rarely enjoying public patronage.[19]

Yet, while growing institutionally, intellectually history had become stuck in a nineteenth-century understanding of its place in the universe of discourse and understanding, as well as, in fact, become stuck in that century. When the staid, post-Victorian world of the American intellect of which history was a constituent part was eventually challenged after World War I by Freud, Marx, Bloomsbury, Paris, and Greenwich Village, historical thought and scholarship largely escaped their enlivening influences. Instead, a kind of intellectual and methodological consensus enwrapped the discipline, to say nothing of the general uniformity of view stemming from the overwhelming Protestant, male, middle-class origins of its members.[20] Intellectual work remained focused on the nation-state and its political and social institutions, policies, and practices. When social history commenced its emergence in the interwar years, it gained little more than a foothold in most departments. Intellectual history was the history of formal ideas, and little non-Western history was yet pursued. It would not be until after 1945, and not with major impact until the 1960s, that real fissures appeared in the disciplinary and professional domains of historians in the United States.

In its impermeability to fresh intellectual currents, academic history was not unique among the disciplines of the humanities and social sciences. A few areas of intellectual culture, especially literature and criticism, did experience something of a split between their practitioners inside and outside the academy, even if no deep schism appeared within university walls themselves. Not so, however, with most other disciplines in the

---

[19] Haskell, *Emergence of Professional Social Science*, 175–177, 235. One can of course make too much of the bland history that characterized early AHA meetings and publications. After all, Turner's epochal paper on the American frontier was delivered under AHA auspices at a special World Congress of Historians and Historical Students at the 1893 World's Columbian Exposition in Chicago, a mere nine years after the association's founding. But the other papers delivered there have also been characterized as unremarkable. Ray Allen Billington, *Frederick Jackson Turner: Historian, Scholar, Teacher* (New York: Oxford University Press, 1973), 124–131.

[20] On the growing discontinuities between historical thought on the one hand and art and science on the other, discontinuities that the author believes to have had deeply injurious effects on the role of historical knowledge in the human sciences, see Hayden V. White, "The Burden of History," in *Tropics of Discourse: Essays in Cultural Criticism* (Baltimore: Johns Hopkins University Press, 1978), 27–50 (originally published in *History and Theory* 5 [1966]: 111–134).

early decades of the twentieth century, including history, whose academic professionals, still consolidating their work in colleges and universities, remained largely inward looking, their scholarship still highly derivative of older approaches pioneered decades before in Europe. Writers of history outside the academy, themselves similarly conservative, clung to the older narrative and civic traditions of their craft. Rare was the case of historians challenging historians (or challenging the entire discipline, as Charles A. Beard did) the way artists threw down challenges to art and many writers started experimenting with style and form.[21] Within history, homogeneity and comity generally prevailed. In fact, after the successful 1907 protest of Jameson and like-minded historians of his generation against the genteel orthodoxy of the AHA's first three decades, the next principal "revolt" from within – the formation in the late 1930s of the Society of American Historians after the AHA refused to create a popular history magazine – arose not over intellectual issues but over the perceived decline in a public audience for history, a matter seen then, as it often is now, as a question of writing style and flair and entirely within the ability of historians to address and solve.

For the first fifty or so years of the twentieth century, then, the basic trajectory of history, directed principally by academics, was never widely in dispute. While issues of ideology, theory, diversity, curricula, and preparation sometimes troubled historians, no authoritative challenge was mounted to the principal elements of academic work – basic preparation for careers in history in university-based graduate programs, a commitment to the advancement of historical knowledge on the basis of evidence, and adherence to a more-than-hundred-year tradition of

---

[21] The conservatism of the forms in which historical knowledge is presented marks the discipline off sharply from the arts if not from the other intellectual disciplines. But see the new presentational forms and approaches to historical subjects conveyed in the journal *Rethinking History*. A selection of articles from that journal has been collected in Alun Munslow and Robert A. Rosenstone (eds.), *Experiments in Rethinking History* (New York: Routledge, 2004). See also Rosenstone, "Space for the Bird to Fly," in Keith Jenkins, Sue Morgan, and Alun Munslow (eds.), *Manifestos for History* (London: Routledge, 2007), 11–18. Rosenstone has been among the leaders in producing the kind of new history he promotes. See *Mirror in the Shrine: American Encounters with Meiji Japan* (Cambridge, MA: Harvard University Press, 1988) and *The Man Who Swam into History: The (Mostly) True Story of My Jewish Family* (Austin: University of Texas Press, 2005). Among the most unorthodox works along this line, combining first-person reflection, imagination, and large metaphor with history, archaeology, and ethnography, is Greg Dening, *Beach Crossings: Voyaging across Times, Cultures, and Self* (Philadelphia: University of Pennsylvania Press, 2004).

method, approach, and subject matter. Archival research, a mild liberalism of view, and a consensus that topics of political, institutional, and diplomatic history formed the core subjects of historical inquiry constituted the usually uncontested ethos of the discipline. Suggesting the widely shared agreement on the fundamental norms of history work, this ethos also guided the work of historians outside the academy. When disagreements over particular matters or challenges to this ethos arose, they were usually contained within academic walls.

Yet this developmental history of history is only part of the story of the American segment of the discipline's growth. It is normal historiography – an account of history's development serviceable as a general guide to history's pre-1950 history in the United States and as an orientation to the discipline's circumstances before then. But it is not the full story, and its partiality makes it of decreasing use in orienting the discipline, its aspirants, and its more experienced practitioners toward the future when history is going through its most momentous changes in a century.

Unfortunately, that full story of history's history in the United States has not yet been fully told, and its pieces are only slowly being put together. We still lack a comprehensive history of the discipline, principally because, as we are now discovering, so much of it took place, even when it took place at the hands of academics, outside the academy.[22] Recent scholarship, especially that conducted by Ian Tyrrell and Robert B. Townsend, has begun to reveal a much more complex historical reality than normal historiography permits us to see in fact existed. We carry in our minds a history of the discipline today, Tyrrell asserts, "without being more than dimly aware of the precedents and battles fought before, and without awareness of the structural conditions that shaped and are today shaping responses" to current issues. What present debates about the discipline's challenges reveal, he pointedly writes, are their "lack of

---

[22] This is a subject that needs to be addressed more directly than it has been. For example, as Eric Arnesen has reminded me, the activities of such nonacademic scholars and activists as W. E. B. Du Bois and Herbert Aptheker brought to the attention of historians subjects that they had routinely ignored. And the Association for the Study of Negro Life and History laid the foundation for the flowering of black history in the late twentieth century. In addition, many of the controversies regarding history in the schools have long been incubated outside schools, colleges, and universities. See Jonathan Zimmerman, *Whose America? Culture Wars in the Public Schools* (Cambridge, MA: Harvard University Press, 2002).

historical depth" and historians' "amnesia over the intellectual history of their own discipline." For as it turns out, despite having gained an impregnable residence in the academy, history work, even that emanating from the academy, was far more institutionally and occupationally diverse throughout the entire twentieth century than has been recognized.[23]

The fact of the matter is that historians never became so professionalized in the academy and so immured in their particular specialties that they gave up trying to reach beyond academic walls to public audiences and reaching beyond the academy to do so. Put another way, if history was being carried out beyond academic walls, what we now term public history was also being energetically pursued from within them – if not by a large number of historians, at least in important ways. Even in the 1960s and 1970s, fresh assaults on academic history, most of them from the Left, did little more than deflect into other channels what were older, oft-tried endeavors to apply history to perceived public needs. Historians' public engagement might ebb and flow over the decades, but their general aspiration to provide a "usable past" relevant to each era's concerns, to serve many different audiences, and to make historical knowledge directly useful long existed side by side with academic work. In fact, academic history always allowed, even if it did not actively encourage, ventures into other kinds of professional activities, especially those directed at conveying historical knowledge to the general public, influencing governmental, industrial, and commercial policies, and maintaining history's role in the schools.

Throughout the first two-thirds of the twentieth century, as Tyrrell makes clear, those ventures were numerous and varied; all represented what was for their time a capacious definition of the discipline and a

---

[23] Much of what follows is indebted to Ian Tyrrell's revelatory excavations of much "lost" history in *Historians in Public: The Practice of American History, 1890–1970* (Chicago: University of Chicago Press, 2005). The quotations are from pp. 21 and 250. See also John Louis Recchiuti, *Civic Engagement: Social Sciences and Progressive-Era Reform in New York City* (Philadelphia: University of Pennsylvania Press, 2007). Necessarily, I emphasize from Tyrrell's rich and multifaceted work only what is relevant here. It is notable, however, that Tyrrell writes nothing about the involvement of historians, if there were any, in the commercial, financial, and corporate worlds before 1970. This dimension of history work in the first two-thirds of the twentieth century cries out for research. The term "usable past" was exhumed from earlier use by Henry Steele Commager in a 1965 essay and used as the title of his *The Search for a Usable Past and Other Essays in Historiography* (New York: Alfred A. Knopf, 1967). The first to use the term may have been Van Wyck Brooks in *America's Coming-of-Age* (New York: B. W. Huebsch, 1915). See Karal Ann Marling, *Wall-to-Wall America: Post Office Murals in the Great Depression* (Minneapolis: University of Minnesota Press, 1982), 72.

broad optimism about the relevance and pleasures of historical knowledge. For instance, in part to equal the success of popular histories written since the nineteenth century by nonacademics, in 1915 Yale University Press commenced the publication under Allen Johnson's editorship of its fifty-five-volume *Chronicles of America* series, a shelf of books so successful that they were adopted for film. Later, historians wrote and publishers issued such similarly popular series as *The American Pageant*, edited by Ralph Henry Gabriel, and *The Annals of American Sport*, overseen by John Allen Krout. Not content to leave outreach only to the conventional means of books, by the 1930s even the AHA was wading with foundation support and the involvement of many leading scholars into the production of radio programs. The 1937 debut on CBS radio of the AHA's *Story Behind the Headlines* formally committed the discipline to the diffusion of historical knowledge over the air, while other historians independently essayed their own radio productions. Furthermore, well before World War II, historians were involved in the production of historical and documentary films.

In addition, they engaged themselves with the nation's public schools. Here the record is mixed, with most historians bemoaning the state of school history without doing much about it. Yet just as they did in reaching out to the public through popular works of history, radio, and then television, for roughly a century some historians tried, albeit with waning enthusiasm, to improve the history that young people received in their schooling. They did so in part because of, in part in disdain of, those who charged historians with having abandoned history in the schools as leaders, practitioners, and – the most cutting charge – professionals who should know what part of the past to teach to young people and how to teach it.

Yet contrary to such widespread and continuing attacks on them, historians never in fact abandoned the schools. Individually, collectively, and through the AHA they grappled energetically well into the 1940s with the challenges facing history's place in the secondary school curricula, reviewed history texts, offered leadership and advice (increasingly not followed) to the schools and their associated organizations, and maintained representation in many bodies, such as the National Council for the Social Studies, and on many commissions, such as those of the College Entrance Examination Board, whose efforts directly influenced the nation's precollegiate classrooms. The AHA itself subsidized and sponsored publication of the *History Teacher's Magazine* and its many renamed successors, and in the 1950s it created its Service Center for Teachers of History, which

began publishing a still useful series of pamphlets on many historical subjects and fields. Academics, including William H. Cartwright, Richard
Watson, and Thomas A. Bailey, took the lead in developing and offering summer and other institutes to teachers. In fact, there was never a
total interruption in the discipline's engagement with schools. One has
to be impressed with historians' repeated efforts to preserve history's
classroom authority and integrity in the face of the many countervailing
external pressures, especially from within the educational establishment
itself, that were slowly turning schools into social service agencies and
increasingly making of the curriculum a means to reconcile young people
to modern life through "social education."[24]

Furthermore, when historians' influence over teacher training, the history and social studies curriculum, and the contents of textbooks waned,
it did so in part because of robust debates among historians themselves,
dating from before the First World War, over such matters as the geographic areas to be covered and emphasized (the United States, Europe,
or the world?) and the emphases of instruction (a Progressive present-
minded focus, a social studies approach focused around civic knowledge,
or patriotic themes?). Nor was it that, once the discipline as a whole
had more or less given up on the schools, individual historians neglected
elementary and secondary schooling. In fact, John D. Hicks, Charles A.
Beard, Caroline F. Ware, Merle Curti, John Spencer Bassett, Harold U.
Faulkner, and many other leading historians kept active their commitment to history schooling throughout their careers. If these and other
historians from time to time fell out among themselves about schooling, thus mirroring debates that were widespread within the discipline
itself, this could be read as much as evidence of history's vitality as of its
confusions.[25]

Historians' efforts did not of course ensure a happy marriage between
academics and schoolteachers or the academy and the schools. Even
if there was never any formal divorce between the two worlds, their

---

[24] Until we know more about teachers' own responses to historians' efforts and can better
assess their own responsibility for the erosion of history's place in the schools, we should
not too quickly condemn academic historians alone for school history's decline.

[25] Even if that vitality was inapposite to the end in view – gaining a firmer place for well-
taught and informed history in the schools. On these matters, in addition to Tyrrell, see
Orrill and Shapiro, "From Bold Beginnings to an Uncertain Future," and for the larger
context Diane Ravitch, *The Great School Wars: New York City, 1805–1973* (New York:
Basic Books, 1974) and *Left Back: A Century of Failed School Reforms* (New York:
Simon & Schuster, 2000).

relationship gradually weakened. And as in most marital separations, the responsibility for this one was shared by both parties. By the 1920s, the National Education Association, flagship organization of the teaching trades, had already unmoored itself from the academy. And try as historians and the AHA might, the professionalization of teaching, if that it be called, brought with it the professional particularism that ate into whatever identification with ideas and their disciplines teachers earlier had possessed. If we measure history teachers' professional identification with the discipline by membership in the AHA, by the 1940s their number had dropped to no more than three hundred.[26] Not surprisingly, given the withdrawal of teachers from its ranks, the AHA and its now disproportionately academic members themselves stepped back from the schools. The association's Committee on Teaching continued its labors, and individual historians continued to undertake episodic work with the schools and their textbooks. But the discipline as a whole reoriented itself away from primary and secondary education.

Historians' involvement with the federal government, starting before the First World War but given focus and clear applicability after the nation's entry into armed conflict, is more widely known and recognized than the work of their colleagues in the schools and media. J. Franklin Jameson, Frederick Jackson Turner, and James T. Shotwell served on the National Board for Historical Service from its 1917 origins. Shotwell, who subsequently headed the historical division of the American Commission to Negotiate Peace (usually known as the Inquiry), brought to his assistance in offering advice about the war's global settlement such other historians as Charles Homer Haskins, George Louis Beer, Wallace Notestein, Dana C. Munro, and James Truslow Adams. Then during the New Deal, Verne Chatelaine, an academic with a Chicago doctorate who served as chief historian of the National Park Service, hired professional historians to develop federal policies for historic monuments and sites and established a tradition of history in the parks that continues to this day. In this way, hundreds of historians gained experience implementing public policy and interacting with their fellow citizens. Similarly, the Historical Records Survey sponsored by the Works Progress Administration involved countless historians in assays of state and local archives and

---

[26] A figure cited in Tyrrell, *Historians in Public*, 143. That figure should be taken only as a proxy for teachers' commitment to the discipline. One should measure it against teachers' membership figures, if available, for other history organizations. But the fact remains that history teachers' identification of themselves as historians as well as teachers has long been far less than ideal.

related resources, and such leading figures as Robert C. Binkley, Theodore C. Blegen, Solon J. Buck (later archivist of the United States), Milo M. Quaife, and Lester J. Cappon held supervisory roles in survey offices.

The Second World War similarly called hundreds of historians into national service in more than fifty governmental bureaus. Among Europeanists and Americanists, Caroline F. Ware, Shepard B. Clough, Kent Roberts Greenfield, Wesley Frank Craven, Samuel Eliot Morison, Irving Bernstein, and Richard W. Leopold recorded wartime actions and provided historical perspectives in civilian and military branches of government. Other historians, including Carl E. Schorske, Sherman Kent, William L. Langer, H. Stuart Hughes, Franklin Ford, and Walter Dorn, served in the Office of Strategic Services. What distinguished their service after 1941 from that of the historians who had earlier involved themselves in the schools and in film and radio productions was that, while they may have been on leave from their academic homes, for the time of their official service they were paid employees of government under official orders.

Yet off-campus history work of this sort, which inaugurated the acculturation of a large number of historians to work that denied them the full range of freedoms they enjoyed in the academy, did not leave a continuing legacy in the postwar era, just as the outreach efforts of historians in the 1920s and 1930s left only a faint memory to guide their successors. The lively and productive involvement of historians in government service during the war in the end failed to protect them against the termination of their service once the conflict had ended, once attitudes toward government had changed, once academic conditions had altered, and once the discipline itself had moved further in directions no longer consonant with its members' public service. Those who had pioneered in the public service of history thus left little to guide others, and those few historians who before the 1970s served in government did so to little professional notice and with little support or recognition from the discipline as a whole. This augured poorly for the day, should it arrive, that academic positions were not plentiful. It also spoke ill of a discipline that should have been more self-conscious of its own history than it was.

Not that historians' many engagements outside the academy, present almost from the start of the discipline's organization in the decades around 1900, were accidental or foreordained. They were neither. They arose directly from specific circumstances, opportunities, and needs – professional history's origins in belles lettres and civic commitment, many historians' determination to establish links to the larger public, and a

continuing concern about the quality of public policies devoid of historical grounding. Consequently, deep into the twentieth century, sometimes
individually, sometimes in partnership and through their learned societies, historians made room in their professional lives for both broad and
targeted interventions into a wide range of arenas outside college and
university walls. Their failure was in taking their initiatives no further –
in not institutionalizing them in the training of graduate students, in not
making more of what they were undertaking in public, in not working
from the start and consistently with government agencies to retain the services of historians. Unlike those who would inherit their aspirations many
years later, they made little of what they had done when in public service
or acting as historians in public (no doubt because their own and young
historians' employment chances were reasonably favorable); instead they
considered their extra-academic work part of their professional obligations and for that reason unremarkable. Like Molière's *bourgeois gen-
tilhomme*, who spoke prose for forty years without knowing it, these
academic historians practiced what would later become known as public
history without being aware of doing so. Their lack of consciousness cost
the discipline dearly.

Consequently, however much these ventures reveal of the desire of
many twentieth-century academic historians to make historical knowledge relevant and appealing to a broad public, whatever they also reveal
of the capacity of the academy to countenance initiatives of outreach and
the receptivity of managers of various media and officers of government
departments to adapt history to varying formats, from the perspective of
our own day, when public history has taken significant strides forward,
the limitations of most pre-1970 public history endeavors are striking.
They depended on external, usually temporary, funding and interest,
which is always difficult to sustain; and the universities at which most of
these historians taught rarely provided incentives or budgets for their con-
tinuation. Those who expended the greatest amount of time and energy
on them (and often on more than one of them at the same time) did not
succeed in institutionalizing them – indeed, rarely made efforts to do so –
so that their efforts remained episodic and did not endure. They created no programs to train graduate students in the public presentation
of history, nor did their projects answer to the employment needs (say,
in historical societies, government, or business) of young historians who
did not choose to pursue academic careers as more formal public history
programs were to respond to the employment crisis of the later twentieth
century. And except for the distinctive, and comparatively narrow, effort

of Allen Nevins and a few others to provide an outlet for the more publicly and literarily inclined historians to write for the general public, none
of these historians successfully proselytized their colleagues to carry on
and broaden their efforts to reach their fellow citizens with their knowledge. In short, they did not take steps to ensure that their examples would
endure and were unable to prevent the costly interruption in historians'
outreach efforts that commenced by the mid-twentieth century. The discipline of history thus remained for two-thirds of a century a discipline
with almost everything emanating from its academic center. It did not
yet resemble the more decentralized discipline, with different nodes of
innovation, employment, and practice, that it would become by the end
of the twentieth century.

The most troubling part of this story is that people dedicated to
knowing and understanding the past largely forgot a major dimension
of their own professional past and instead had to reinvent their discipline's involvement with their fellow citizens rather than building on earlier achievements.[27] Having forgotten, they could not gain nourishment
from the past or adapt the achievements of one age to another. It was, of
course, to be expected that when the reinvention of public involvement
started to take place in the 1970s, it occurred under circumstances different from those of earlier in the century, and its enduring and often novel
results arose from the particular needs of that later era. But much time
and effort were lost in the reinvention.

But why the intervening amnesia? Why did historians let lapse their
previous efforts to affect public policy, the schools, and public debate, and
why did they forget what they had earlier done? For one thing, the Second
World War disrupted the discipline as it did everything else and, except
for government service, sharply curtailed historians' long engagement
with other professions and occupations. For another, the large number
of discharged military personnel who sought graduate degrees in history
under the GI Bill entered college and graduate school during the early
phases of the prosperous, classic era of the research ideal, and the training of graduate students in all disciplines now gave priority to research
over teaching and outreach. These older students also matriculated for
graduate education at a time when the reputation of the natural and
physical sciences had reached heights never before known and when the
norms of science had permeated most corners of the intellectual world.
This new emphasis on objectivity, rigor, and reason as the standards of
empirical and theoretical research in all disciplines pushed ideological,

---

[27] I take up that process of reinvention and its consequences in Chapter 5.

artistic, and belletristic – that is, humanistic – norms and aspirations toward the margins. Research now, more than ever before, heavily outweighed teaching and service in the mission of a larger proportion of colleges and universities. The criteria for promotion and tenure followed suit. After 1945, graduate school matriculants, many of them veterans and somewhat older than normal, were in no mood or position to delay pursuit of their doctorates, and they carried their commitment to research above all else forward into their mature careers. To this list should be added the relative inattention given in graduate programs to the discipline's history, structure, and operations in favor of historiography – the study of the history of particular subjects and themes. All of this suggests the weight that academic professional culture and practices exerted over the discipline's other needs.

This state of affairs could last only if nothing jarred it or called it into question. And that shift in orientation was likely to happen only when the postwar generation of historians had significantly passed midcareer and when a younger generation of aspiring historians had entered the scene in the midst of war and the women's and civil rights movements while recognizing the utility of historians' involvement in public debate and public life. Yet it was only when young historians' employment opportunities shrank sharply in the 1970s that there emerged the need, in addition to the circumstances, to find new uses for historians' knowledge and skills. By then, however, most senior faculty members had had little experience, save for wartime service, in professional outreach, and few of them considered passing on that experience to others. Younger historians would be more or less on their own in reinventing their public roles.

Regret about the discipline's lapse of memory and purpose should not be taken as a wholesale condemnation of it or of the research universities at which historians are prepared. Throughout the era in which history was withdrawing from public engagement, it was also in other ways greatly strengthening itself, and the two processes were not unrelated. During the postwar decades, the ongoing intellectual work of the discipline – its research-based discoveries, the emergence of new subject fields, the development of fresh interpretive schemes, and the training of aspiring historians – was never at issue. Criticized the discipline might be for overspecialization, ideological homogeneity, and the poor writing of its practitioners, but no one could dispute the fecundity of historical thinking, the growing complexity of historical argumentation, the high plateau of monographic and interpretive scholarship, and the availability of outlets for publication, presentation, and debate. New history research centers came into being, as did new ongoing research seminars and cross-disciplinary projects that led to extraordinary gains in knowledge of the past. Greatly increased understanding, mastery, and application of the technical and theoretical foundations of the discipline were the happy result.

That result, however, exacted a cost. Such was the uniformity of view among historians, especially among those in the academy who enjoyed the greatest security and preferment, that well into the 1960s one could prepare to be a historian without being exposed (except in a rare university department or in the classrooms of an unusual historian) to any major alternatives to reigning intellectual orthodoxies or to major alternatives to an academic career. Universities did not see themselves as the homes of diverse, even clashing, intellectual cultures but instead as the residence of knowledge and thinking that, while open to challenge and correction, had stood the test of time. Aspiring historians were expected to join in this kind of intellectual work and prepare themselves to be academics like their professors, and most did so. This intellectual and professional imprinting, in which young historians modeled themselves after their senior professors who welcomed the tribute almost as a matter of nature, was never at issue. Yet this rather undifferentiated academic culture, the expectations it fostered, and the ideological and disciplinary cohesion it represented probably could not have lasted much beyond the mid-1960s. In the event, it did not. By 1970, the force and progress of new intellectual winds and professional realities were undeniable and, as it turned out, irresistible. In fact, it is difficult now to imagine the convulsive changes within history in the late decades of the twentieth century not taking place, given how comparatively placid were the roughly two decades of American intellectual and university culture after 1945.[28]

Since 1970, that culture – its institutions, disciplines, and practitioners – and the careers that can grow from the pursuit and application of knowledge have diversified to a degree unparalleled previously.[29] No

---

[28] See Thomas Bender, "Politics, Intellect, and the American University, 1945–1995," in Bender and Carl E. Schorske (eds.), *American Academic Culture in Transformation: Fifty Years, Four Disciplines* (Princeton: Princeton University Press, 1997), 17–54, and Louis Menand, "College: The End of the Golden Era," *New York Review of Books*, October 18, 2001, 44–47, a fuller version of which is "The Marketplace of Ideas," *ACLS Occasional Paper*, no. 49 (2001).

[29] I say this in the face of the alternative argument of Louis Menand and Henry Louis Gates, Jr., *The Marketplace of Ideas: Reform and Resistance in the American University* (New York: Norton, 2010). My point here concerns not curricular and ideological conformity and rigor mortis but rather the topics, types of work, venues, and practitioners of history.

longer can we relate history's history in linear fashion – as if all of its practitioners had a single goal in mind, as if understanding proceeded in a teleological and unidirectional manner, and as if the fruits of research and teaching were foreordained – in the past as well as now. In the twenty-first century, we live in a more diverse intellectual universe. Politics, theory, and belles lettres have entered historical discourse in new ways. Thanks to the work of Clifford Geertz, Thomas Kuhn, Hayden White, and French and German theorists, much of it starting to make its influence felt in the 1960s, interpretation, relativism, challenges to disinterestedness, perspective, context, contingency, diversity, and concerns for the relevance of knowledge are now the common currency of historical research and debate.[30] The discipline, whose contents, methods, and approaches seemed so firm throughout the quarter century after 1945, now has spongy boundaries and houses subjects and discourses unimaginable forty years ago.

The consequences of this diversity for knowledge and for careers in history are not yet fully apparent. Practiced in so many professions, for so many purposes, in so many kinds of places, and by so many kinds of minds, history may permanently have lost its previous protection against changes in intellectual fashion, ideology, and method. But then its range is now so large and its practitioners so far-flung and diverse that it can continue to welcome and gain from all kinds of approaches, interests, and temperaments while maintaining its general perimeters, conventions, and standards. Surely the discipline of history has become capacious enough to beckon all its practitioners, more than it used to, to be true to their various interests, concerns, and gifts.

---

[30] This literature is now enormous. But see, for example, Hayden V. White, *Metahistory: The Historical Imagination in Nineteenth-Century Europe* (Baltimore: Johns Hopkins University Press, 1973) and *The Content of the Form: Narrative Discourse and Historical Representation* (Baltimore: Johns Hopkins University Press, 1987).

2

The Structure of the Discipline of History

Like much else in the world, the discipline of history has taken the sed-
imented form of the times in which its major institutions and practices
came into being. How it functions now is the result not of decisions made
yesterday but of long-ago events, decisions, and actions whose full significance could not be foreseen and whose layered consequences continue
to be many and diverse. We live with those consequences in the structure
and ways of a discipline grown increasingly complex. Yet while historians are likely to function best and to make choices consonant with their
interests and skills when they understand the discipline's organization in
relation to the sequence of its development and when they can locate
themselves in its present configuration, there exists not even an introduction to the structure of history in the United States. I know of no work
that explores how the discipline is shaped, why it came to have the organizational structure it does, what problems arise from its current form,
and what might be done about them. As a result, historians typically enter
on their careers without understanding how the discipline's institutional
structure affects their ways and with a kind of easy acceptance of the
discipline's given shape and practices. When they then gradually accu-
mulate an understanding of their particular worlds of work and develop
critical postures toward them, they often do so without seeing the discipline whole or engaging themselves with its totality. This chapter tries to
present an outline of that whole discipline, especially of its institutional
structure and operations. But because it is the first such attempt, and
an attempt made in the absence of a substantial literature, it is a sketch
only, intended more as an orientation to its subject rather than as a full
exploration of it.

It would be easy enough to assume that the institutional origins of history in the United States were to be found in the colonial colleges. But that assumption would be wrong. Well into the nineteenth century the early colleges' curricula, which were centered on philosophy, classical languages, and mathematics and almost entirely prescribed, made no room, except for some ancient history and exemplary lessons drawn from the past, for history as an independent subject. History was taken principally to be moral philosophy teaching by example (moral philosophy being roughly what we know today as ethics) and a literary art instrumental in teaching rhetoric and oratory. Although by 1830 some direct history instruction had been introduced into the course of study, in 1881 only eleven men held history professorships in the nation's growing number of colleges and universities.[1] Baccalaureate colleges long remained, in institutional terms, rudimentary, and they contained no departments of history or of any other subjects. No men holding themselves out as professional historians peopled college and university faculties, although the first hint of what lay ahead came with Jared Sparks's appointment in 1838 as McLean Professor of Ancient and Modern History in Harvard College.

To the degree that historical study was institutionalized at all by the middle of the nineteenth century, that study found its principal lodging place in state, county, and local historical societies. Although the germ of the independent discipline of history in the United States is usually dated to the founding of the American Social Science Association (ASSA) in 1865, the discipline's institutional origins are more accurately found in the historical societies created decades earlier when history was not even an organized subject of inquiry, much less a discipline. The Massachusetts Historical Society, founded in 1791 through Jeremy Belknap's initiative, was the first of these societies, the New-York Historical Society under John Pintard and the American Antiquarian Society under Isaiah Thomas its successors in 1804 and 1812 respectively. While it is customary in the context of their now greatly expanded collections and professionalism to dwell on the limitations of these institutions in their

---

[1] The standard history of the collegiate curriculum since the colonial founding of American colleges is Frederick Rudolph, *Curriculum: A History of the American Undergraduate Course of Study since 1636* (San Francisco: Jossey-Bass, 1977). The figure for history professors is from p. 177. See also Julie A. Reuben, "Going National: American History Instruction in Colleges and Universities," *OAH Magazine of History* 21 (April 2007): 33–38. A full history of the subject of history in the college and university curriculum is very much needed.

early decades – their filiopietistic orientation, their focus on local elites, and their restricted, male memberships – they and those founded in subsequent decades housed the earliest, formal collections of manuscripts, books, and other printed materials in the United States (some of them now among the largest in the nation and world) devoted expressly, though not exclusively, to the historical past. They also ventured on the earliest programs of publications devoted to that past. It is difficult to imagine our knowledge of the first 250 years of American history being what it is today without these institutions' collections and the efforts of the men of learning and vision who founded them.[2] Equally important, history's initial location in these societies, as well as in the genealogical associations being founded by the mid-nineteenth century (the first being the New England Historic Genealogical Society, established in 1845), marked history in the United States with two characteristics it has never lost.

First, the early historical societies gave history a substantial antiquarian and hereditary cast, for these institutions served the purpose, as they continue in some measure to do, of maintaining the historical consciousness of the elites who founded them and preserving the records of the existence and achievements of the nation's highest governing and social strata. This reflection of original elite values remains cast into the core of historical studies in the United States even when, as in the case of such venerable institutions as the New-York Historical Society and the Historical Society of Pennsylvania, these societies have taken on the additional roles of museums and have become sites for generous and effective historical programming of all kinds for students, scholars, and members of the general public in a more open and democratic culture. In addition, while it would be incorrect to say that in these societies can be found the roots of what today we know as public history, their founders and members' families were exhibiting by the patronage of their earliest collections and publications a strong regard for historical memory and a powerful interest in organizing community identity, even if their interests were those of the gentry of which they were members. If such historical consciousness no longer holds the field unchallenged, it remains the case that a large proportion of Americans who think of history at all associates it with research into the bloodlines of families, the preservation of the records of great men and women, and the celebration of locales and communities

---

[2] The standard work is Walter Muir Whitehill, *Independent Historical Societies* (Boston: Boston Athenaeum, 1962), a stylish, implicitly celebratory, now increasingly outdated, but nonetheless invaluable and exhaustive source of information about these institutions.

of descent rather than with the search for analytical understanding of the past.[3]

In the second place, along with the early school and college curricula in which lessons from the past were embodied, the societies' collections and their patrons strengthened in Americans' historical consciousness an enduring nationalistic, regional, and moralistic coloration. The societies' emphasis on the nation's origins and their assumption of each state's and region's exceptionalism is scarcely surprising, any more than that the collections of historical societies were created and mined to establish the attainments of the talented and public-spirited men who had founded them with the same zeal in which their kind helped lead the early nation. But not until the twentieth century would these venerable themes of national and regional distinctiveness and the heroism of the nation's founders be subjected to sustained criticism, and then thanks little to the societies' members and leaders themselves. These institutions instead helped place strong and lasting historical shoring beneath regional and sectional identities and, in so doing, contributed both to the nation's division in the nineteenth century and to the regional loyalties still woven into the fabric of Americans' historical consciousness.

Regional differences themselves eventually distinguished some historical societies from others. The great figure in setting many societies, especially those founded west of the original seaboard states, on a fresh course was Lyman C. Draper of the State Historical Society of Wisconsin, founded in 1846 and the first such institution to receive state financing. This society and the others founded in its train were purposefully established to be public institutions that received government appropriations, and they were often affiliated with state universities. Some of them, like that of Wisconsin, saw their collections surpass most others in size and scope. This last feature assured them the later attention of academic historians and their students and gradually drew to the societies' collections people whose scholarship led American historiography away from its eastern orientation and toward a more national and inclusive perspective.

All of these societies together, those as different as the Massachusetts Historical Society and the State Historical Society of Wisconsin, helped establish the American circumstances by which history would become

---

[3] I borrow the term "communities of descent" from David A. Hollinger. See "Amalgamation and Hypodescent: The Question of Ethnoracial Mixture in the History of the United States," *American Historical Review* 108 (December 2003): 1363–1390.

an organized realm of knowledge. To be sure, European intellectual culture was itself developing in that direction for reasons often distinct from American conditions and would no doubt have led American men of letters, in the absence of any historical societies, to create an organized, more national discipline on their own. Nevertheless, the diffusion and deepening of formal historical knowledge and practice were surely aided by the gradually spreading influence of the societies and the increase in their collections. It would take the emergence of university departments (themselves reflective of the increasing definition of specific areas of knowledge and inquiry), changes in the collegiate curriculum, and the rise of the research ideal in American universities to push the institutionalization of history into its next phase.[4]

That phase was not completed all at once. Separate university departments devoted to distinct subjects of study came into being only in the post–Civil War decades and developed slowly – the first appearing at Harvard, then at Cornell and Johns Hopkins, and gradually elsewhere. Cornell established the first department of history in the United States in 1881, although Harvard claims its own in 1839.[5] These departments, plus a growth in land-grant institutions, a steady rise in collegiate enrollments, the emergence of the elective system, and the accompanying development

[4] Omitted from this history are museums. As Steven Conn, *Museums and American Intellectual Life, 1876–1926* (Chicago: University of Chicago Press, 1998), argues, an older object-based historical epistemology lodged in museums and characteristic of the historical house movement and the collection of material sources was overtaken and replaced by a Continental university-based academic system that effectively laid claim to being the principal site of the production of new knowledge. When the discipline of history emerged, it did so within institutions given over to an emphasis on books and written sources rather than within those that stressed visual and built products of human agency. This is not to say that museums continue to play a secondary role in the creation of historical knowledge and understanding. In fact, some of the greatest advances in historical understanding now originate in the study of material culture and art; and the broadening of historical subjects now studied, changes in the preparation of historians, and the utilization of new methods available in new media will surely accelerate the growth in museums' roles and the use of artifacts in historical research and teaching.

[5] Rudolph, *Curriculum*, 125–126, 144. There exists considerable confusion in the sources about the dates of the earliest academic departments. Laurence R. Veysey, *Emergence of the American University* (Chicago: University of Chicago Press, 1965), 320–321, has the earliest departments in existence by 1880. Rudolph notes the existence of departments at Harvard in 1872. The Harvard department's claim of a much earlier date (connected no doubt to Sparks's appointment as the university's first professor of history) is contained on its Web site. But does the appointment of a single history professor mark the establishment of a department as an institution?

of the capstone undergraduate subject major laid the groundwork for the creation of ever more teaching positions and professorships, which, a half century later, had become the bedrock of the discipline of history as they had of all disciplines.

Academic departments of history did not inevitably take on the centrality they now possess. They did so because of the near monopoly over the training of professional historians they gained after their emergence, as well as their almost total independence from external influence. Once they securely gained that monopoly (no later than the first three decades of the twentieth century), they never lost it and hold it to this day. Which is not to say that they rule their professional world unobstructed or unchecked: visiting committees can suggest alterations to a history faculty's undergraduate curriculum or its approaches to graduate instruction; university promotion and tenure committees can refuse to approve a department's nominees for permanent professorships; and, in the absence of strong departmental leadership and solid collegiality, an institution's central administration can even put a department in a receivership of sorts to return it to institutional and intellectual health. But on the whole departments are free to structure and implement their programs with little interference from outside. Their independence is of lasting consequence not just to their members but also to their students. For when postcollegians decide to become historians – professionals who will seek salaried employment as historians (rather than, say, as journalists or writers) – they necessarily make themselves dependent on a particular subset of historians, academics senior to themselves, who alone are authorized by public authority and alone legitimated by other historians to grant doctoral degrees. The resulting dependency of these graduate students on their professors, who inculcate their students with the standards, ethos, knowledge, and skills of the academic dimensions of historical scholarship, and until recently with those alone, has had lasting consequences for the discipline.

Rarely acknowledged is what normally happens to aspiring historians as a result of this required immersion in academic norms in academic settings in circumstances of dependency: it brings with it an early and thoroughgoing acculturation to an academic career – a particular occupational track – as distinct from a career as a professional historian – an encompassing category that embodies many occupational paths. However much a department may try to introduce its graduate students to the varieties, public as well as academic, of history work, the ideal of what a historian should be is quickly set in place. As much as the realities of the discipline of history have changed and broadened in recent years, that ideal is what is presented to students from the first moment of their studies: the research-oriented professor who lectures, leads seminars, and guides dissertation research and writing. "This is what historians do," is the un-uttered message of the professor's stance. "This is what a true historian is, not someone who is committed to study of the past and diffusion of knowledge about it in any number of ways and settings, but someone like me – a professor of history with tenure." Rare are the historians who, after having completed their graduate education, do not ever afterward adjust their work and calibrate their estimation of themselves to this ideal – that of those who teach them in graduate school. Psychological adaptation to the ideal is almost inescapable, and those who do not adapt to it often carry the mark of having somehow abandoned the only true aspiration for a historian throughout their careers. One's *Doktorvater* or *Doktormutter* is always the ghost at later banquets.[6]

This rapid and permeating acculturation process – usually unremarked and, though gradual, also probably ineluctable – may be said to be the principal socializing consequence of the departmental location of graduate education in history. The department is both the site of origin of what are taken to be the principal aims and achievements of historians and the negative reference point against which so much criticism, from both within the academy and without, is directed. Just because this kind of professional preparation has been located in academic departments since the emergence of research universities does not mean that a monopoly of preparation must always remain there. Yet it would be difficult to find reason to remove graduate education from university departments or to create institutions that would join departments in that responsibility, and none is likely to emerge. The university history department, the home of history's principal scholars and the seat of its intellectual power, is likely to remain well into the future the institutional center of gravity of the entire discipline. Any alterations in the discipline's practices and arrangements must therefore be sought within university departments.

---

[6] I write this with due regard for the fact that not all history departments inculcate the research and professorial ideal to the same extent. Fortunately, a variety of institutions and departments cover the American landscape. Nevertheless, the central tendency of post-1950 developments in the preparation of historians has been in the direction of greater emphasis upon the professorial ideal; only in the past quarter century has that tendency diminished somewhat and a greater recognition of the diversity of historical pursuits made itself felt in Ph.D.-granting institutions.

Historically, that has proved about as easy as making the United States Senate once again into a deliberative body.

Because the history department is the *locus classicus* of history's major modern intellectual developments and because it monopolizes the formal preparation of historians, most historians assume that any hope of changing the discipline's ways and assumptions must reside there. Yet those hopes, frequently expressed in reports and proposals emanating from the American Historical Association (AHA) and Organization of American Historians (OAH), have proved to be misplaced, just as the assumption that scholarly associations deeply affect faculty and academic life does not stand up to scrutiny. Most of the discipline's significant changes in recent years – the entire public history profession, the production of historical films, initiatives to apply history to public affairs, and the use by historians of new electronic media being only four examples – have developed entrepreneurially and without appreciable professional reward inside departments of history.[7] And despite the urgings of the major professional associations, changes in the ways departments prepare aspiring historians have been glacial. Yet the sharp, and possibly permanent, darkening of the academic employment prospects of aspiring historians is likely to bring increasing pressure upon departments to change their graduate programs.

A telltale sign of the difficulties involved in altering departmental ways is the fate of the most recent AHA report on graduate education.[8] That report, the result of months of deliberation by a specially appointed committee of AHA members, recommended that university history departments significantly alter the education of their graduate students, especially to prepare them to be skilled classroom instructors and knowledgeable and trained public historians. The report, backed by the AHA's authority, thus represented the discipline's considered views that

---

[7] The principal exception to the withholding of professional reward for innovations in new media is the Center for History and New Media within the department of history at George Mason University. There may be others. Their number is likely to grow.

[8] Published as Thomas Bender et al., *The Education of Historians for the Twenty-First Century* (Urbana: University of Illinois Press, 2004). As significant as is this volume, I believe it deficient in not being broad enough in its conception of the ideal contents of a preparation for a career in history, which would include many of the matters taken up in this book. The same limitations mark Thomas Bender, "Expanding the Domain of History"; Joyce Appleby, "Historians, the Historical Forces They Have Fostered, and the Doctorate in History"; and William Cronon, "Getting Ready to Do History," all in Chris Golde, George E. Walker, et al., *Envisioning the Future of Doctoral Education* (San Francisco: Jossey-Bass, 2006), 295–310, 311–326, and 327–349.

graduate training should be updated to reflect the current realities of historians' responsibilities as teachers and citizens as well as scholars. It made its case by urging university departments to prepare every student to be a capable teacher and a historian able to apply historical knowledge to matters outside the academy – that is, to make an emphasis on teaching and public outreach as important a part of graduate education as the traditional emphasis on research and published scholarship. The AHA followed up the report's issuance with workshops for departmental chairs. But only a few of the nation's major history departments have followed the report's recommendations. Those of the report's two senior authors, Princeton and New York University, as of this writing have not. That they have not done so suggests the likelihood that, to the extent that the discipline changes, it will continue to alter itself outside of, and not within, history departments.

Of course, the AHA report itself makes clear that departments by no means monopolize the institutional life of historians or provide to historians the only cues to professional action. The AHA itself, today the largest, as well as oldest, organization of professional historians in the United States and arguably the most important historical organization in the world, is the principal institution that may be said to equal university departments in its influence over the way history is taught and practiced in the United States. In fact, the discipline's growth to maturity during the twentieth century took place principally around these two poles – academic departments of history and the AHA. In the previous chapter, I outlined how the AHA had grown out of the American Social Science Association – or rather had come into being once the limitations of the ASSA had become apparent to the slowly growing cadre of professional historians. The demise of the ASSA symbolized the failed aspirations of those who hoped to link together the nonscience branches of knowledge so as to promote their intellectual and practical utility. One of the consequences of the ASSA's failure was that from then on history, like the other disciplines, would organize itself independently of the others – not however without a slow loss in public usefulness that it did not begin to regain for another seventy-five years.

While the AHA's growth, in both size and authority, was incremental, its immediate advantage over individual departments of history was its convening capacity – its annual meetings and its ability to draw on members to join together, as they have since the AHA's earliest years, to address issues the AHA identified as important to the discipline. These issues related, in the words of the AHA constitution, to "the promotion of historical studies, the collection and preservation of historical manuscripts, and for kindred purposes in the interest of American history and of history in America." The AHA's advantage over other historical institutions was also its catholic membership; no other history association gathered to its ranks historians who studied and taught all subjects of history – subjects that would greatly enlarge their number during the twentieth century. While its authority had to be earned, in another respect, too, the AHA started with a singular advantage – its congressional charter. That warrant, rarely (perhaps too rarely) used, gave it claim to speak, as no other historical institution so legitimately could, for the general interests of history in the United States. Also, because its charter required the AHA to maintain its offices in the nation's capital and originally to submit annual reports to Congress through the secretary of the Smithsonian Institution, the AHA, though an independent organization, began its life with the blessing of the national state.[9]

Perhaps because of its congressional charter, no doubt because of the nature of its membership throughout roughly the first seventy-five years of its existence (largely male, always gentlemanly, and long consistently of one mind about the proper subjects of historical study and about approaches to them), the AHA usually moved and spoke with majestic prudence. That ensured its reports and statements a respectful, often obliging audience, even if they also invited criticism for their caution. When, for instance, starting in the late nineteenth century and continuing well into the next the AHA offered historians' views on the state of history teaching in the schools, its proposals carried enough weight to influence education policy makers in and out of government. Sometimes prudence was the outward manifestation of internal division, as it was when the AHA was gradually withdrawing itself from involvement in the schools. Often, however, prudence was the natural result of the association's governance structure. Because members of its council were elected to staggered terms, frequent turnover on the council prevented the AHA from moving swiftly on any particular matter. Sometimes a council that appointed a committee or commission to review a certain subject was not the same council that received that body's report. The result often could be irrelevance or inaction.

The association's governance structure, combined with its overwhelmingly academic membership, tended also to divert its attention, especially in the middle years of the twentieth century, from issues that were not

---

[9] The AHA now publishes its annual report, still submitted to Congress, on its own.

clearly academic – or at least defined at the time as central to history's enterprise in the United States, which usually amounted to the same thing. It could act only when its members, concerned about a growing issue of importance, pushed the AHA to take steps to address it. For instance, only when sharp internal divisions in 1970 over whether the association should take a formal position on the war in Vietnam became disruptive were steps taken to update the AHA's structure and operations; only after the formation of the National Council on Public History in 1979 did the AHA begin to concern itself with current public history issues. And once historians of a particular subject, like historians of science, formed their own association and drifted away from the AHA, the AHA tended to lose interest in the subject of the new organization, as it did in the history of science. Such developments would prove to be a loss for the AHA, for historians, and for specific subjects of historical inquiry.

Only after a significant restructuring of the association's governance in the early 1970s did issues pertaining to teaching and professional affairs gain coequal status within the AHA with research (if not throughout the discipline) by the creation of three, distinct governance divisions.[10] That restructuring has enabled the association to respond more effectively than it otherwise might have to the growing number and salience of challenges affecting history's increasingly broad and complex interests in the United States and elsewhere. These have included the growth in government regulations and policies regarding public archives, changes in the professional fortunes of aspiring young academics, the emergence of public history as a career line of professional historians, and mounting concerns once again about the quality of history teaching in the schools.

From the start, the AHA published historical scholarship and documents as part of its annual reports. Gradually, however, the *American Historical Review* became the focus of the association's publishing function. Today we naturally associate the *AHR*, as a child to its parent, with the AHA. But that was not always so. The journal, now the most important and comprehensive historical serial in the world and the principal tangible benefit of AHA membership, was not conceived within the

---

[10] I was an instigator of sorts of that restructuring through an AHA review board, appointed by AHA president Joseph R. Strayer and chaired by Hanna Holborn Gray, and was one of its members. The review board's history and report can be followed in James M. Banner, Jr., and S. Frederick Starr, "Proposals for the Reform of the American Historical Association," *American Historical Association Newsletter* 8 (November 1970): 12–17; 9 (October 1971): 1ff.; 9 (November 1971): 1ff.; 10 (March 1972): front matter; 10 (November 1972): 2–44; and 11 (November 1973): 1–37.

AHA's womb. Its founders – academics Albert Bushnell Hart and George Burton Adams – created the journal on their own and, with the assistance of its first managing editor, J. Franklin Jameson, embodied in it from the start the severe academic cast and standards that it has possessed ever since. Only slowly, largely because of its financial difficulties, did the *AHR* fall under the auspices of the AHA, which, after years of increasing subvention, gained ownership of the publication in 1915. That development, as much as anything else, signaled the AHA's own transition into a fully professionalized, largely academic organization, and from then on the AHA and its flagship publication became twinned in historians' minds as the discipline's most influential American institution and scholarly journal.

The association's comparatively large individual membership – which is now close to fifteen thousand – as well as the quality and authority of the *AHR* brought to the AHA the early support of historians of all research and professional commitments. The AHA's size and the breadth of its members' scholarly interests also tended to insulate the AHA, although never fully, against some of the ideological divisions that often caused more difficulty to other organizations. But the AHA's broad membership also exacted a cost as specialization mounted. A few history organizations – like the Mississippi Valley Historical Association (MVHA) and the History of Science Society – devoted to the pursuit of particular, though broad, subjects had existed before the Second World War. But by the 1960s, the AHA could no longer satisfy the narrowing, increasingly technical and theoretical scholarly interests of historians whose growing numbers mirrored the growth of American higher education in the same years. Most subjects of history, as of other disciplines, now had enough adherents to support specialized organizations. Accordingly, many historians tended to join these subject-specific associations in preference to the AHA, while the AHA itself failed for many years to respond effectively to this threat to its own catholic mission and institutional interests. Thus, while the AHA was able to maintain and slowly expand its programs and responsibilities in the face of disciplinary splintering, it reached the point that, at the opening of the twenty-first century, fewer than a third of the historians practicing professionally in the United States are AHA members.[11]

No doubt the principal cause of the AHA's inability to draw a larger percentage of historians to its ranks has been this spread of

---

[11] I owe this fact to Robert B. Townsend.

specialization.[12] The creation of new organizations has kept pace with
the disintegration of the discipline's original large, nation-based subjects –
Europe, the United States, politics, and diplomacy – into more confined,
more intensively pursued fields of and approaches to history. The AHA
now lists almost 115 organizations among its affiliated societies, a number
that, even so, excludes some organizations. Specialization is also attested
to by the existence of more than four hundred peer-reviewed English-
language history journals throughout the world. Historians are therefore
more likely to join, say, the OAH, the Alcohol and Drugs History Society,
the Urban History Association, the National Council on Public History,
the Society for Romanian Studies, or the Historical Society and to read
those organizations' scholarly and other publications than they are to
join the AHA and read the *AHR*. So while nonmember historians may
attend AHA annual meetings and read the *AHR* in their libraries and thus
gain the benefits of both, many do neither.

Historians who identify themselves disproportionately with their specialties risk cutting themselves off from some of the larger currents of the
discipline and weakening the more comprehensive institutions of it. Yet
all seem to accept the costs. The AHA itself has accommodated to specialization by extending a kind of loose affiliation to most other history
organizations, which can meet under its umbrella during AHA annual
meetings and whose members can thus benefit from the meetings' book
exhibits, employment interviews, scholarly papers, and professional discussions, as well as the corridor talk that is so woven into the fabric of
the discipline. And those who are not members of the AHA can offer
plausible justification for remaining outside its ranks: not every issue of
the *AHR* or every annual meeting of the AHA is of equal interest to
each historian, and no historian, especially a younger one, can escape
the necessary choices regarding the use of limited disposable income and
time. In addition, the AHA itself may have failed to make its best case
for membership and support and to adopt policies that would make joining it more advantageous and necessary than it now is. Nevertheless,
that so small a percentage of historians supports the discipline's major

---

[12] Although I emphasize specialization here, no one can be unmindful of other factors
at work reducing the felt necessity of AHA membership. Historians' economic circumstances always require choosing among competing goods, in this case professional
memberships. Where the AHA alone used to be able to provide subscriptions to the
AHR, that journal can now be accessed through electronic copies of the journal on
the Web and in institutional libraries. And what historians expect and want from their
professional associations has changed over the years.

institution testifies to the weakening of the original cosmopolitanism of their discipline.

Not surprisingly, many of the organizations that symbolize the gradual fragmentation of historical interest have achieved considerable influence themselves. Unquestionably, they have done do so by virtue of their contributions to learning and to professional needs, and any regret about some of the consequences of onrushing specialization must be tempered by recognition of the extraordinary gains in knowledge that specialization and its accompanying institutional diffusion have brought in recent decades. The principal segment organization of historians in the United States has since 1907 been the OAH, which represents the interests of historians of the United States and can be considered with the AHA as one of two major organizational pillars of history in the nation. This is not surprising, inasmuch as roughly 40 percent of all doctorates granted annually in the United States go to historians of the United States; and, measured by discrete field, the largest percentage of undergraduate history courses taught in American colleges and universities concern various aspects of American history.[13] It thus seems natural that the most numerous group of historians in the United States has an organization that represents its subject and those who pursue it and that the OAH has taken on most of the characteristics of the discipline's senior organization, the AHA. The OAH publishes the world's most authoritative journal in American history, the *Journal of American History*, founded in 1914 as the *Mississippi Valley Historical Review*.[14] Like the AHA, it convenes annual meetings, offers a diverse set of benefits to members, manages a wide array of programs for academics, teachers, and public historians, and is active in the defense of history's interests in the United States and throughout the world. Many aspects of its history, such as its gradual withdrawal of attention from the teaching of history in the schools, an early emphasis, then its recent return to this critical matter, and the slow broadening of its range to encompass all subjects of

---

[13] Robert B. Townsend, "Survey Shows Sizable Increases in History Majors and Bachelor's Degrees," *Perspectives* 42 (April 2004): 17–23. Only world history and Western civilization courses come close, and only they surpass American history courses in the size of average enrollments. These figures, the latest, are from 2002.

[14] Lest it seem that the *Review*'s founding was a consequence solely of the development of the MVHA, its founding must also be seen as an artifact of the professionalization of the discipline and the disaggregation of institutions that had been under way since the nineteenth century. The *Catholic Historical Review*, the *Journal of Negro History*, and the *Hispanic American Historical Review* were all founded in roughly the same era – between 1915 and 1917.

American history, parallel similar changes in the AHA. In a like fashion, the OAH's membership, like the AHA's, failed soon after its founding to lend support to public history and the popularization of history, which created a lengthy hiatus in its attention to history's larger public, to which it has now returned.

Yet even though it is difficult to imagine the world of history in the United States without the OAH, it is worth wondering whether the OAH's founding could have been avoided and the institutional structure and authority of the discipline left with greater coherence and strength. Evidence suggests not, for regional strains could probably no more be limited in a national organization than they could in a continental nation. After all, the Pacific Coast Branch of the AHA had emerged in 1903 to give historians along the Pacific Coast, for whom travel to the east for AHA council and annual meetings was often impossible, an association of their own; similarly with the independent Southern Historical Association, which the AHA chose, after its experience with the Pacific Coast Branch, not to bring under its umbrella at its founding in 1934. Closer to our own time, in 1961 historians of the American West founded the Western Historical Association at roughly the same time (in 1961) as the Mississippi Valley Historical Association acknowledged its having become the principal organization of Americanists and took on its new name. Regional interests – intellectual, institutional, and professional – were and are not to be given up.[15]

The conventional narrative of the OAH's inception has it that a group of historical society directors, taking umbrage at the AHA's neglect of American history west and south of the Appalachians, founded the Mississippi Valley Historical Association in rectification of northeastern bias.[16]

---

[15] The history of the Pacific Coast Branch of the AHA is laid out in an unpublished paper by Albert L. Hurtado, "Herbert E. Bolton and the Rise of Professional History in the American West," paper presented at the annual meeting of the Western History Association, St. Louis, Missouri, October 11–14, 2006, which the author has generously lent to me. The topic of regionalism within the larger discipline of history remains a subject in need of further exploration, to which Hurtado's paper makes a substantial contribution, as does his *Herbert Eugene Bolton: Historian of the Borderlands* (Berkeley: University of California Press, 2012).

[16] What follows is much in debt to Michael Kammen, "The Mississippi Valley Historical Association, 1907–1952," in Richard S. Kirkendall (ed.), *The Organization of American Historians and the Writing and Teaching of American History* (New York: Oxford University Press, 2011), 17–32. Kammen's is one of a number of essays, all together constituting notes for a full history of the OAH, contained in this work. See also John R. Wunder, "The Founding Years of the OAH," *OAH Newsletter* 34 (November 2006): 1, 6, 8.

Partially valid, that story is more complicated. Surely eastern snobbishness played a role. In such a way as to throw paradoxically into high relief the comparative cosmopolitanism and historiographical breadth of their western colleagues, by 1900 many eastern historians were openly depreciating western history and at least by implication the work of historians in and of the American West like Frederick Jackson Turner and Herbert Eugene Bolton. As a result, acting like an uncomprehending imperial power, the AHA leadership failed for years fully and happily to incorporate western historians, respond to their transmontane concerns, or include noneastern and non-European subjects in the AHA's annual meeting programs (although the AHA acknowledged the problem by allowing the formation of the Pacific Coast Branch of the organization). In addition, the AHA, despite repeated protests from the westerners and while giving the MVHA a place on the AHA annual meeting program for many years, stubbornly kept insisting that the MVHA become a branch of the AHA, subordinate to its governance. The AHA also long resisted shifting its annual meetings even occasionally from the East to accommodate the westerners' situation. Had the AHA adopted greater *suaviter in modo* in place of *fortiter in re*, it is possible that the largest fracture in history's American institutional structure could have been avoided. That it was not avoided has deeply affected the discipline ever since by adding strongly to the institutional fragmentation that has accompanied intellectual specialization.[17]

This specialization of intellectual interest and endeavor, as well as of professional activity and location, was probably bound to lead eventually,

---

[17] This account leaves out the Southern Historical Association, founded, as was its journal, the *Journal of Southern History*, in 1934. (A Southern History Association came into being in 1896 but gained no lease on life.) Like the OAH (and like the Western Historical Association), the SHA commenced its life as a regional association. And while it has remained more of a regional association than the OAH and draws a high proportion of its membership from the American South, it, too, has broadened its reach over time. Its annual meetings, for instance, are broadly inclusive. Regionalism has also deeply inflected the historiography of the United States. A recent study of one dimension of regional distinctions in interpretations of American history is David S. Brown, *Beyond the Frontier: The Midwestern Voice in American Historical Writing* (Chicago: University of Chicago Press, 2009), a study centered on the American history originating in the history department of the University of Wisconsin. Brown's book can also be looked upon as a history, of sorts, of a history department. Other histories of the discipline's great departments are sorely needed. But for a start see William Palmer, *From Gentleman's Club to Professional Body: The Evolution of the History Department in the United States, 1940–1980* (published by the author, 2008). A related work is Palmer, *Engagement with the Past: The Lives and Worlds of the World War II Generation of Historians* (Lexington: University Press of Kentucky, 2001).

even if not in 1907 or originating with American history, to the discipline's eventual institutional splintering, especially as the definition of the discipline became more expansive and the interests of history and historians more complex and far-reaching. For how long were historians to exclude from the roster of history's institutions historic sites like Mount Vernon or the Gettysburg battlefield, living museums like Colonial Williamsburg, presidential libraries, history museums like the Chicago History Museum (formerly the Chicago Historical Society), "subject" museums like the Baseball Hall of Fame, and great research libraries like the Huntington Library? For many years but not, as it turned out, forever. The present strength of the discipline has grown in part from the number and diversity of the institutions that have become integral to it.

That diversity has advanced so far, however, that halting, even if not reversing, the discipline's institutional as well as intellectual fragmentation remains one of the large challenges before all historians. While many of the circumstances, such as the earlier avoidance by eastern historians of historical questions of interest to those west of the Appalachians, that brought about the discipline's earlier institutional fissioning have passed, inertial historical forces work to maintain the discipline's current structure. If benefits come with institutional diversity – such as the vitality of the smaller associations and their ability to draw historians of like interests – so also do costs. Especially in the case of the AHA and OAH, the overlap, sometimes the duplication, of programs and projects create significant financial inefficiencies and heightened costs for both organizations. And the necessity on the part of many historians, especially younger Americanists, to choose membership in only one of these two large organizations causes each to have fewer members than it might. It cannot be expected that the AHA and OAH will merge, but it is noteworthy that the matter has not been a subject of sustained discussion in my professional lifetime. Nor have the benefits and costs of folding back into the AHA some smaller historical organizations been widely considered.

Institutional diversification has reflected more than intellectual specialization. Over decades, the discipline has segmented itself and its members into sectoral as well as subject-specific organizations. Those who define themselves as, say, historians practicing principally in local museums and historical societies can join the American Association for State and Local History (independent of the AHA since 1940), those serving as historians in the federal government can associate themselves with the Society for

History in the Federal Government (founded in 1979), and public historians have their own organization in the National Council for Public History (founded also in 1979). Woman and minority historians have gained support as well as intellectual and professional benefits from their own organizations, like the Coordinating Council for Women in History, the Berkshire Conference of Women Historians, and the Association for the Study of African American Life and History. These groups have helped define the particular professions and interests of their members and have created and sustained their broad professional identities, often in distinction to the heavily intellectual, academic focus of the discipline's older organizations. But in their specific emphases, however justified, these groups, like the AHA and OAH before them, have created a splintering of program and activity that always risks hollowing out the center of the larger discipline. The challenge to them and those who join them is the reverse of the AHA's, which over the past forty years has had to expand its identity beyond its previously largely scholarly focus to incorporate the increased professional and other diversity of its members and their interests. The organizations that attract members by the kind and place of their work now must endeavor more energetically than they do to involve themselves to greater effect in the discipline's core intellectual work and to make contributions to that work commensurate with the knowledge and experience of their members.[18]

The discipline and its many institutions do not exist isolated from the larger intellectual and professional universe of its practitioners. They reside within a complex and populous institutional world, many of whose organizations concern themselves with issues relating to schooling, higher

---

[18] I write this in particular reference to the National Council for Public History. The contents of the *Public Historian*, the journal of the NCPH and in its early years the location of major statements about public history and of that profession's principal early intellectual contributions to history, is a case in point. In recent years, its intellectual contributions to the larger discipline have declined, and one finds in its pages few, if any, debates among public historians. It may be that major contributions in public history that otherwise would have been published in the *Public Historian* are now appearing in other journals (like the *Journal of Policy History*), which would be a good sign even if it reduced the weight of the *Public Historian*'s contents. But if so, those articles concern more academically appreciated subjects and not articles that address directly such matters as the conduct of public history, how public and academic history intersect, the application of historical knowledge to public affairs, and the like. The result is that the journal itself does not now possess the intellectual heft it earlier did. Consequently, it is not read as widely as it otherwise might be.

education, the humanities and social sciences, government, and the public welfare. The two transdisciplinary organizations, both focused on the support of research, most involved in supporting the creation of historical knowledge are the American Council of Learned Societies (ACLS) and the Social Science Research Council (SSRC). The former, founded in 1919, has long involved itself in promoting scholarship in the disciplines of the humanities, bringing together American learned societies for common purposes, and representing and advancing American humanistic scholarship abroad. While many of the projects completed under its auspices – the multivolume *Dictionary of American Biography*, its successor *American National Biography*, and the correspondence of Charles Darwin being among the most notable – have deservedly won it renown, its most significant, steady boon to research is the fellowships it offers to junior and senior research scholars, including many historians.[19]

The ACLS has also long concerned itself with scholarly communications, area studies, and the translation of scholarly works, and it has joined in promoting the use of electronic media for research and the dissemination of scholarship. Most recently, it has ventured into supporting off-campus work by humanists through a program of public fellows. Its most notable institutional achievement was its leadership in the 1960s of the campaign to create the National Endowment for the Humanities (NEH). But while the humanities in the United States would be weaker than they are without the ACLS, one must regret that it has not since its founding appreciably broadened its deliberations and outreach to include individual scholars and teachers. Its annual meetings, open principally to representatives of its constituent societies and to a few invited others,

---

[19] Because it has so little direct impact upon history in the United States and because it is more reflective of current trends than influential in promoting them or historical practices generally, I exclude from consideration here the International Committee of Historical Sciences. The committee is, however, a constituent element of the institutional framework within which historians practice, and it would do no harm to the discipline were its activities more widely known and influential. On its history, see Karl Dietrich Erdmann, *Toward a Global Community of Historians: The International Historical Congresses and the International Committee of Historical Sciences, 1898–2000*, trans. Alan Nothnagle (New York: Berghahn Books, 2005). Because of space limitations, I also exclude from consideration such institutions as the National Humanities Center, the Center for Advanced Study in the Behavioral Sciences, and the Woodrow Wilson International Center for Scholars, academic centers like the Davis Center for Historical Studies at Princeton and the Charles Warren Center for Studies in American History at Harvard, and research libraries like the John Carter Brown Library at Brown and the Huntington Library, each of which offers residential fellowships to historians and thus offers critically important sustenance to historical research.

fail to have any significant or felt influence on the large population of humanities practitioners, which, among other things, attenuates individual historians' sense of being part of the larger world of the humanities.[20] The council publishes little that might keep humanists informed about developments, debates, and forthcoming developments in the humanities generally, although these are often the subjects of its invitation-only annual meetings and of discussions among the operating officers of its constituent groups. And at a time when the National Endowment for the Humanities has reduced its emphasis on academic scholarship and the support of libraries and research institutes and instead increased its funding for public programming and American history, the failure of the ACLS – indeed, of its constituent societies acting together – to reassert its leadership toward restoring balance to NEH programs is a grave disappointment. In short, achieving superbly its chosen missions, the ACLS remains too much a mid-twentieth-century institution in the new conditions of the twenty-first century.[21]

The Social Science Research Council, founded in 1923 shortly after the ACLS, parallels the ACLS in bringing together the disciplines of the social sciences, including history, in pursuit of research on pressing social issues and in pursuit of solutions to them. Over the years, its programs have opened up research on such diverse topics as financial markets, foreign area studies, migration, and technology. The SSRC has carried out its work largely through working groups and conferences of social scientists and by offering fellowships to young and more senior scholars to support their research. Unlike the ACLS, it convenes no annual meeting; but like the ACLS it operates like an insiders' club. Regarding historical studies, the SSRC is notable for having sponsored two classic reports that can be said to have inaugurated history's half-century engagement

---

[20] I do not recall, for instance, ever reading in the newsletters of the AHA and OAH any reports by those two organizations' representatives to the ACLS about the presentations and debates that take place at ACLS annual meetings or within the meetings of its constituent societies' executive directors, even though these issues are often of critical importance to historians. This was the case when I was a member of the ACLS Board of Directors and remains so today. Should anyone wonder about historians' ignorance of the welfare and benefits of this critically important institution if they are told nothing about it?

[21] In the late 1970s and early 1980s, I was involved, as was then ACLS president Robert M. Lumiansky, in an effort to create these and other additional resources for the humanities through the American Association for the Advancement of the Humanities. For a review of that project and its failure, see James M. Banner, Jr., "Organizing the Humanities: AAAH's Vision Ten Years Later," *Change* 21 (March–April 1989): 45–51.

with social science learning.[22] For roughly three decades after World War II, SSRC fellowships supported historians' application of social scientific and statistical methods to historical research. And the broadening of that research and the teaching that accompanied it beyond history's previous focus on the United States and Western Europe was inconceivable without the SSRC's backing of language training and travel and fellowship support for young historians who subsequently became leading scholars of non-Western places and people. Sometime around 1970, however, the affair between history and the social sciences began to wane, and by the end of the twentieth century, with the emergence of social and cultural history to prominence, the influence of theories conceived largely in a humanistic vein, and the emergence of a more critical and political edge in much historical scholarship, history had lodged itself again firmly and thoroughly within the humanities, where it remains today. As a result, the SSRC's work seems less central to historians' concerns than it used to be.

The nature and structure of these two institutions – led by scholars from their constituent disciplines and, in the case of the ACLS, including representation from its member organizations – keep them at a remove from most historians' professional activities. That has its benefits, the principal one being the relative insulation of the ACLS and the SSRC from the variable winds of disciplinary trends, ideology, and immediate professional needs that affect their constituent societies. But it also exacts its costs. Historians have no clear stake in the two organizations' welfare. Aside from those few involved in ACLS and SSRC governance, historians also have little influence over the two organizations' programs or directions. Top-down institutions in an open, democratic intellectual culture, they exist without much support among individual historians and other professionals and thus stand at risk in the event of difficulties in their own affairs. The discipline of history, like all the others, would be stronger were the institutional defects of the ACLS and SSRC remedied.

Of the government institutions that affect history, none has more influence than the National Endowment for the Humanities. A federal agency whose chairman and council members are nominated by the president

---

[22] See *Theory and Practice in Historical Study: A Report of the Committee on Historiography* (New York: Social Science Research Council, 1946), and *The Social Sciences in Historical Study: A Report of the Committee on Historiography* (New York: Social Science Research Council, 1954). A history of the SSRC – Kenton W. Worcester, *Social Science Research Council, 1923–1998* (New York: Social Science Research Council, 2001) – can be found at http://publications.ssrc.org/about_the_ssrc/SSRC_History.pdf.

and confirmed by the U.S. Senate, the NEH has by far the largest budget of any single institution devoted exclusively to the humanities in the United States. Its peer-review process, though often the subject of complaint, exceeds all others in the humanities in its depth, rigor, and quality (except on the few occasions when it has been corrupted by politics). For history and historians alone, its special grant categories, such as those that provide funding for the digitization of newspapers, for summer institutes for school and college teachers, and for the editing and publishing of letterpress editions of the papers of significant historical figures, underwrite endeavors that would not otherwise exist. Its support has, for example, strengthened research institutions and libraries; its funding has inaugurated the publication of the landmark volumes of The Library of America; and its subvention of state humanities programs has greatly influenced the growth of what has become known as the "public humanities." Its positive influence on the humanities and on the discipline of history, except when those who chaired it were captive of ideological camps, has been incalculable.

Yet if the ACLS and SSRC are generally impermeable to historians' influence even though they provide often-critical support to historians' research, the NEH, whose programs more pervasively affect history, is even further beyond swaying. Its professional staff members are keenly aware of intellectual and other developments in the disciplines of the humanities, and they do their best to insulate their grant-making efforts against anything save strictly professional considerations. But their influence over NEH programs is limited by always-threatened congressional intervention into the agency's affairs, especially through the federal budget process, and, since the 1980s, by ideological intrusions into agency decision making. While humanists' fears of political meddling are probably overdrawn, such has been the history of extraprofessional criteria affecting agency decisions, both large and small, that the NEH may never be able to rid itself of the suspicion of political influence, whether from liberal or conservative national administrations and their appointees to NEH governance.

The importance to historians' work of other federal agencies, especially the National Archives and Records Administration, the Smithsonian Institution, and the Library of Congress, equals that of the NEH.[23] All three have vast research collections and distinct programs (like the National

---

[23] These do not by any means exhaust the federal bureaus whose activities are critical to historians. These include, for instance, the State Department, whose continuing publication of volumes of *The Foreign Relations of the United States* makes important

Historical Publications and Records Commission of the Archives) whose work directly supports historical research. Rare is the historian anywhere in the world who does not use their resources at some point. But with them as with the NEH, historians are beneficiaries and users of their collections rather than professionals who exercise much influence over them or are engaged as staff members in their affairs (except through the few representatives that sit on their advisory councils). The principal means that historians possess to affect them is through the lobbying organizations historians have helped create and that have gained at least modest collective leverage over the budgets and actions of these agencies.

The discipline's modern lobbying efforts grew out of the creation in 1976 of the National Coordinating Committee for the Promotion of History (NCCPH), a creature of a number of history organizations, which focused at its origins on addressing that era's employment crisis and on reaching out to historians outside the academy. Its efforts in those regards were among those leading to the founding of both the Society for History in the Federal Government and the National Council on Public History. When in 1981 historians like others in the humanities were faced with sharp reductions in funding for the NEH, the NCCPH turned its attention more directly to lobbying. It was joined in the same year by the National Humanities Alliance, which provided the disciplines and associations of the humanities, including many historical organizations, with their first general lobbying force in Washington.[24] Since then, the NCCPH, subsequently renamed the National Coalition for History, has grown into an effective, respected lobbying organization, the only discipline-specific lobby in the humanities.[25] Now numbering more than seventy history and archival organizations, the coalition represents

contributions to the history of international relations, as well as the historical offices of most cabinet-level departments and other agencies and of the two houses of Congress.

[24] I have written an account, "The National Humanities Alliance: A Memoir" (1998), of the early years of the alliance. Manuscript in the author's possession and in the files of the alliance.

[25] The coalition characterizes itself as "the voice of the historical and archival professions in Washington, D.C." and, organized as a strictly nonpartisan, educational organization, is not technically a lobbying organization. Nevertheless, its energetic representation of history's interests in Washington and elsewhere entitle it to be considered a lobbying force. On the early history of these efforts, see Arnita A. Jones, "Bookends," *Perspectives on History* 48 (February 2010): 5–6, and Page Putnam Miller and Donald Ritchie, "History's Lobbyist: An Interview with Page Putnam Miller," *Public Historian* 32 (May 2010): 31–50. Miller succeeded Jones as head of the coalition.

the discipline before Congress and executive branch agencies and in the states. Through direct lobbying and the coordination and encouragement of associations' and individual historians' efforts to affect legislation and rule making, its efforts over the years have helped protect funding for the NEH, the National Archives, the National Historical Publications and Records Commission, and other federal agencies concerned with history. Equally important, it has often decisively influenced the federal regulations and procedures that govern such critical matters as the declassification of official records, their availability under Freedom of Information Act rules, and the governance of presidential libraries. While the coalition's activities are relatively unamenable to the influence of individual historians (in large part, again, because the coalition is not an organization of them), every historian in the United States at one time or another benefits from its efforts. All of those efforts have been of vital importance to the discipline, whose general welfare would be gravely compromised without them.

While the conventional stopping place of a review of history's institutions would be with those organizations that support history academically and professionally, such a terminus has never made sense. For just as pre-collegiate teachers of history who participate in the discipline's larger world have every reason to expect themselves to be considered historians, so their institutions – schools – ought to be considered part of history's institutional structure. Yet where to place the nation's schools and their teachers in an institutional genealogy like this one is unclear, and because of that the omission of schools from consideration here might go unnoticed.

Although it took many decades after 1870 for schools and colleges to articulate the roles of each in relationship to the other, those roles never became stable or satisfactory. To create some kind of ordered integration between school preparation and the collegiate arts and sciences course of study, the nation's colleges and universities had to abolish their preparatory departments in deference to public and private high schools and establish admissions requirements (those in American history, at the University of Michigan in 1870, being among the first) that would impel schools to set their own curricular standards. Coincidentally, the growth in the number of high schools, with their emphasis increasingly on useful knowledge instead of the classical curriculum, pressed colleges in their turn to adopt their curricula to developments in secondary schooling.

For all this, few teachers in the schools followed their academic counterparts in joining, as professionals, the community of intellectual discourse that was supplanting the more casual atmosphere of the old-time
colleges and universities and that might under other circumstances have
done so in the schools. College admission requirements may have helped
improve somewhat the content of high school history courses – as the recommendations of the so-called Committee of Ten in 1892, the founding
of the College Entrance Examination Board in 1910, and the inauguration of Advanced Placement tests later also would do. But few schools
of education became the sites of robust intellectual endeavor equal to
their neighboring university departments in the arts and sciences, nor
did mastery of the knowledge of a discipline ever emerge as a principal
requirement for school teaching or a central aspiration of schoolteachers. Consequently, by the eve of World War II the schools and their
faculty members had effectively removed themselves from membership
in the nation's larger intellectual world. Coincidentally, academic historians were turning their backs on their colleagues in the schools in a
self-reinforcing cycle of recrimination and frustration, and history's many
institutions for decades gave up trying to hold teachers, even the most
aspiring and intellectually gifted ones, within their orbits, to say nothing
of their membership. It is for these reasons that, while some teachers of
history have managed to rise above the disappointing intellectual level
of too many of their schools and colleagues and participate actively and
creatively in their discipline, the schools themselves, as institutions, still
cannot easily be considered part of the structure of the disciplines, surely
not that of history. For this reason, too, one of the greatest tests facing
American culture is to find ways to bind the nation's schools to the world
of thought. It would be a new day were schools and their teachers, as well
as more colleges and universities and their faculty members, to adopt that
aspiration as their own.[26]

But because too few schools and teachers make the push to do so, it is
left to particular organizations and programs devoted to that mission to
try to pull teachers and schools along and support those that seek support
while encouraging academic historians to enlarge their own understanding of their responsibilities to history in the schools. The NEH has long
provided funding for summer institutes for teachers. The Gilder Lehrman
Institute of American History is an example of a private organization

---

[26] A review of the changing relationship between school and collegiate curricula is found
in Rudolph, *Curriculum*, chap. 5.

that, along with other activities, offers summer and other programs to teachers of American history. The always provisional Teaching American History program of the Department of Education (as of this writing without current funding), which has involved many academic and off-campus historians, has offered some promise of binding local schools to their neighboring colleges, universities, libraries, and historical societies through multiyear projects. But no organization more consistently tries to enlist teachers in their own professional development than the National Council for History Education (NCHE). Founded in 1990 to implement recommendations of the report of the Bradley Commission on History in Schools and taking upon itself the challenge of bringing historians in schools, colleges, and universities together to confront common problems, the NCHE, an individual membership organization, has from its creation sought through its annual conferences, summer institutes, and other programs to inspire and help develop in teachers, especially those of American and world history, the knowledge and commitments that will lead them to think of themselves as historians. Swimming against powerful contrary tides, the NCHE has become an increasingly influential force in bringing at least some teachers back into more productive contact with the larger discipline and in protecting the interests of history in the classroom.[27]

Unfortunately, that cannot be said of the National Council for the Social Studies (NCSS), which had earlier emerged from the AHA itself. For many decades, rather than being an accessory of the disciplines (history, political science, economics, sociology, and psychology) of which its subject can be composed and rather than making those disciplines partners in its own work, the NCSS has instead disappointed those who hoped that it would commit itself adequately to the intellectual strength of its members and the subjects they teach. After 1945, the NCSS instead came to seem an obstacle to the improvement of history teaching in the schools. As a result, most historians abandoned it. Instead, through the AHA and OAH, in the latter's *OAH Magazine of History*, and in *The History Teacher* published out of the history department of California State University at Long Beach, historians have continued to try to influence

---

[27] The Bradley Commission – named after the foundation that funded it, formed in 1987, and composed of leading historians – assessed the conditions in the nation's schools that impeded sound history instruction and urged reforms in history teaching that would improve that instruction. The commission published its influential recommendations in the 1988 report *Building a History Curriculum: Guidelines for Teaching History in Schools* (Washington, DC: Education Excellence Network, 1988).

the quality of teacher preparation and instruction, extend to committed teachers opportunities to work in collegial harmony toward the improvement of history teaching, and keep individual historians involved with educational issues.[28] Meanwhile, some historians, including members of the NCHE, concerned with the state of history in the schools have taken steps independent of the two principal professional associations to try to reinstate history as a distinct and independent subject in the school curriculum free of the social studies. And all along, individual historians, many of them eager to assist the schools and their history teaching colleagues in them, have created efforts to remedy what they have believed to be defects in teacher preparation, in-service continuing education, and instructional methods.[29]

This does not mean that historians have been blameless for the situation in the schools.[30] In addition to abdicating many of their earlier accepted responsibilities for working with teachers, they have often (but recently less frequently) absented themselves from the roiling public debates over history instruction and from playing a part in their own communities' efforts to improve history instruction. Often, they have let their organizations stand in where their own individual efforts might have made a difference.[31] But it does mean that, since the 1980s, an increasing

[28] For a history of *The History Teacher*, see William Weber, "The Origins of *The History Teacher*: Reforming History Education, 1960–1975" (forthcoming in the *History Teacher*, kindly lent to me in manuscript by the author).

[29] The exemplary institutional efforts in this regard have been the Social Science Credential Program and the Seamless Partnership of the history department of the California State University at Long Beach in league with that city's unified school district. That history department has also served as one of seven sites of the California History/Social Science Project, which offers teacher-led in-service programs year-round. I know of no other such comprehensive and enduring partnership between a history department and school system in the United States. On one project to strengthen history education, see William Weber, "The Amherst Project: Reform of History Education, 1959–1972" (the text of a forthcoming essay generously lent to me in draft by the author).

[30] See Diane Ravitch, "History's Struggle to Survive in the Schools," *OAH Magazine of History* 21 (April 2007): 28–32, and Robert Orrill and Linn Shapiro, "From Bold Beginnings to an Uncertain Future: The Discipline of History and History Education," *American Historical Review* 110 (June 2005): 727–751.

[31] An exemplary instance of historians and teachers, as well as students, intervening in issues immediate to them was the 2010 effort, led by Holly Brewer, to oppose changes in North Carolina's school curriculum that diminish the place of history teaching. See "Real History Reform" at http://realhistoryreform.org/. Historians' individual involvement in the "history wars" and in more recent controversies over history instruction is difficult to assess. Many did and do so, as did and do the organizations of which they are members. One has only to cite the loud protests of the AHA, OAH, and other organizations against the promulgation of new, backward-looking history standards in Texas

number of historians in all educational arenas have been attempting to create among teachers a sense of disciplinary membership and commitment and to focus their efforts on strengthening their own knowledge of history as an independent subject distinct from the Rube Goldberg contraption of indiscriminate components and approaches that social studies has become.

A brief review like this of the discipline's institutional structure can do little more than suggest history's modern organizational complexity. The growth over a century's time in the number of organizations seeing to history's many interests has provided an institutional home – beyond those provided by immediate places of work – to every historian who has sought one. Scarcely any of history's needs now go unmet or its interests unrepresented for lack of an organization devoted to them. Many of these institutions have integrated their work together so that history and historians can speak, if not with a single voice, at least more concertedly and with more authority within the larger culture than was the case a half century ago. And the proliferation of historical associations has given all historians one organization or more in which their own professional interests can be satisfied and their ideas tested and implemented.

In large part because of history's institutional growth, however, much overlap of effort, with a corresponding duplication of activity and expense, now exists. That all historians can find specific institutions to express or represent their individual interests has also resulted in their often taking little interest in organizations, as in subjects, beyond their particular specialties. Institutional proliferation has thus intensified, while it has reflected, the narrowing of historians' professional views and interests. In addition, our era's general inhospitability to institutional thinking and endeavor – in this case deepened by the general, even if now slowing, intellectual turn away from political and institutional, toward social and cultural, history – has sapped from the institutions that exist some of the support and engagement from which they would otherwise benefit.

in 2010 as well as their efforts to reduce the ill effect on history teaching of the federal No Child Left Behind law. On efforts to address the latter challenge, see "Consensus Recommendations for a Well-Rounded Education" at http://www.ascd.org/news-media/Press-Room/News-Releases/Well-Rounded-Consensus-Recommendations.aspx. Unfortunately, there exists no easy way that individual professional historians can track and exchange information about individual efforts, both successful and otherwise, to improve history instruction, standards, and understanding. The best forum for that is the NCHE.

Equally consequential, historians are unlikely to encounter, either during their graduate schooling or later in their careers, any encouragement to involve themselves in institutional work, nor are they offered professional incentives or rewards for doing so. As I also suggest elsewhere in this book, the service ideal on college and university campuses remains confused, and the benefits of being active in professional affairs beyond a particular campus or organization are never great or clear. Until the service ideal is more clearly defined and articulated, it must therefore be left to each historian to determine how to be professionally engaged in the institutions of the discipline.[32]

In the meantime, each historian's entrepreneurial inclinations and sense of professional responsibility will have to determine how history's institutions can be employed and reformed. The opportunities for individual involvement, the frequent need for institutional improvement, and the always-existing need for institutional inventiveness will continue to attract some historians. Others will prefer to let their colleagues govern in their name the institutions that deeply affect their work. Whatever the case, the pursuits of historians in the United States will continue to be shaped by the organizations that historians themselves have built and the ones that they will continue to create.

[32] See Chapter 4.

3

A Multitude of Opportunities

Sites, Forms, Kinds, and Users of History

When people conceive of becoming historians in our era, it is difficult for them to imagine how many types of work a career in history can entail, in how many places it can be pursued, the forms that the results of historical thinking can take, and the number and variety of the audiences desirous of historical knowledge that exist. Moreover, historians in the seedtime of their careers often fail to learn – because they are rarely prepared to see – how the choices that they face are necessarily determined substantially by each other. The kind of history work one undertakes, say as college faculty member or museum curator, affects the freedom of choice of one's intellectual pursuits, just as the audiences to which one seeks to appeal, say film viewers or readers, affect the ways in which the fruits of one's knowledge are presented. While this may go without saying, the preparation of historians in fact rarely takes these interlocking considerations into account even though they all hold freighted consequences for the larger discipline as well as for individual historians.

Without doubt, the principal choice each historian must make is the kind of history work to pursue. Yet despite the significant broadening of professional historical pursuits in the past fifty years and the increased prospect of having one's professional self-respect remain intact outside the academy, the gravitational force of all history preparation continues to draw historians overwhelmingly to careers as academic faculty members. Precisely because of this force, the most searching examination of one's own hopes, talents, and personality ought to go into a choice of profession; becoming an academic should not occur by default. Nevertheless, that most aspiring historians envisage themselves as academics without

much thought should not be surprising. It was around the academic ideal
that professional history first took form in nineteenth-century Germany.
Those who prepare other historians – the knights of the discipline – are
themselves faculty members who serve at the lectern and seminar table
as exemplars, albeit usually of one kind only, of what historians can
do and become. Alternative models of historians – professional knights
errant – are rarely seen in graduate school classrooms, and if, as some
do, nonacademic historians teach graduate courses in universities, when
they do instruct others they serve in the role of what students know and
expect; that is, they serve as faculty members. Thus, after years of time
already spent in classrooms with school and college teachers, in graduate
school young historians' acculturation to their professional careers com-
mences usually unknowingly with the firm imprint of "faculty member"
on their aspirational template. After that, academic work is an ideal difficult to change or erase. The challenge is not that of freeing oneself from
that aspiration but rather of freeing oneself from an automatic response
to it.

In urging that the decision to become an academic be conscious and
not made by default, I mean no derogation of an academic career. On
the contrary: the academy might be stronger than it already is were there
fewer historians who felt that they were academics principally for lack of
earlier preparation for other alternatives. Moreover, at a time when the
number of doctoral recipients in history is once again out of synchrony
with the number of academic positions available, academic careers cannot and will not absorb all available historians.[1] It therefore behooves
individual historians to be resolute in their evaluation of all kinds of
history work and to do so by taking into consideration the fit between
aspiration, temperament, institution, and work.

As for the particular benefits and attractions of an academic life, they
are well known. More so than in most professions even if not totally,
academic historians can pursue their intellectual interests freely as well
as, once tenure is gained, with relative immunity from others' pressure.
While their days are full – of teaching, administrative work, reading,
and research – their schedules are comparatively flexible; and, for many,
summers are available for research and writing. Perhaps in more than in

[1] See Robert B. Townsend, "Feds Report Rising Undergraduates and Declining PhDs in
History," *Perspectives on History* 47 (May 2009): 8–9, and *Digest of Education Statistics,
2003* (Washington, DC: National Center for Education Statistics, 2004), online at http:
nces.ed.gov/programs/digest/do3/list_tables3.asp#c3. As so often, I am indebted to Robert
Townsend for leading me to the data in the *Digest*.

any other profession of history, an academic historian lives in the world of ideas and can spend more time devoted to the pursuit of knowledge than off-campus historians can. At an increasing proportion of American colleges and universities, a historian works among colleagues who are deeply engaged in their subjects; and when they are not in proximity to large and great libraries, they are likely linked electronically to journals and to collections elsewhere. Students, especially undergraduates, provide the satisfactions of the young; at their best they are absorptive, eager, and excited. Graduate students are open in other, more intellectually serious aspects to their teachers' influences; and if they resist or rebel, they often do so in formative ways. An academic life offers a combination of the eremitic and the social; an academic historian can hide away in intellectual solitude or embrace and engage the world – the world as represented by academic institutions, active intellectual conversation and combat, and the additional activities, such as consulting or film making, even "punditry," that academic work often opens to its practitioners.

Yet for all the many satisfactions of an academic career, not all historians, their dispositions and aspirations rightly understood, choose to become academics. For many, the path to tenure, always thistly, proves exhausting and embittering, even when successfully negotiated. With few exceptions, academic historians work independently of each other rather than as members of groups, a mode of endeavor more characteristic of the social, natural, and physical sciences; and for many historians the solitary demands of research and writing are neither attractive nor fulfilling. Some find life with adolescent undergraduates trying and infantilizing. Many colleges especially are located away from urban centers, other academic institutions, and the large libraries and depositories of books and manuscripts so essential to historical research (although this obstacle is diminishing by virtue of the World Wide Web). Increasingly, the isolation of some colleges makes difficult or untenable academic work for those historians whose spouses and companions also work, especially when academics cannot, as they might have forty or fifty years ago when academic positions were plentiful, move from one institution to another in search of a preferred position. The spousal challenge comes up in another way: because fewer academic institutions exist than, say, businesses and because historians cannot easily be sole practitioners of their profession, as can attorneys and accountants, academic historians are more institution-bound than many other people and cannot easily move elsewhere to satisfy the needs or desires of a working partner.

Yet the complications of dual-career relationships have only added a new complexity to the many older challenges of academic careers. As early as the 1920s, historians began to feel immured in out-of-the-way places. The professorial ranks at the large research universities had reached a kind of plateau and been filled, and salary increases had consequently stalled.[2] Many historians began to feel a sense of isolation and, without electronic communications, airline travel, and research support, faced professional conditions far more exacting than today's. In the early twenty-first century by contrast, research opportunities, sources of support, travel and communications, and meetings and research programs have so greatly expanded (even if they are not ideal) that geographic distance no longer entails professional isolation. One has only to look at the geographic and professional diversity of the recipients of research and travel fellowships to know that a quiet revolution in academic opportunities has taken place.

This revolution does not, however, mean that all historians can, or should choose to, pursue academic careers. While every historian will continue to be trained at a research university, not all historians need any longer set their sights on teaching at a university or college or, in fact, on teaching in a history department. Yet to college and graduate students, other opportunities to be historians are often unknown, unseen, and unheralded, obscured in the classroom penumbra of teachers and professors in history departments. Nor do all of these opportunities fall under the rubric of public history. Existing in mounting numbers, they hold increasing promise of yielding benefits of knowledge, practice, and understanding that redound to the benefit of history, historians, and the general public.

Take, for instance, the opportunities within the academy itself but outside four-year college and university history departments.[3] Such is the overidentification of history with those departments that it is difficult for historians to recognize the extent to which history is and can be pursued, and historical knowledge gained and conveyed, by historians located in other parts of institutions of higher education. Historians have long had berths on faculties of law, education, business, religion, and medicine from which they have carried out their scholarship and

[2] Peter Novick, *That Noble Dream: The "Objectivity Question" and the American Historical Profession* (Cambridge: Cambridge University Press, 1988), 169–170.
[3] I have here chosen to single out a few select berths for historians outside history departments. To this list should be added university and special collections librarians and academic program directors. I take up some others in Chapter 5.

enlarged their students' understanding of their professions.[4] Often they enjoy joint appointments in their institutions' history departments and thus have easy access to their history colleagues, and they are free to participate in every aspect of the community of historians. The decided advantage these historians possess over historians in history departments is direct acquaintance through their students and immediate colleagues with practitioners in other professions and thus more widely throughout society. Their influence on others is thus less confined to a single professional population than that of most historians; the opportunities for their participation in legal, medical, and business matters are greater than other historians'; and they can then introduce into their historical studies knowledge from other walks of life more extensive than the more limited practical knowledge of many of their fellow historians. Theirs is often a wider intellectual and professional terrain than that of history department members.

Also now firmly within the academic universe as a result of their remarkable growth since 1950 are the community colleges, whose contributions to education remain too little appreciated and whose historians still must struggle against prejudice born of the days when many community college faculty members did not hold doctoral degrees. But that day is passing, and an increasing number of community colleges are bringing fully trained professional historians into their ranks. In fact, at nearly 50 percent, the proportion of community college historians with Ph.D.s now greatly exceeds the proportion of Ph.D. holders teaching other subjects in those same institutions, among whom only one-quarter hold doctorates. In addition to holding out a warmer welcome for fully trained historians, some community colleges are also encouraging (and also paying tuition for) existing faculty members to get their Ph.D.s, and these institutions are also offering M.A.-level courses to their students in conjunction with "senior" institutions nearby so that their faculty members can escape the taxing demands of repeatedly teaching freshman and remedial courses at their two-year institutions. As they tighten their academic standards, try

---

[4] Among those have been Alfred D. Chandler at the Harvard Business School, Hazel W. Hertzberg at Teachers College, Columbia University, David J. Rothman at Columbia Medical School, William Novak at the Law School of the University of Michigan, Christopher J. Tomlins at the Law School of the University of California at Irvine, and Annette Gordon-Read at Harvard Law School. Many others could be named. A useful discussion of the advantages and challenges of holding a position as historian in professional schools is "Interchange: History in the Professional Schools," *Journal of American History* 92 (September 2005): 553–576.

to accommodate historians with serious scholarly aspirations, and appeal to students (especially older ones) who seek to study with fully trained professionals, community colleges are becoming increasingly attractive to those who wish to pursue research while enjoying the fruits of intense teaching.[5]

Within the boundaries of the college and university world lies also that close cousin of academic history: academic publishing. Historians too frequently overlook the intellectual and other satisfactions of scholarly publishing, whose practitioners are often thought mistakenly to be nothing but handmaidens of their supposedly more intellectually weighty academic colleagues. Little could be further from the truth. Those who seek out and acquire manuscripts for university and other scholarly presses play a key role in the nourishment and creation of knowledge. By knowing as much about intellectual developments in particular fields as academics, they are as surely involved in the world of ideas as college and university faculty members. They identify promising scholars and writers, encourage the writing and completion of scholarly work, help shape scholars' manuscripts as they are being written, select those who evaluate submitted manuscripts, and represent manuscripts for their presses once they have been accepted for publication. In addition to identifying promising work and nurturing scholarly careers, the acquisitions editors of university presses also play a major part in defining new fields and strengthening existing ones. They do so, for instance, by establishing book series on particular subjects, committing their presses to scholarly specialties, and then taking a lead role in finding scholars to undertake research in those areas. No one who has worked among scholarly publishers or published with a scholarly press will be a stranger to the professionalism and knowledge of those who bring scholarly works into being.[6]

It might appear that employment within scholarly presses would exhaust a historian's energy and prohibit active engagement in research and writing. But such has not proved to be the case. Many university and scholarly press editors themselves hold doctorates in history.[7] Numerous

---

[5] See Emily Sohmer Tai, "Teaching History at a Community College," *Perspectives* 42 (February 2004): 31–32, and Tai, "Research and the Classroom: A View from the Community College," *Perspectives* 44 (November 2006): 41–44.

[6] For the United States, we could use a study like that of Leslie Howsam, *Past into Print: The Publishing of History in Britain, 1850–1950* (London: British Library, 2009).

[7] An exhaustive list is of course impossible to construct. But five who come immediately to mind are Lewis Bateman (of Cambridge University Press), Jonathan Brent (formerly of Yale University Press), Robert J. Brugger (of the Johns Hopkins University Press), Aida

are the examples of historians who, as scholarly editors and administrative officers of presses, continue to publish their own historical works. The determination and aspirations of these historians without doubt are key. But so is the particularly appealing and serious atmosphere that is consonant with the production of books. While historians tend to look at books only as the vehicles for their words and knowledge, that is not so for the acquisitions and copy editors, the designers, the sales and marketing specialists, and the printers of books. For the best of them, a book is a tangible object, all of whose parts, not just its contents, are integral to its desired quality. The publication of scholarly and learned books therefore has a concreteness that teaching and research do not. Book publishers and editors aim to produce artifacts, an aim that some historians find more congenial than teaching and undertaking scholarship. Why should they not pursue that aim?[8]

Artifacts – those produced by others and not by themselves – are also the delight and focus of museum historians. Their "students" are viewers, their employers the institutions that house as well as teach about the past. For historians who chafe at being restricted to audiences of young people in classrooms and who seek to influence the understanding of a wider public, the design and preparation of museum exhibits provide satisfactions that no teaching berth can. This is especially so in an era in which museology is undergoing many changes, and the presentation and interpretation of artifacts are being deeply affected by electronic media, reconceptualized, democratized, and opened to diverse interpretations. No less than classrooms, museums are increasingly the sites of spirited debate, and their historical curators are finding themselves engaged in the intellectual world's most significant contests. What used to be staid, ethnocentric, reclusive, and fusty institutions are today among the culture's most open and lively.[9]

No one will fail to notice that all of these locations of history work are formal institutions that employ historians. Given that most historians

---

Donald (of Harvard University Press), and Lynne Withey (director of the University of California Press).

[8] Academic publishing, a distinct branch of publishing, possesses its own journal, *Scholarly Publishing*, in which publishers, editors, and others involved in the preparation of scholarly books present and debate developments in their particular occupation.

[9] Catherine M. Lewis, *The Changing Face of Public History: The Chicago Historical Society and the Transformation of an American Museum* (DeKalb: Northern Illinois Press, 2005), provides not only an illuminating picture of changes in a single museum but a solid idea of the kinds of considerations that go into exhibits and of the sensitive relations between academic historians, museum officers, and curators.

work within an institutional setting, that emphasis is justified. Yet historians can also engage in history work, albeit with considerable difficulty and risk, as independent professionals – as self-employed practitioners of history analogous to many attorneys and psychotherapists. While the paths of independent endeavor are fraught with difficulty, no historian is obliged by the nature of history itself to labor professionally within some organizational structure. Like many crafts, history work is portable and adaptable, even if not easily vendible. Furthermore, unaffiliated history work comes in many forms, each suitable to distinct personalities and aspirations. Frequently, the term "independent scholarship" is summoned to denote the work of historians who have no institutional affiliation, and organizations to encourage and support the work of unaffiliated scholars have sprung up under that name.[10] Yet, more accurately described as independent history work, the opportunities for resourceful historians free of institutions go beyond scholarship to consulting and contract work, although it is usually independent scholars of history who feel most keenly the lack of libraries, colleagues, and students that independence can entail.

What marks off independent historians from others are the grit and risk taking involved and the exchange of easy access to libraries and colleagues for the freedom to work as one wishes and can. Because a small number of well-known independent historians (most of whom consider themselves writers) become people of decently comfortable means because of their successes, it is easy to relegate the circumstances and travails of independent historians to a footnote to the main story of salaried historians. Yet that depiction of the matter is neither warranted nor accurate. Since the 1970s, a sizable proportion of historians thrown on their own devices comprises people who, in better times, would have found secure berths on college and university faculties and within other institutions. Many of them were women just gaining doctoral degrees for whom no suitable academic or other positions, because of both their gender and the economy of the day, were to be found. Their determination to pursue their work without benefit of academic cover and to create institutions of support and sodality to carry them through difficult times was then a matter of great concern to the discipline and of urgency to them. And even if those who were not forced to give up their work in history were

---

[10] The principal such organization is the National Coalition of Independent Scholars, which publishes the *Independent Scholar*. The coalition's Web site (http://www.ncis.org) lists similar organizations throughout the United States.

gradually absorbed within academic and other ranks, their plight, as well as the kinds of careers they pioneered, remains worthy of note.

In fact, still inadequately heralded, these independent historians have found it possible to produce published scholarship through normal publishing channels. They have created scholarly seminars for themselves – most often, not surprisingly, in populous cities where most of them are located. (Those in rural areas or small cities without a core of like-situated historians have had a much more difficult time of it.) They have managed to get themselves onto the programs of the meetings of scholarly associations. The inventiveness of those who wished to be what were just then becoming known as public historians was analogous. They became independent consultants, some of them setting up consulting firms. They wrote the histories of companies and organizations. They formed film companies. In doing so, they created new career paths, parallel to academic ones, which are widely followed today. Not that the ways of independence were easy, for they were not and probably, but for the wealthy, never will be. A few academic historians and their departments responded to the difficulties of independent historians by creating berths for them, frequently as adjunct professors or scholars in residence. But rarely did most academic historians assist these innovative and often struggling colleagues, and too rarely do they do so now. Developing ways to welcome independent historians as participants in academic settings and, conversely, to lead academic historians to learn from independent ones remains the unmet obligation of college and university teachers and scholars of history.

If decisions about the kinds of history work to pursue and where to pursue it are critically important, so are related decisions about the audiences to which historians can offer their knowledge. The academic conventions that have long embodied the assumption that the only legitimate audience for historical scholarship is one's academic peers – not the "generally informed citizens" who seek new knowledge and historical guidance through books and magazine articles, not those (like history "buffs") who possess a passionate interest in some part of the past and thirst for knowledge of their beloved subjects, not government or corporate officials who may need to use historical knowledge for policy purposes – are no longer workable. Larger, more diversified, and more discriminating audiences make that clear. Yet despite the severe limitations and costs of the assumption that historians' preferred audience ought to remain the one composed of their academic colleagues, it remains the case that that assumption made possible most of the twentieth century's dramatic gains in historical knowledge and understanding as well as some of the world's highest achievements in historical learning – achievements represented by books and articles rooted in the deepest scholarship and presented principally to audiences of academic historians. Without monographs and journal articles written by academics for academics, without specialization and reliance on the work of other scholars (made visible by use of the often-derided footnote), historical knowledge would have remained part of the world of amateurish speculation and not become a constituent part of human understanding based on substantiated evidence, interpretation subject to evaluation and revision, and openness to addition.[11] In addition, without monographic scholarship the popularizers of history – nonacademic writers and filmmakers especially – would not have had at their disposal the knowledge that lends their work what credibility it has. Taken as a whole, therefore, the advances represented by scholarship directed principally at audiences of peers amounted to an extraordinary gain in human knowledge and understanding.

Graduate education in scholarly research, however, means that historians' typical initial experience is with audiences of graduate student peers and professorial instructors – academics all. Formative professional encounters with these two audiences, plus early career exposure to teaching undergraduate students, marks aspiring historians' consciousness with the ideal of the academic audience as not only the highest but the principal, if not sole, legitimate audience for their work. This misconceived and increasingly anachronistic ideal results in what Thorstein Veblen called "trained incapacity," many historians being rendered incapable of conceiving of their work as having any interest or utility to anyone beyond academic walls. Too many historians quickly forget that while colleagues and undergraduates constitute legitimate and essential audiences for them, others have a legitimate interest in the contents, quality, and method of presentation of their work. The trustees who authorize historians' salaries, the officeholders who vote their budgets, the viewers who see their films, the visitors who attend their exhibits, the businesspeople who hire their skills and knowledge, even the average informed readers who wish to read and use their most abstruse and specialized work cannot, except at the risk of history's place in the general culture,

---

[11] On the history and significance of footnotes, see Anthony Grafton's learned and elegant *The Footnote: A Curious History* (Cambridge, MA: Harvard University Press, 1997). Pertinent as a lament is Gertrude Himmelfarb, "Where Have All the Footnotes Gone?" in *On Looking into the Abyss: Untimely Thoughts on Culture and Society* (New York: Alfred A. Knopf, 1994), 122–130.

be ignored. To think that they can safely be overlooked is an especially dangerous misconception in an open society and representative democracy, which relies for its very existence on the availability of knowledge and the jousting of differing informed views. So while for two centuries history has kept company with academic audiences and will wither if it does not do so, to limit the availability of history principally to such audiences is a grave mistake.[12]

If, however, it is a mistake, it is one attendant on the growth of history as an intellectual discipline. Shrinkage during the twentieth century in the intellectual universe of academically trained historians and in the audiences for the knowledge created by them was, if not inevitable, surely not surprising. But it occurred at considerable cost. Academic peers were likely to know more about specific subjects than most nonacademic members of the public and therefore to be in the best position to gain yet more knowledge of these subjects from fresh research. Yet the confinement of so many historians' audiences to academics often cut historians off from general intellectual currents and the unfettered and often exhilarating questions and concerns of a wider variety of minds and perspectives than could be found in the academy. That relative isolation also led many historians to assume that what was of greatest interest to them was, and should be, of intense interest to everyone else.[13]

Even after the discipline began to diversify after 1960 and people of greatly wider origins and interests became historians, this isolation and a uniform allegiance to the academic ideal failed to dissipate in any appreciable measure. Yes, here and there, especially in public history programs, some recognition of the need for historians to approach nonacademic audiences was to be found; here and there – one thinks of Richard Hofstadter, Oscar Handlin, C. Vann Woodward, Christopher Lasch, Staughton Lynd, and William Appleman Williams, more recently Simon Schama, Tony Judt, Stephanie Coontz, Stephen J. Pyne, John Lewis Gaddis, Laurel Thatcher Ulrich, Linda Colley, and Niall Ferguson among

---

[12] I write this with due regard for the gradual advance of academic historians' engagement with nonacademic audiences. On this matter, see, for example, Eric Arnesen, "Historians and the Public: Premature Obituaries, Abiding Laments," *Historically Speaking* 9 (November–December 2007): 2–5. A different view of the same matter is Ian Mortimer, "The Art of History," and the replies following in *Historically Speaking* 11 (June 2010): 12–19.

[13] That assumption could be seen at work especially in the 1980s and 1990s, when novel theories of historical change and understanding, most borrowed from abroad, were greatly in fashion in academic circles but served to render some history inscrutable to the average person.

others – academic historians succeeded well in reaching the larger public.
But in all graduate programs and most departments a concern for audiences had to vie for time and attention with conventional preparation.[14]
And even where formal training and practice in developing a repertoire of
presentation skills for a variety of audiences were available, the absence
of incentives and recognition for outreach beyond academic circles continued to inhibit the spread of training in writing for a wider public. In
the face of these enduring realities then, what considerations should historians inclined to try their hands at approaching nonacademic audiences
have in mind as they do so? What does it take to attract and engage nonhistorians in an era of population diversity, fragmentation of audiences,
and multiplicity of media?

Every distinct kind of presentation to every audience in every distinct
medium must be understood to be a discrete kind of art, each needing to
meet the particular requirements of the medium in which it appears and
of the audience to which it is presented. Many structural realities, such
as the length of television documentaries and the size of historical society
exhibits, are established by the nature of the case and scarcely affected
by historians' desires. Some demands of form and content, as in an after-
dinner talk to a group of history "buffs," are intrinsic to each setting and
audience. Take, for instance, the op-ed articles now standard on most
newspaper editorial pages. Unlike scholarly journal articles or reflective
essays in magazines, most op-eds (distinct from longer feature articles) are
no more than eight hundred words long. Such enforced brevity requires an
economy of statement, a tautness of expression, and a focus of argument
rarely appropriate in longer texts. Themes must be few, sentences short,
and nuance sacrificed to unqualified statement. Above all, op-eds must
by their very name convey argument; the author of an op-ed must take
a stand. Also, because op-eds are directed to newspaper readers, they
cannot contain references to scholars or to scholarly literature, and they
must be written in colloquial, not academic, English. The authority of
these texts resides with the weight and force of their writing, not with
their authors' display of erudition, and their success depends on adherence
to the conventions of the form. All who have tried their hands at op-eds
know how difficult they are to craft and how much practice they demand –
as well as how hard it is to place them with newspapers already inundated

---

[14] One among possibly other exceptions is a course in academic and professional writing
within the Professional Development Program at the University of Texas, Austin. The
course aims to prepare graduate students to write for nonacademic audiences.

with them.[15] If they are to write op-eds that are published, historians have to master that particular form as they do any other, as well as to submit themselves to its structural and journalistic conventions.

Analogous challenges face historians who, for example, appear as commentators in films, where pithiness of spoken expression is also essential; as "pundits" on news programs, where analysis must often give way to stories and information; or as historic site interpreters, where myth, memory, and politics often vie with known facts. Approaching the highly segmented general public as if its members compose a uniform mass possessing the sensibilities of an academic audience, practiced in academic ways and attracted by the footnoted page, is a grave mistake. One cannot assume that audiences of nonhistorians have the developed interest in historical subjects or the attention spans to tolerate long, erudite excursuses on topics dear to many historians' hearts. Each audience has its particular composition and desires, of which no historian can be heedless without risk, and the means historians choose to present knowledge strongly determines whether their audiences will gain that knowledge. To ignore these differences in audiences, or to fail to consider in advance the requirements of the particular means employed to put history before them, is to court failure.[16]

All of this is to say that attention, as either student or experienced historian, solely to scholarly and published means of expression is a kind of professional obtuseness. To think that the book-length or journal monograph is the sole means of presenting knowledge or, equally pertinent here, that the subject of history, not also the varied means of its presentation, constitutes the sole justifiable subject of study and practice and that attention to the varied means of its presentation is of less significance, is self-defeating. Such an assumption hazards what all historians ought to desire: the wide acceptance of accurate historical knowledge and the deep reflection about the past by citizens at large. To gain that acceptance, it cannot be assumed that among the various media only books are fit subjects of study in their own right. Those topics which have come to be known as "the study of the book" and "reader response theory" by their very names imply a disassociation from the study of other media

---

[15] Guidelines for writing op-eds that use historical knowledge to contextualize current events, as well as examples of the genre, can be found on the Web site of the History News Service, www.historynewsservice.org/.

[16] Many historians know these realities; and good editors, especially at trade presses, will not let them forget them. The fact remains that they are learned along the way and are not the stuff of professional preparation.

by which knowledge is transmitted. The ways in which various modes of presenting history affect their audiences ought to be legitimate subjects of study and conscious practice, too. They have not yet become so – at least not among historians.

Historians have to keep in mind that audiences are deeply affected by the form in which history is presented to them. Those who listen to a lecture usually have little chance to question the lecturer, and those who view a film of history are similarly left on their own to absorb what they have seen. By contrast, students in a seminar, spectators on a tour, or court officials being presented with expert scholarly testimony can be actively engaged with those who are presenting historical knowledge. Audiences differ also in the level and intensity of their engagement. Some are inert, and little can be done to activate them. Others are irrepressible. Some, not to be moved with new knowledge, resent and are angered by those who present alternative perspectives on the past. Others seek out history precisely because of their openness to new knowledge. One audience wants confirmation; another may need shaking up. For these reasons, for example, it is probably not wise to address a group of Turkish Americans with growing evidence of Turkey's complicity in the death of thousands of Armenians in 1915 (as critical as such broadened understanding in that community may be) because they are not yet likely in this era to have open minds on the issue. Yet the presentation of fresh understanding about aspects of the American Civil War to eager members of the Civil War Roundtable is likely to meet a more enthusiastic response. Each situation requires distinct decisions about aims, methods, and voice. Whatever a historian's principal pursuit, each audience encountered – whether pupils in school or experienced adults on cultural tours – will be demanding in its own way. All historians have to calibrate the subtle distinctions between what they might like to offer, what the public wants, and what, in some cases, the public may need in the way of knowledge. Historians who are not sensitive to these differences and approach audiences as if they were all the same will fail in their intended aim of conveying knowledge of the past effectively to others.

Historians must also be acutely sensitive to the language in which they convey their knowledge. Unless historians do not care how their work is received, they cannot ignore the value of colloquial language. The use of such words and expressions as "trope," "gendered," "alterity," "sub-altern," "to privilege," and "to valorize," even more widely accepted and older words like "liminal" and richly connotative and more easily explicable terms like "master narrative," none of which are part of colloquial conversation, quickly cause difficulties when spoken before or written for audiences whose members cannot be expected to know what they mean. One has to assume as a working principle that an audience understands colloquial English but not its academic third cousin. The perils of what has been called "cliobabble" are genuine, far more serious in fact than the often ignorant derision of self-appointed critics make them seem to be. Obscurantist language defeats the aim of diffusing knowledge; it runs the danger of losing, often of earning the ridicule, of readers and auditors; it puts at risk the larger reputation of historians and intellectuals; and it stands in the way of conveying the knowledge that an open society requires. Most historians know this, but reminding themselves and their students and colleagues of it is never amiss.

There is of course a place for technical language in specialized academic work just as there is room in common speech for slang, and in this regard, too, historians must approach each audience in their own voices, not ones donned for each occasion. How, after all, could we have come to know what we understand about so many historical subjects without detailed exposition and sometimes the most specialized vocabulary? Critics often confuse works of synthesis, which should be written in colloquial English, with works of discovery and argument, which may more appropriately be couched in technical language. Yet it behooves all historians to be more keenly aware than many of them are of the impact of their chosen words on audiences beyond those to which they direct their most specialized work. Their aim should be Orwellian lucidity and directness, and they should keep in mind that the use of hermetic language poses the same danger as elitism – a gulf between them and their prospective audiences of readers, auditors, and viewers.

Such reflections, risking the truistic, might have been less necessary fifty years ago, when audiences were smaller, more homogeneous, and less active and when the media available for presenting history were less numerous and diverse. Nor would they be appropriate here were graduate programs in history suitably designed to introduce students to these basic realities and to provide opportunities for experience with them. But if the discipline of history is seriously to engage the citizenry in the adventure of historical ideas in all their multiplicity and significance, then reminders of such fundamental, if elementary, principles are warranted – and greatly in need of application by all historians concerned about the vitality of public culture.

The tendency to ignore such considerations starts early. It is imbedded in graduate training, when few question the monopoly that the presentation of research in a single medium and in particularistic language holds over a student's preparation for a career in history. When taught to convey to peers the fruits of research in printed scholarly form, students are not acculturated just to publish those research results; they are also by implication taught how not to convey it and to whom not to present it. A huge weight of convention lies behind publication as the sole legitimate means of scholarly presentation. The catch phrase "publish or perish" would be less subject to debate and less a barrier to aspiring historians of different dispositions were it to be replaced with the admonition to "satisfy peers about your ability to pursue research and present it effectively in a form of your choice to any chosen audience, or perish." For we have confounded the ideal of disseminating knowledge with a particular means of dissemination – publication in print. Is it not true that, especially since the 1970s, many historians have published *and* perished – that is, not been able to find and hold a professorial berth? And does the world of history lack examples of some whose reputations have failed of enhancement for producing work of little significance but of much bulk? Not to publish may be to risk one's professional standing, but to publish too much may also be to perish on the fields of low audience reception.

The requirement that one's researches be published was not designed to create a small mountain of work bearing each historian's name but to ensure that historians would be motivated to produce enduring contributions to knowledge – of which publication in books and journals used to be the sole means but no longer is. The problem is that whereas the media for the presentation of knowledge have broadened, the criteria for professional advancement and recognition have not. So while the faculty members of doctoral-degree-granting institutions who determine entry into the academic profession and advancement through it are often involved in producing history for public audiences, while they prove themselves skilled at it and find it rewarding, and while most now quite readily acknowledge that one can make major contributions to understanding through media other than books and journal articles, they have not yet altered academic criteria of appointment and advancement, especially to the tenured ranks of history faculties, to take into account achievements in other media.

Until the current systems of scholarly evaluation on the one hand and incentive and reward on the other are somehow altered for all humanities and social science disciplines that train practitioners in universities, one will not be able to blame academic historians alone for fixing their eyes on conventional means of presentation, even when academic positions make up a decreasing proportion of the professional berths that historians occupy. Until standards of evaluation broaden (especially in college and university departments) and professional reward takes in new forms of scholarly presentation, each will similarly become increasingly irrelevant to much history work. Nevertheless, we cannot also lose sight of the need to continue to judge all history work first by its quality as history and only then as art. Making appropriate changes in the system of evaluation and reward, ones that recognize history produced outside the academy as well as history produced from within it for nonacademic audiences in new forms, remains one of the major unmet needs facing historians today.[17]

Yet, while altering the academic reward system so that achievement in the creation and diffusion of historical knowledge for a wide variety of audiences and not just academic peers can be recognized is certainly called for, to await such changes is to perpetuate some of history's most vexing problems. If the challenge of historians' audiences is to be met, then academic historians especially will have to alter fundamentally their stance toward a public thirsty for historical knowledge. Too, they will have to accustom themselves to the fact that, willy-nilly, nonacademic audiences, as demanding in their particular ways as academic peers, will suffer no patronizing lectures about what ought to interest them, nor are they likely to tolerate a single academic voice in which history is presented to them. They will seek what they wish and need to know in the form and manner in which they wish and need to know it, and historians' failure to respect their freedom to do so will cost more than their audiences' attention; it will risk the utility of history itself.

Among the discouraged reflections to which Theodore S. Hamerow was given after a long and distinguished professional career, he ventured the disenthralled view that "scholarship can offer no guarantees for the solution of social problems." To their solution, he concluded, history had become "irrelevant." He had also come to doubt the proposition that history offers something "for the education of the citizen, the conduct of the

---

[17] The literature on this vexed matter is large and often polemical. The most penetrating and sober review of the issue, one that contains an essential history of attempts by the AHA and allied organizations to address it, is James B. Gardner, "The Redefinition of Historical Scholarship: Calling a Tail a Leg?" *Public Historian* 20 (Fall 1998): 43–47, and the resulting discussion in the *Public Historian* 21 (Spring 1999): 84–97.

government, or the guidance of the community."[18] Few will challenge what is implicit in Hamerow's beliefs – that the successful application of history to public affairs and the effective presentation of historical knowledge to members of the general public is often difficult, never guaranteed, and frequently the cause of deep frustration. Yet all historians must cling to the possibility that in ways unplanned and unforeseen historical knowledge enriches the culture of an open society and makes possible a deeper and broader understanding of life than ignorance allows. To realize that possibility, indeed to be a historian in the fullest sense of the word, one has to struggle against understandable pessimism and seek out every audience that might be open to the adventure of historical ideas.

When we turn from audiences to media, further professional complexities arise. Historians have traditionally defined themselves by what they produce, and what they have traditionally produced are books and articles, mostly scholarly. After all, one of the chief consequences of the transfer of serious historical endeavor from the province of skilled amateurs to that of trained professionals, which took roughly seventy-five years after 1875 to complete, turned out to be the intimate linking of scholarly publication to academic advancement and consequently to academic audiences. The process of embedding the German model of academic research in research universities and wresting the authority to determine what constituted "legitimate" historical inquiry away from amateurs required the creation of new professional conventions, among which the demonstration of professional qualifications through the publication of research validated by peers became uppermost. As a consequence, most historical work moved from the desks of belletristic writers to those of academic scholars, and published scholarship, appearing in both journal- and book-length monographs, came to be the measure by which the achievements and quality of individual historians were judged. Not surprisingly, most historians bent every effort to conform to these new conventions, which by the middle of the twentieth century had become secure and nearly universal in the United States.[19]

---

[18] Theodore S. Hamerow, *Reflections on History and Historians* (Madison: University of Wisconsin Press, 1987), 3, 12.

[19] This is a radical foreshortening of a long and complex process. The best history of the matter is John Higham, *History: Professional Scholarship in America* (Baltimore: Johns Hopkins University Press, 1963; rev. ed., 1989). On the history of historians' struggle over defining their stances on audiences, see especially Higham's fourth chapter.

Once the historical monograph became the principal medium for the presentation of historical scholarship and (a coincident and related development) once the principal dependable form of salaried historical work became a professorial appointment, academic norms came rapidly to suffuse all practices of history, and adherence to academic expectations soon came to determine all professional progress. By the late nineteenth century, for example, universities would not grant doctoral degrees – the initial step in professional advancement – unless their aspirants had first published their dissertations, often by underwriting the cost of publication themselves. Even after universities abandoned that requirement, recipients of doctorates were expected to have their dissertations or revisions of them published soon after their degrees were in hand, face rustication to some outpost of academia, or, worse, experience the end to all hopes of an academic career in history. Academic publishing had gained a lock on professional aspirations and norms.

But with changing professional and cultural conditions, that near monopoly of approach and evaluation was bound to loosen, as it slowly has. Now, other forms of history in other media are emerging to salience as both professionally acceptable and publicly useful, and older forms of presentation are being adapted to new media. It is likely – indeed, it will become increasingly necessary for the health of the discipline – that historians adapt to new media, use them, and, equally important, develop the means and standards to evaluate their quality just as they long have evaluated books and articles. By the very nature of the new media – unceasingly changing and driven almost entirely by internal dynamics and commercial advantage – this adaptation will have to be continuous even as historians themselves innovate with new media and make it serve them, not vice versa. What is more, anything that I write here will rapidly be rendered obsolete; only the most general observations will remain relevant to historians' work.

The most consequential new medium for historians has of course proved to be the World Wide Web. It may be that Web-based new media would have elicited innovations in the presentation of knowledge and information on their own. But significant alterations – some would say a continuing crisis – in the circumstances of publishers have played a large role in the search for new ways to convey historical research and instruction. In addition, falling library budgets, the never-ending escalation in the number and costs of scholarly, especially science, journals, and the decline in library and individual purchases of scholarly monographs have driven scholarly and other publishers to seek new ways to make historical and other knowledge available. University presses, themselves under stress because of the changing economics of publishing and the ending in most cases of their home universities' subventions, have responded in part by trying to capture more "mid-list" books from commercial presses.

The danger facing historians, like all others who must adapt to strikingly new circumstances, is that they will be guided by the approaches and conventions of the past rather than imagining new ways of practicing their craft called for, even if not yet imagined, by the new media. It is probably too soon to know which approach will win out. But to date, the principal one has been that of adaptation rather than novelty. For instance, experiments in electronic publishing have consisted chiefly of presenting print documents in digital form. In addition to the digitization of conventional scholarly journals like the *AHR* and *JAH*, both by their publishers and through JSTOR and the History Cooperative (the latter suspended), online journals have made their appearance. So have "e-books," both under the nonprofit sponsorship of the AHA, the ACLS, JSTOR, and the University Press Content Consortium and commercially through firms like Xlibris and Amazon.com, which allow authors to publish their own books, register their ISBN numbers and copyrights, and have their works appear on book retailers' Web sites so that anyone can order copies electronically or on paper.[20] Some books have been published simultaneously on compact discs as well as in paper covers, those discs sometimes containing material not found in the printed work. The advantage of electronic books (which can also be printed out and read as texts) is that they can be of any length, can embody photographs, maps, and other illustrations in numbers difficult, because expensive, to include in most printed books, and can include still and moving images, music and other audio content, and hypertext links that lead to related literature and Web sites. They can also be revised in the light of new literature and findings, and their electronic publication leads to instant worldwide access. These advantages of electronic publishing have in effect taken "books" well beyond their long-stable codex form and given historians the opportunity to provide source and illustrative materials to

---

[20] For a selective list of electronic journals, see Joel D. Kitchens, "Clio on the Web: An Annotated Bibliography of Select E-Journals for History," *Perspectives* 38 (February 2000): 34–39. The list of e-journals has no doubt grown longer since then, but, as Kitchens has himself indicated in conversation with me, he has not updated his census nor has he or I been able to locate a more recent tabulation. The History Cooperative can be found through www.historycooperative.org, JSTOR through http://www.jstor.org.

readers never before possible. It is difficult to imagine historians not exploiting these advantages in increasing numbers and yet-unforeseen ways.

The AHA ventured into e-book publishing in 1999 with its Gutenberg-e project, a fellowship and publication program funded by the Andrew W. Mellon Foundation. The project awarded generous sums to young historians chosen in rigorous peer-reviewed competitions to produce scholarly e-books that were published by Columbia University Press. In the end, the series numbered thirty-five e-books. While more time and experience are needed before a full assessment of history e-books can be made, it is already clear that this initial experiment in e-book publishing was at least not a failure. By the evidence, these early e-books have been reviewed conventionally along with published books in scholarly journals, and they are finding their way into the historical literature.[21] But whether over time they will be cited comparably with other monographs and whether they will prove able to sustain themselves without external subvention (which the Gutenberg-e Project originally received) remains to be seen. In its final project evaluation, the AHA judged the project to be a "qualified success" because roughly two-thirds of its e-book authors had received tenure or held tenure-track appointments, which, reported the AHA, indicated "that there is no substantial [professional] risk for publishing an on-line monograph." However, in a sign of the challenges in getting historians and other scholars to adapt to e-publications, the Columbia University Press, contrary to its original plan, in the end published archival copies of the works; the e-books themselves proved far more complicated and time-consuming to produce online than anticipated; and rather than creating a viable business model for e-book publishing, online publication did not reduce the costs conventionally associated with preparing books for publication. So while electronic book publication is likely to have some growing impact on historians' work, it does not

---

[21] See, for example, the review of Joshua R. Greenberg, *Advocating the Man: Masculinity, Organized Labor, and the Household in New York, 1800–1840* (New York: Columbia University Press, 2006), a Gutenberg-e book, in the *American Historical Review* 113 (June 2008): 829–830. Ominously, however, the book originally carried a price of $49.00, and access to this and other titles was severely restricted and costly. Since then, the press has made possible free and open access to these works. In the end, however, these particular e-books will likely prove but a minuscule part of the larger market for electronic books, a market now being rapidly accelerated by Amazon.com, Apple, Google, and other companies, as well as by the introduction of such electronic readers as the Kindle, Nook, and iPad. University presses are also making available an increasing proportion of their lists in electronic form.

yet hold out promise of addressing the complex economics of scholarly publishing.[22]

On the whole, however, electronic communication has enlarged the stage on which historians can act and made possible new and distinctive contributions to both scholarly progress and public understanding. Take,

[22] The AHA's final, detailed Gutenberg-e report, as well as earlier ones, can be found at http://www.historians.org/prizes/gutenberg/background.cfm. It is not without significance that the AHA's main criterion for judging the effects of e-books was their consequences for tenure and advancement decisions. The Mellon Foundation's reflections on the project are contained in Donald J. Waters and Joseph S. Meisel, "Scholarly Publishing Initiatives," in the foundation's annual report for 2007 (at http://www.mellon.org/news_publications/annual-reports-essays/annual-reports/). See also Patrick Manning, "Gutenberg-e: Electronic Entry to the Historical Professoriate," *American Historical Review* 109 (December 2004): 1505–1526, in which Manning writes, "As those in academic life find themselves having to become accustomed to the multiple platforms for the information they collect, so also may they have to learn to present their results in a wider range of forms." Links to all Gutenberg-e books can be found on the AHA Web site. Many challenges remain. They include determining the sponsorship and publishers of e-books, Internet problems such as changing and wandering URLs, incompatible servers and browsers, and fees for archiving, subscriptions, and downloading. On such matters, see, for example, Michael O'Malley and Roy Rosenzweig, "Brave New World or Blind Alley?" *Journal of American History* 83 (June 1997): 132–155 (reprinted in Rosenzweig, ed., *Clio Wired: The Future of the Past in the Digital Age* [New York: Columbia University Press, 2011], 155–178), and Nicholas Evan Sarantakes, "So That a Tree May Live: What the World Wide Web Can and Cannot Do for Historians," *Perspectives* 37 (February 1999): 21–24. On the ACLS Humanities E-book collection, see http://www.humanitiesebook.org/intro.html.

Scholarly publishers have become increasingly troubled by finding themselves, as some see it, being surrogates for promotion and tenure committees, which in effect make their decisions regarding tenure and advancement hinge on the decisions of publishers' own peer reviewers and editorial committees, especially when the economics of publishing are discouraging the publication of many monographs that previously would have seen print. Some have suggested as a solution to this crisis that colleges and universities accept articles as well as books as evidence for advancement and that these institutions themselves underwrite at least part of the costs of books published by university presses so as to separate the decision to publish from the economics of publishing. A cogent discussion of the pros and cons of these two approaches is [Carlos J. Alonso], "Editor's Column: Having A Spine – Facing the Crisis in Scholarly Publishing," *PLMA* 118 (March 2003): 217–223. Another development, one that is only going to make things more complex for young historians, is the growing inclination of doctorate-granting universities to put accepted dissertations online. While this makes all contributions to knowledge widely available, it particularly threatens young scholars in the humanities, whose general form of publication is the book. The discussion of this crisis has been far more spirited within literature and language disciplines than within history. In fact, history lacks the kinds of publications, enjoyed at least by literature (through *PMLA* and *Profession*), in which professional matters can be discussed and debated at length. The AHA's *Perspectives in History* (formerly titled *Perspectives*) and the *OAH Newsletter* and its more recent *OAH Outlook* do not routinely carry these discussions, which are also excluded from most history journals.

for instance, the edited lists and Web sites of H-Net, the online connecting point for humanists and social scientists like historians and the librarians and archivists whose work is so central to historians' endeavors. Through H-Net lists, scholars and teachers around the world communicate publicly with each other about the specialized topics that define each list. Permanently archived and increasingly cited, these discussions have become part of the discipline's scholarly literature, which specialists ignore at their peril. But perhaps even more important than providing communication among historians about scholarly and professional issues (which include new methods, technical scholarly matters, reading lists and bibliographies, teaching ideas, and the like), H-Net lists have greatly improved the evaluation of books by carrying reviews that are longer and more searching than customarily short journal reviews, that contain citations and active electronic links, and that give historians practice in writing the kind of extended review essays that until recently appeared in only a few publications, such as the *New York Review of Books*.[23]

As the versatility of H-Net makes clear, the growing variety of media through which historians can convey their work has enlarged the forms of writing they can employ, the diversity of their written texts, and, consequently, the audiences they can reach. It would be too much to say that, collectively, historians have fully utilized the modes of presentation available to them or sought out all the audiences they might. Yet discrete efforts by an increasing number of historians are now numerous enough to suggest that the discipline of history is beginning to move into a new phase of its own history. Many of these efforts are directly the result of the emergence of new media and the techniques associated with them; some arise from the development of the new profession of public history, while others are fresh applications of old ways. But many take the different, less academic, and less institutionalized form of trying to find ways to carry historical knowledge directly to the nonacademic public, to apply academic learning to public affairs, and to provide historical knowledge in more popular form to people who are not historians. All represent a welcome development. Yet if history is in the early stages of a period of experimentation at the end of which historical knowledge and historians themselves come to occupy a different and larger position in American intellectual life, more historians who imagine what not yet is but might be will have to involve themselves in experimenting with new ways to carry history beyond academic boundaries.

[23] Full information about H-Net can be found through http://www.h-net.org/about.

Few historians have more fully recognized the opportunities open to historians and history through new media than the late Roy Rosenzweig and his colleagues at the Center for History and New Media at George Mason University. Their vision of historians' role in the development of professionally and intellectually applicable uses of new media is both powerful and optimistic. Rosenzweig wrote of a new world of "unheard of historical abundance" while cautioning historians about ignoring the digital revolution at their peril. Throughout his writings – and there has yet been no one more authoritative on these matters than he – Rosenzweig saw digital history as inaugurating an era of democratic, open, cooperative, and participatory history work, a wired future that serves scholarship, public knowledge, and teaching. To this end, he and his colleagues have invented and developed an extraordinary range of computer programs, Web sites, and educational tools to which no doubt they and other historians involving themselves in this new electronic world will continue richly to contribute.[24]

Like an increasing number of historians and others involved in what is called the "digital humanities," Rosenzweig envisaged a developing professional world that welcomed and used historical knowledge for public and civic ends. Such endeavors, however, would not be unprecedented, for well before history became institutionalized in colleges and universities, most historians wrote for general audiences of informed and interested readers, not captive students or professionalized scholars. Yet between that day of classic amateurism and today's search for means to give historical knowledge more utility and appeal – a means to keep the tide of academic historical writing from destroying history's longtime standing as a branch of literature – another effort intervened. Its diffuse and unclear influence is instructive.

That effort grew out of frustration with the standardization of professional evaluation and purpose attendant on history's development as an academic discipline as well as the prejudice that rendered most non-monographic forms of presentation suspect and of lesser professional status among academics. That prejudice came to mean that only those

---

[24] Most of Rosenzweig's most influential essays on history in the digital world are contained in *Clio Wired*. The quotation is from p. 6. It should be noted that some of the essays in this volume were coauthored. Surveys of historians' use of new media for scholarly and instructional purposes in 2010 is contained in Robert B. Townsend, "How Is New Media Reshaping the Work of Historians?" *Perspectives on History* 48 (November 2010): 312–336, and Townsend, "Assimilation of New Media into History Teaching: Some Snapshots from the Edge," *Perspectives on History* 48 (December 2010): 24–26.

historians who had first proved themselves as academics writing for academic audiences were considered legitimately free to write for the general public in popular forums like magazines without loss of professional stature, and even some of them faced criticism for doing so. As a consequence, by the 1960s public historians were scarcely noticed by academic professionals or recognized by the scholarly and professional organizations that give structure to the discipline of history.

Not that the stranglehold of academic norms on the definition of professional legitimacy had ever fully escaped challenge from within academic walls. All along, a few university historians – and here I draw my examples only from among historians in the United States – had become widely known and admired by the general public for the force of their arguments and the grace of their writing. Such academic historians as James Harvey Robinson, Charles A. Beard, Harry Elmer Barnes, and Samuel Eliot Morison actively sought and gained a wide readership for their sharply different visions and approaches to history; others, like Garrett Mattingly and Peter Gay, who were quintessentially academic in their professional roles, came to enjoy a public following for the power and grace of their writing even when their books often concerned recondite subjects and were learned in every sense of that word. Their successors – let the names of James M. McPherson, William H. McNeill, Tony Judt, David Levering Lewis, Heather Cox Richardson, James T. Patterson, Simon Schama, and Joyce Appleby stand in for all of them – have been equally ambitious and influential. Their successes can be read as evidence that a public for grand history continues to exist when historians write for it. Their successes can also be read as implicit protests against historians' neglect of their potentially large audiences.

One of these more broadly gauged historians, Allan Nevins, originally a journalist and then a member of the faculty of Columbia University whose works enjoyed a wide popular following, decided in the late 1930s to confront head-on what he considered historians' increasingly self-defeating stance in relation to their audiences. Joined by a few others, in 1938 he challenged the AHA to create a popular history magazine. Angered by the rebuff his proposal received from the association, Nevins and others founded a still-existing organization, the Society of American Historians. The society's aim was, as it remains, to bring academic historians together with journalists, publishers, editors, and independent writers of history in a membership of elected fellows who were skilled writers. They were to celebrate and encourage the writing of serious historical works the public would enjoy as well as learn from. By 1954, along with the American Association of State and Local History, the society was able to raise funds to inaugurate publication under the editorship of James Parton of *American Heritage*, an appealing, hardbound magazine that seduced the eye while trying to engage and capture the mind. Nevertheless, Nevins's hope of proving that a substantial proportion of the reading public would extend itself to read (if not study) works of history if only those works were presented in lively and graceful prose was not fulfilled by the magazine. Most often found on the coffee tables of well-off consumers and history "buffs," filled with articles by skilled academics and writers who hold back from offering subscribers the challenging findings and interpretations that they simultaneously present to their students, the magazine continues to enjoy a large number of subscribers. In addition, the Society of American Historians keeps alive the flame of good writing even without appreciably affecting the discipline or the writing of American history. If anything, these facts suggest that alterations in the ways historians perceive their role and the health of their discipline will have to happen otherwise.[25]

Nevins, however, proved prophetic in his concerns about the loss of history's audiences. If not all historians were walking away from their potential readers or giving up trying to make historical knowledge useful, other factors were at work to keep historians and the general public apart. The expansion of higher education and academic faculties in the quarter century after the Second World War intensified the identification of historical studies, as it did the other constituent disciplines of the humanities and social sciences, with the academy. In addition, even while by some measures – the number of works of history published and purchased and the viewership of films and television programs devoted to history – the

---

[25] On Nevins's efforts, see Higham, *History*, 80–84; Novick, *That Noble Dream*, 194–197; and Roy Rosenzweig, "Marketing the Past: *American Heritage* and Popular History in the United States, 1954–1984," in Susan Porter Benson, Stephen Brier, and Roy Rosenzweig (eds.), *Presenting the Past: Essays on History and the Public* (Philadelphia: Temple University Press, 1986), 27–49. In the 1980s, the AHA again looked into sponsoring a popular magazine of history but concluded that doing so was infeasible. It is not surprising that so many of the historians who sought a broad readership for their works held faculty appointments at urban universities, or that members of the Columbia faculty in New York City, home to both the principal American publishing houses and probably the most lively and demanding consumers of ideas in the United States, constituted the largest concentration of them. Unfortunately, the Society of American Historians has not played the larger role in the discipline that, by the authority and quality of its membership, it could play; ever expanded its membership to include historians of the entire world; or made its mission the celebration of the best historical writing about any subject.

public's interest in history remained manifest and extensive, many of the foundations on which historical knowledge relies in modern society were weakening. Less history (even in its watered-down form of "social studies") was being taught in school classrooms, and much of what was taught there was uninspired. As the social sciences (especially economics and anthropology) grew in favor over history and as vocationalism made inroads into the arts and sciences generally, a smaller proportion of college undergraduates was majoring in history. Public support for higher education and for the humanities generally was eroding.

Perhaps worst of all, the loss of authority of demonstrable fact and considered reflection rendered displeasing if not incomprehensible to many people a subject to which both were central. More and more members of the public began to complain (some of them with clearly political intent) about the irrelevance of historical knowledge, indeed about the irrelevance of historians. To make matters worse, as they succumbed to the seductive blandishments of corporate popular culture, itself freshly assertive by virtue of new media that elevated entertainment over knowledge, many people withdrew themselves from access to the historical information and sources of historical knowledge to which by taste or need they might have remained attached. Audiences themselves began to splinter into special interests, into "buffs," into ideological groupings. Historians, indeed all intellectuals, could no longer easily ask of or count on their prospective audiences, whether they were students, readers, museumgoers, or park visitors, to make a decent effort to understand what they had to say.

Except for some prescient historians like Nevins, until recently too few others recognized and fewer still paid more than lip service to all of these dangers facing history's place in the general culture, wherever those dangers may have originated. Even now too many historians remain uninvolved in efforts to confront the dangers to their discipline.[26] Surely few graduate programs in history, except those designed specifically for students desirous of pursuing careers in public history, have altered their focus on preparing aspiring historians, as if their audiences must and will be only academics. As a result, decades after Nevins and his colleagues

---

[26] That the AHA has once again taken an interest in altering the preparation of graduate students is chief evidence of this concern. See Thomas Bender et al., *The Education of Historians for the Twenty-First Century* (Urbana: University of Illinois Press, 2004). Its predecessor study, which did so much to shape graduate education in history during the latter decades of the twentieth century, is Dexter Perkins, John L. Snell, et al., *The Education of Historians in the United States* (New York: McGraw Hill, 1962).

essayed the first steps to stem the loss of history's audiences brought on by the triumph of the German model of research and writing, the problems they identified have now grown into a major test for historians. Fortunately, however, this one has begun to lead more historians than previously to reconsider the many conventions of their intellectual world that contribute to that crisis and to seek a fresh understanding of history's place in contemporary culture.

In some respects, everything that is now being undertaken in the name of public history constitutes one approach to that crisis. Yet specific projects, whose purposes suggest the range of these efforts and the variety of intentions behind them, indicate the breadth of innovations that are being essayed. Some of them are directly linked to current events; others have use in classrooms. While each differs in its intended audience, all seek to create or recapture part of history's larger following through different outlets in a number of different media. They hint at a future now only dimly perceived.

The earliest of these endeavors was the current-events-related History News Service, which Joyce Appleby and I inaugurated in 1996 as a syndicate of professional historians that provides op-ed articles to newspapers and wire services throughout North America. The second was *Talking History*, a series of weekly half-hour public radio programs, instituted by Bryan F. Le Beau in 1998 and, until its suspension, produced under the auspices of the Organization of American Historians. The programs conveyed audio reports about history in the news, commentaries on history topics, and interviews with historians. The place of *Talking History* has more recently been filled by two newer projects. One is *BackStory*, a history-themed radio show produced out of Charlottesville, Virginia, by Brian Balogh, Edward L. Ayers, and Peter S. Onuf but, so far at least, confined to subjects of American history. A second is New Books in History, a series of audiocast interviews produced and carried out by Marshall Poe and distributed to subscribers and available for download over the Web.

Another initiative, the 2001 brainchild of Rick Shenkman, is the History News Network, a Web-based source of articles both written expressly for the network and republished from other sources. HNN, a consolidator of historical news, is designed principally but not exclusively for journalists' use and claims to be the only Web site given over to articles relating history to public events. Two analogous endeavors have focused their aim chiefly but not exclusively at classroom audiences. One is Common-place, which styles itself as "a bit friendlier than a scholarly journal, a bit more scholarly than a popular magazine." Inaugurated in 2000 by Jill Lepore and Jane Kamensky, Common-place is a Web site devoted – through short essays, interviews, exchanges between scholars, and other written texts – to American history before 1900. The second is George Mason's Center for History and New Media, which is pioneering in the use of the Web for research and teaching.

A final experiment in outreach is the series of briefings for members of Congress and their staffs established in 2005 by the National History Center. In these briefings, historians present to their audiences the historical origins, context, and implications of policy matters being considered and debated in both houses of Congress and place expert historians into association with Congress in the conviction that historical knowledge is critically important in the design and implementation of public policies.[27] The National History Center is itself a promising new institutional endeavor that is attempting to add resources to the discipline as a whole. Implementing a 1901 vision of J. Franklin Jameson, the center, located in Washington, D.C., and a formal initiative of the AHA, is also sponsoring lectures to foreign policy experts in conjunction with the Council on Foreign Relations, as well as weekly seminars for policy and opinion makers and historians that bring historical knowledge to bear on public policy making. And it has laid the groundwork – through a series of books, summer institutes, and other programs – for what in the future, with the addition of fellowships and scholarly seminars, will constitute in effect an institute for advanced study in history. The Center is one of the more promising institutional initiatives of recent years, one however that will require much time fully to develop.

---

[27] The URLs for these efforts are as follows: History News Service – www .historynewsservice.org, Talking History – http://talkinghistory.oah.org; BackStory – http://backstoryradio.org and http://newbooksinhistory.com/; History News Network – http://HistoryNewsNetwork.org; Common-Place – http://www.common-place.org. David Nord has recently taken over as director of the History News Service. To this list might be added the History Channel, which offers a kind of history-related television entertainment. The only one of these projects not to emerge from academically trained historians and the only commercial venture among them, it presents to its viewers its own productions, historical film footage, and old movies, most, but not all, related to historical subjects and issues. It should be noted that, as with so many history-related productions also carried by affiliates of the Public Broadcasting Service, films shown by the History Channel are rarely produced or directed by historians themselves, who, instead, are used as commentators, perhaps as consultants, but not as the principals behind the films. The same appears to be the case with the *History Channel Magazine*, a magazine of history for the general reader (alas, depressingly thin of substance), inaugurated in 2003.

No review of our era's promise for the diffusion of historical knowledge and of the availability of new means to reach beyond academic borders can overlook the growing influence of Web logs, or "blogs" written by historians. Dating to the late 1990s and not yet having achieved their full professional and public potential, blogs are not easy to define. At their best, they compose a method of distributing informal, often personal, increasingly professional ideas, reflections, critiques, and news to those who access them on the Web. Often dismissed because of the undisciplined and amateurish use to which so many blogs are put, history blogs must make their way in an electronic universe filled as much by tawdry and insubstantial content as by serious work. Yet some blogs written by historians have become widely followed, authoritative, and cited along lines analogous to the postings on H-Net listservs. Moreover, the open-ended nature of the Web allows the most serious history blogs to take a myriad of forms and concern a wide array of subjects. History bloggers can highlight new findings and thinking about narrow topics, present historians' views on particular subjects, write pseudonymously as well as openly, and offer diary-like reflections and commonplace book entries as well as formally written texts. Most importantly, their readers can respond with comments and thus contribute to ongoing discussions. Fortunately, there is some evidence that the readership of serious history blogs, infinite in prospect, is, while small in comparison to those on popular subjects, an attentive one spanning the world. Whether this audience can help make history blogging an accepted, respectable means of communicating historical knowledge among both amateurs and professionals remains to be seen. But no one concerned with the future of historical communication can afford to ignore this new use of a young medium.[28]

To all of these projects and approaches can be added the more diffusely designed efforts, relevant to many disciplines as well as to history, to

---

[28] Historians who blog have not yet offered much by way of explanation of their intentions and achievements, nor have they adequately explored the limitations of the genre and its practitioners. However, two useful, if informal, introductions to blogging are Ralph E. Luker, "Were There Blog Enough and Time," *Perspectives* 43 (May 2005): 29–32, and Manan Ahmed, "The Polyglot Manifesto," History News Network, May 22, 2006. The blog Cliopatria, which Luker founded and is now integrated with the History News Network, maintains a registry, with links, to over fifteen hundred history blogs around the world and offers annual awards, chosen by independent judges, in recognition of the highest-quality blogs. Some of the better and most widely followed among them include historian Joshua Micah Marshall's Talking Points Memo (about contemporary American politics); Eric Alterman's Altercation (about current affairs); and historian Juan Cole's important Informed Comment (about the Middle East).

provide incentives to scholars to involve themselves in public culture. The National Endowment for the Humanities, both directly and through its state humanities councils, has long funded endeavors that feature scholars, including historians, who carry humanistic knowledge to a wide range of audiences. The Woodrow Wilson National Fellowship Foundation has underwritten a few graduate students to design short-term projects that convey the results of their research outside the academy. In a related effort, the foundation has also been supporting efforts by faculty members to join in collaborative projects with local cultural groups and to introduce "public scholarship" into doctoral programs. Whether these efforts will bear the lasting fruit hoped for by their sponsors, and what that fruit may be, is still unclear. But their existence is much to be welcomed.[29]

History is not going to begin even to approach the outer bounds of the possible until more historians see the invention and pursuit of outreach efforts as part of their professional responsibilities and as integral to their work as historians. As in so many other regards, clear and satisfactory incentives and rewards – fellowships, compensation, promotion, prizes – to those historians who undertake them will be necessary, and not just in academic settings, before experimentation becomes more common. But one set of conventions, one set of standards, incentives, and rewards, cannot, and should not, replace the other. Instead, we should hope for the addition of new criteria to those we conventionally use to evaluate historians' work and their contributions to the discipline, and those criteria should surely include the quality of what historians do to convey historical knowledge beyond their colleagues and immediate students and how they do so. That will no doubt require a new way of looking at peer review. While most of the history conveyed by outreach projects is subject to varying degrees of review and editing, none of their contents is, in the conventional use of the term, peer reviewed. In fact, because their aim is to provide the public with material based on historical scholarship relevant to current debates, their content's very timeliness makes almost impossible the use of the careful, time-consuming, hard-to-administer conventional peer-review process known to all historians. Notwithstanding this fact, little has been done to broaden or diversify the grounds customarily employed to judge the quality and aptness of the products

---

[29] Part of this story concerns the role of public intellectuals, which I take up in Chapter 5. One university-based and broad-gauged project aiming to link universities and the wider public through the arts and humanities is Imagining America (http://www.ia.umich.edu).

of historians' increasingly varied work. And nothing is likely to be done until such outreach projects grow in number, authority, and note.[30]

But given the ethos of the discipline (or the discipline's particular set ways, for which the French term *déformation professionelle* is apposite), such a transfiguration is unlikely anytime soon. And the discipline's ways are not the sole obstacles historians face: the book review sections of daily newspapers are disappearing, and the few remaining weekend book reviews are now far less substantial than they used to be; trade presses issue fewer books and promote even those less than before; and not all university presses have stepped in adequately to publish and market what commercial presses now do not. Therefore, while calls, like those of Nevins, for major changes in the way historians behave and carry out their work have their place in alerting people to what is needed, realities external to the discipline will have to change, too, before historians claim a larger share of public attention. But the continued accumulation of additional resources through discrete innovation is likely to be the most promising route to change. In fact, the discipline finds itself further developed in its engagement with the public than it was a quarter century ago – surely further developed in outreach efforts than any other discipline in the humanities, although quite unaware of that comparative strength – precisely because of separate initiatives on the part of individual historians working independently of each other. None of their initiatives alone represents, nor do all together constitute, a frontal attack by history professionals on the audience problem; few have originated from within the discipline's scholarly or professional societies. But perhaps this is the way

---

[30] Joyce Appleby and I tried to take this consideration into account in the covering memorandum to History News Service authors that accompanied the dispatch of their distributed op-eds to them: "We have been asked occasionally how to note work for HNS on a professional record. Because there's no guarantee of publication and because, as you know, our standards are exacting, we believe that HNS acceptance and distribution of a piece is an important professional event in and of itself. Therefore, you might wish to record a distributed HNS piece as follows: '[Title of article], distributed to more than 300 metropolitan daily newspapers and news services in the United States and North America by the History News Service on [distribution date].'" More significantly, the AHA, OAH, and National Council on Public History have developed approaches that history departments can use to evaluate public history scholarship. The report, "Tenure, Promotion, and the Publicly Engaged Academic Historian," issued in June 2010, as well as an accompanying white paper can be found at http://ncph.org/cms/wp-content/uploads/2010/06/Engaged-Historian-White-Paper-FINAL1.pdf. It is also pertinent here that scholars in a number of disciplines have begun to experiment with Web-based peer review by which scholarly works can be evaluated more quickly and broadly than by traditional peer review. The consequences of such a system, were it to spread, would likely be great.

it should be – that individual historians working by themselves and not in the name of institutions invent ways in which historical knowledge can be applied to extra-academic issues and circumstances.

As Rick Shenkman of the History News Network has argued in a robust justification of historians' engagement in all of these kinds of projects, peer review cannot be the sole concern of those who seek to discover and satisfy nonacademic audiences. Whether or not their work is considered suitably academic by academic historians and rewarded accordingly, historians must endeavor to speak to nonacademic audiences in ways those audiences can accept. Historians cannot claim their authority simply because they are scholars; they cannot write for the general public simply for the satisfaction of having met what they consider a professional responsibility to the general welfare. Nevertheless, Shenkman writes, "Neither can the fact that they are scholars deprive them of the right to weigh in on matters of vital public importance. Indeed, the fact that they bring to the public debate a special expertise and sensibility derived from their studies is all the more reason to give them a hearing. Leaving the public square to people who lack the scholar's knowledge diminishes democracy."[31]

Unfortunately, the muscular assertion of this truth does not remove the barriers to the realization of broadened audiences. It does not alter the canons or procedures of peer review. Nor does it direct attention to the equally critical matter of historians' preparation or to the means by which credible assessments of public outreach efforts can be made.[32] All of these barriers will have to be attacked to improve history's place in public culture. It remains to be seen whether historians will have the collective will to attack them.

---

[31] http://hnn.us/articles/982.html.

[32] I stress here the matter of credibility. For decades, foundations and the NEH have routinely asked recipients of their funds to submit reports of the success or failure of their projects, including public projects. Not surprisingly, few grantees report failures or limitations. It may be that all efforts to reach out to nonacademics are intrinsically valuable, especially in an open society. But this does not obviate the clear need for better means to measure failure and success.

4

The Academic Trinity

Research, Teaching, Service

Although the proportion of academics among professional historians continues slowly to decline, a solid majority of all practicing historians remains employed as faculty members, and more than 60 percent of the known doctoral recipients in history continue to become academics, at least at the start of their professional careers.[1] Equally significant, although an increasing number of historians pursue nonacademic professional work, academic standards continue to be those against which history work is measured in all the occupations in which history is practiced. Even were academics to become a minority among historians – a situation not so unthinkable as it was thirty or forty years ago – it is highly unlikely that standards born in the academy and long proved in their utility both there and elsewhere would become irrelevant to practicing historians, whatever the nature of their work. So thoroughly do academic norms permeate the entire discipline of history, so deeply do they influence the ways in which all efforts at historical understanding are regarded, that no historian can escape their influence. Even those who spend their entire professional lives outside the academy, including those

---

[1] One survey indicates that roughly 70 percent of history graduate students definitely seek academic positions, a proportion exceeded only by graduate students in philosophy. Only about a half of those surveyed indicated, however, that such a hope was realistic. These and other figures, as well as the reasons for the attractiveness of academic careers to aspiring historians, are set forth in Chris M. Golde, "The Career Goals of History Doctoral Students: Data from the Survey on Doctoral Education and Career Preparation," *Perspectives* 39 (October 2001): 21–26. Given the decline since 2001 in the availability of academic openings, it may be that the figures then cited by Golde have changed substantially.

who, as writers of history without doctorates, often scoff at academic conventions and writing, are forced by the strength of academic standards to pay rough obeisance to them. No history work is now conceivable without adherence to these standards.

In most respects, across the entire academic spectrum the strongest of these norms – the creation of knowledge, its diffusion by publication, and the critical evaluation of both by peers – is the research ideal. It is central to the academic enterprise, and it has come to characterize academic work for most people who know little else of a professor's world. Yet research, publication, and criticism hardly exhaust the range or categories of expectations that shape academic work or academic influences on historians' professional lives. Other expectations and responsibilities, to which most historians are acculturated to some degree early in their careers by virtue of their graduate education in university history departments, equally affect how historians conceive of their work even if that work does not require the uniform application of these other norms. These other expectations and responsibilities, those of teaching and service, may be said, along with research, to constitute the Academic Trinity of the historian's world, the triune presence in the working lives of those who have been prepared for their professional careers as historians in modern research universities. It is to the Academic Trinity that historians-in-training are led to believe that they should consecrate their working lives even if, in the end, some elements of it prove inapplicable to their work. Unquestionably, the majority of historians who make their careers in the academy is powerfully affected by the Trinity and cannot escape its influence. Equally important, each academic historian, even if implicitly, enters into a solemn covenant to bear faith and witness to it.

Not surprisingly, however, not even all academic historians feel equal dedication to the constituent elements of the Trinity. Variances in fidelity to those elements are attributable to the diversity of individual historians' talents, temperaments, and aspirations, to the different rewards that are offered for adherence to each, to the nature and ethos of particular academic institutions, and to a general failure to resolve some fundamental confusions about them. For instance, while the public mission statements of virtually all research universities, private as well as public, pledge commitment to research, teaching, and service, it takes novice historians little time to understand that, even where a premium is placed upon teaching, academic culture usually, if not uniformly, emphasizes research over teaching and service in most tenure and advancement decisions and that universities themselves are largely responsible for the sharply different weights placed on each. This asymmetry of incentive and reward, arising from the superimposition of the German tradition of advanced research training on the Anglo-American baccalaureate teaching college and the uneasy commingling of both with the public service ideal of American public universities, has for decades occasioned intense public debate. Its critics charge it with putting undue emphasis on faculty members' research at the expense of both the quality and intensity of their instruction and of their efforts to use knowledge in service to the community. In fact, criticism of universities for neglecting teaching in deference to research is probably as old as the modern university itself. Yet it has never been entirely clear to what degree the charges of imbalance in faculty members' distribution of their time are valid, whether any serious damage to students results from whatever imbalance may exist, and how, if at all, a correction in this state of affairs, to the degree that it is warranted, might be carried out.

Of greater importance to academic historians, however, is the never-addressed, fundamental confusion attached to the Academic Trinity itself. Distinction is rarely made between its application to institutional missions and individual careers. As made clear by Laurence R. Veysey, since their origin over a century ago research universities have combined within their missions a commitment to research, teaching, and public service (and have been joined in doing so in the second half of the twentieth century by many collegiate institutions).[2] But by virtue of developments

---

[2] Laurence R. Veysey, *The Emergence of the American University* (Chicago: University of Chicago Press, 1965), esp. part I, is a superb, and still the best, study of the coincident and often warring claims for the precedence of research, teaching, and service from the very origins of the modern American university. As Veysey points out, in the late nineteenth century, when the research university as we know it came into being, it was the rather diffuse concept of culture, considered as cultivated taste, that competed with pure research and public service for priority among the goals of university education. A century later, when these distinct goals had concluded a never easy peace of sorts, teaching in its broadest sense, and not just teaching to create cultivated intelligence, had supplanted culture as the third of the three basic missions of higher education. Two fine studies of issues germane to this topic are Roger L. Geiger, *To Advance Knowledge: The Growth of American Research Universities, 1900–1940* (New York: Oxford University Press, 1986), and Geiger, *Research and Relevant Knowledge: American Research Universities since World War II* (New York: Oxford University Press, 1993). Always apposite are three classic works: Charles Homer Haskins, *The Rise of Universities* (New York: Henry Holt, 1923); Clark Kerr, *The Uses of the University* (Cambridge, MA: Harvard University Press, 1964); and Daniel Bell, *The Reforming of General Education: The Columbia College Experience in Its National Setting* (New York: Columbia University Press, 1966). See also David Riesman and Christopher Jenks, *The Academic Revolution* (Garden City, NY: Doubleday, 1968). Two idiosyncratic works on related matters are William Clark,

never to my knowledge analyzed by historians, throughout the twentieth century these same institutional missions have come to be applied to individual faculty members as personal responsibilities. It is no longer only the individual college and university that must exhibit dedication to the creation of knowledge, the instruction of students, and service to the larger world; it is also each appointee to a faculty who is expected to do so. Whereas it is relatively easy to see how an institution might, through the natural dispersal of effort by its many faculty and research staff members, make contributions to research and scholarship, to teaching, and to public service, it is not so clear why these norms are expected to be met by each individual faculty member, how each can do so, and what allowances should be made for choices made between them.[3]

Enduring published scholarship – the result of research – surely constitutes the glory of Clio's discipline. Without the masterful volumes of the ancients like Herodotus, Thucydides, Livy, and Tacitus, medievalists like Ibn Khaldun, early modernists like Montesquieu, Voltaire, and Edward Gibbon, then of academics as diverse as Leopold von Ranke and Henry Adams, Friedrich Meinecke and Fernand Braudel, to say nothing of countless other more recent historians' great monographic and synthetic studies too numerous to mention here, we would be without knowledge and understanding of the world before our time and mired in a mythic, and therefore useless, understanding of our own lives. It can also be said without fear of contradiction that, lacking published historical thought, historical understanding of any respectable weight does not exist. It should therefore occasion no surprise that many historians' greatest aspirations are fixed on the creation of enduring works of

Academic Charisma and the Origins of the Research University (Chicago: University of Chicago Press, 2006), and Anthony Grafton, *The Footnote: A Curious History* (Cambridge, MA: Harvard University Press, 1997). These last two works suggest the existence of a large research frontier on the history of historical practices.

3 As will quickly be apparent, this chapter is less a guide to the academy than a set of reflections on its ways for historians who might be part of it. For guides to academic life generally, two useful works are A. Leigh DeNeef and Craufurd D. Goodwin (eds.), *The Academic's Handbook*, 3rd ed. (Durham: Duke University Press, 2007), and John A. Goldsmith, John Komlos, and Penny Schine Gold, *The Chicago Guide to Your Academic Career: A Portable Mentor for Scholars from Graduate School through Tenure* (Chicago: University of Chicago Press, 2001). I should emphasize, too, that the wide range of types of collegiate and university institutions in the United States, a range that gives each institution warrant to define its particular role in the larger academic galaxy as it wishes to, allows a diversity of emphases among the elements of the Trinity. I am trying here to present the general picture only.

scholarship and that greatest professional recognition flows to those few who succeed best at this monumental task. In those for whom teaching brings greater satisfaction and fulfillment, the promise of job security arising from proven scholarship is a strong motivating force toward publication.

In the modern world, great works of historical thought – indeed all works of historical scholarship – are the products without exception of deep and skilled research. No acceptable product of history is conceivable without fidelity to the research ideal. Every person who claims the title of historian is expected to be proven as a research scholar before anything else. In fact, so great is the magnetic force of the research ideal, so deeply embedded is it in the world of intellectual endeavor, that it may seem unnecessary to do more than to acknowledge its strength and then move on to more problematic matters. Yet, as with all ideals, this one has not been without attack or difficulties, especially as higher education has changed since 1945.

As constituted largely by unspoken convention, the research ideal embodies the conviction that, published scholarship in one of its many modern forms being the fundamental skill and emblem of a historian, one is not validated as a historian without demonstrating the ability to carry out research in primary sources and to relate that research to others through peer-reviewed writing.[4] For universities (even those that emphasize their teaching functions) and an increasingly large proportion of collegiate institutions, in practice this has come to mean that faculty members are expected to compose published scholarship growing from research. But expectations governing how often a given faculty member should produce scholarship and in what form it should appear – whether, for instance, only books and journal articles constitute acceptable scholarship, or book reviews, films, curated exhibits, even online magazines and exhibitions – differ from institution to institution. Yet the principle of published scholarship in some form, proven in its ability to ground historical knowledge in interpreted evidence, remains the principle norm to which all aspiring historians, whatever the profession in which they will choose to practice history, must adhere.[5]

---

4   The writing does not have to be published. One is taken to be a trained historian by virtue of having written a dissertation, approved by a committee of faculty members, even if neither that dissertation nor anything derived from it appears in print.

5   I emphasize here the internalized norm of publication fully cognizant of the external forces pressing on academics to publish. They include above all departmental and administrative pressures to gain high rankings in National Research Council and *U.S. News & World Report* surveys.

In practical terms, for graduate students in training at universities with doctoral programs the research ideal means that the receipt of the doctorate requires the completion of a dissertation that proves the student capable of carrying out research scholarship and meriting membership in the ancient and honorable company of scholars. An assumption behind this requirement at its creation in the nineteenth century was that Ph.D. recipients would join faculties on which they would be expected to carry out historical research. Yet over time, the demonstration of scholarly abilities in a particular discipline has become a requirement for careers in history outside the academy as well. Why this should be so is not hard to see. Every historian needs to have acquaintance with the existing literature in particular fields and subjects. Each must learn how to find, evaluate, and use historical evidence. Each must gain practice in producing written scholarship based on that evidence, whether that scholarship be in the classic form of books and articles or in less venerable formats such as film treatments, Web sites, exhibit plans, or government reports. Historical scholarship being of deep utility in every kind of history work, anyone claiming to be a historian who lacks the knowledge and skills of research (even if that knowledge and those skills were not gained in a Ph.D. program) is not a historian.

The research ideal also embodies acculturation to academic norms of criticism and competition. While both norms can be carried too far, they are nevertheless central to academic professional life. Some historians are adept at competition and revel in the robust give-and-take of intellectual combat among specialists; others by disposition flee from active engagement with other historians and are sometimes reluctant even to publish their work in book form for fear of public reviews. Nevertheless, it is because academics are, in Thomas L. Haskell's words, "immersed in a subculture of competing practitioners who expose and correct one another's errors that their opinions possess greater authority than those of amateurs." Citing Alvin Gouldner's characterization of "the world of intellectuals and scholars, in which the duty to criticize and be criticized is probably more deeply ingrained than anywhere else," Haskell goes on to call the academic world "an occupational subculture that tends to be acutely status conscious, but which also tolerates greater candor and higher levels of criticism and conflict than would be thought acceptable in most human communities."[6] Thus, for better or worse, most academic

---

[6] Haskell's full and nuanced reflections on the role of professional competition and criticism are to be found in Thomas L. Haskell, "The New Aristocracy," *New York Review of Books*, December 4, 1997, 47–53.

historians accept as a given the existence of debate and criticism, enter into both with a certain gusto, and see these characteristics, at least when not excessive, as central to their enterprise.

Yet while such norms are commonplace within academic walls, they are not universally accepted outside and are often assailed. Attacks on the research ideal arise from two principal sources. One comes from members of the public, especially political figures seeking ingratiation with voters, who claim that research has assumed too high a role in higher education at the expense of teaching and service. Faculty members, they argue, should devote less time to their scholarship and more to students and citizens, and graduate students should be better prepared to teach and serve than they now are. While neither of these arguments is without merit, neither do they constitute an attack on the research ideal itself. A correction in what is at times an imbalance of incentives and rewards on campus might be achieved without any danger to the general pursuit of research there; and, when warranted, steps to correct the imbalance can be taken. Yet no one has found a way substantially to reduce universities' emphasis on research, short of removing all scholarly research from universities and placing it instead in freestanding research institutes that welcome no students and award no degrees, and none is likely to be found.[7] Nor can a major reduction in the emphasis on research be achieved without serious damage to research in all disciplines and a corresponding slowing in the advance of knowledge.

A second line of attack against the research ideal originates with those few aggrieved historians who have been disappointed in finding the employment they wish and blame the norms of the academy for their difficulties. While fortunately not widespread, this criticism, too, is largely irrelevant to its target. It is not training in the arts and methods of research per se that are at fault but rather the general preparation of historians, which, as this entire book argues, stands in need of considerable reform. After all, these critics (largely public historians) themselves apply – indeed, they must apply – the very research skills they have gained in their doctoral studies to the public history work they do. Rather than attacking the sway of research, these critics would do better trying to ensure that all public history meets the highest standards of research

---

[7] Or not found at least in the United States, except in rare cases like the Institute for Advanced Studies. National academies are common in other nations, and these academies' members pursue research, often for the benefit of the national state, without responsibilities for students. In them, research and service are conjoined; teaching is absent.

and justifies itself, if further justification be needed, as a variety of history practice coequal in strength and contribution to academic history.

Another source of resistance to research can be found among those who wish simply to teach and not to undertake research or to publish scholarship during their professional careers as historians. Occasionally, their resistance takes the form of proposals to create a distinct academic degree that would recognize competence in, although not mastery of, a particular intellectual discipline along with its distinguishing requirement: demonstrated ability to offer skilled instruction in the discipline of choice. This degree, senior to a master's degree, would not require the completion of a dissertation for its award. While one can understand this proposal's appeal to some people, it remains the case that a teacher of history who has not tried to carry out some research, participated in some summer institutes, attended some professional meetings – that is, ventured in some way to learn how research scholars of history work and think – will probably never have a full understanding or appreciation of how written history and the meaning embodied in it is created. It is therefore difficult to see how such a person can knowledgeably teach history to anyone except perhaps to those too young to need to know how historical meaning emerges from facts – namely, to pupils in elementary and middle schools.

Fortunately, a proportion (always too small) of practicing schoolteachers of history always struggles to secure, and succeeds against heavy odds in securing, their doctoral degrees, producing published scholarship, and maintaining membership in the intellectual community of history. Increasingly, too, these schoolteachers are recognized by scholarly and professional associations as constituting not only a rich resource of mind and skill but also the core of a distinct profession – that of school teaching – greatly in need of intellectual revitalization. As a result, a growing number of programs – sponsored and underwritten by the National Endowment for the Humanities (NEH), a few foundations, and some universities – sustain the aspirations of these few scholarly schoolteachers. If these efforts are maintained or, better, if they spread, the influence of research, or at least of research aspirations, in the professional lives of secondary school teachers will increase and their students everywhere will benefit. For this reason, too, an intermediate degree might prove harmful by removing an incentive for published scholarly research among schoolteachers.

In any event, because of the proven centrality of the research ideal to so many professions, modern universities the world over, and by late twentieth-century extension many undergraduate colleges in the

Anglo-American system, have become inconceivable without the creation and advancement of knowledge at their center.[8] Whether the progress of learning through scholarship is pursued in the belief that knowledge is its own end or that it must prove its utility – debate about this matter is unlikely ever to be stilled – universities and colleges have become the principal sites of the creation, evaluation, and diffusion of knowledge and understanding. This is not to deny that novelists and poets, independent scholars, and the employees of freestanding research institutes, museums, corporations, and government agencies have often proved themselves to be as productive of new knowledge and understanding as academic scholars. But it is at universities that the overwhelming majority of new knowledge is constituted and – a critically important consideration – subjected to demanding criticism; and, most importantly for the discipline of history, it is there that most of the new historical understanding we continue to gain comes into being.

It is therefore to universities that aspiring creators of new knowledge are most readily and naturally drawn, and it is from within them that have emerged the standards and procedures by which new knowledge is both created and evaluated. Universities are the institutions where are to be found those men and women who, in proximity and often in concert, seek to advance knowledge in their fields and where such efforts are protected by the independence of the institutions, by their policies of advancement and tenure, and by the code of academic freedom by which they govern themselves. It is little wonder that the research ideal, born and nurtured in these universities, is the one to which historians of all kinds most often hitch their aspirations.

In addition to being the principal location of historical scholarship, the research university assures its sway by its near monopoly over the accreditation of trained people in most fields of professional and intellectual endeavor, including history. Without a doctorate – or its analog in related fields, such as the LL.D., M.D., and Ed.D. – without certification that one has completed a course of study recognized as complete and legitimate by similar institutions and by peers in the same discipline, professional status is not assured and professional positions are hard to come by. This very fact lends a kind of urgency to universities' unquestioning emphasis on research skills to the near exclusion of every other. One must

---

[8] The classicist Benjamin Jowett is said to have declared of research at Balliol College, Oxford, of which he was master, "There will be none of that in my college." No one could get away with asserting something similar in the United States today.

learn, so the assumption goes, to *do* history (or sociology, biology, or the law) before one can teach or practice it; one must learn to produce works of history before one can legitimately expect to be called a historian.

Historians cannot, and therefore should not try to, resist the gravitation of the research ideal. Each is called instead to decide how the ideal is applicable to particular aspirations, dispositions, and work. While many historians will from time to time tire of monographic writing or historiographical disputes or grow frustrated with the spread of scholarly specialization, having the practiced capacity to produce research scholarship will always prove essential to any kind of professional practice in history. The habits of mind created by training for research remain the foundation of every kind of history work. Every historian would be wise to seek to possess and maintain them.

Because historical research has proved such a boon for human knowledge, it is easy to mistake it for the sole or highest good of history work, at least in academic and related circles. Yet it is neither. For just as historians who freely enter the academy make themselves subjects of the research ideal, so they place themselves in liege to teaching, the second constituent element of the Academic Trinity and, because teaching long preceded research as an honored occupation, the oldest. While most academics are, at one time or another in their careers if not throughout them, research scholars, they are also teachers, most of them of undergraduate students and, in universities, also of graduate students.[9] Earning pay for giving instruction to students rather than for carrying out research, academics are teachers by virtue of their contracts of employment. While some scholars have always sought, and a few have gained, exemption from teaching duties, never have university and college teaching and research effectively been divorced, and rarely has anyone tried to divorce them. Every academic must plan to teach. And in teaching, every academic must necessarily find a way to resist, at least part of the time, the magnetic pull of research.[10]

---

[9] Significantly, the desire to teach seems to hold a higher appeal for those history graduate students (88 percent) desirous of entering the academy than the desire to undertake research (77 percent). Golde, "The Career Goals of History Doctoral Students."

[10] In the United States, exemption from teaching has taken the form of the sabbatical, more recently the separately funded research, leave (which must be applied for), and the exceptional nonteaching research professorship. A small proportion of researchers, especially, but not exclusively, in the sciences and medicine, work in independent research institutes such as the National Institutes of Health, the Battelle Memorial Institute, and Resources for the Future and, as they are colloquially known in the social sciences, in "think tanks" like the Brookings Institution.

Because teaching and research have always been understood as dynamically related, each complementing and replenishing the other, the obligation to teach has been twinned with responsibilities toward research since the birth of research universities in nineteenth-century Germany. It was not of course until well into the twentieth century, and not uniformly in every university even then, that research was expected of every academic. Even today there remain academic islands of "pure" teaching, largely at small baccalaureate colleges, in a sea of research college and university faculties, and the balance between teaching and research varies from institution to institution and among categories of institutions. Many four-year colleges and public universities place great emphasis on teaching while supporting faculty members' research. But generally speaking, if one now chooses to be a teaching historian only, it will have to be in a secondary school or on a small, sectarian, or two-year college faculty. Otherwise, teaching must be managed as part of the Academic Trinity.

The marriage between teaching and research is most often explained as necessitated by the link – psychological as well as intellectual – between having a thought and expressing it. One does not fully understand, perhaps not fully possess, a thought until it is written or spoken. Additionally, it is only by speaking and discussing ideas that they take on their fullest form and are thoroughly understood. Thus, teaching is a way of completing the process of thinking. It is also commonly, and surely validly, argued that it is by teaching as much as by writing that ideas are communicated to others, that teaching, especially when it is embodied in a person who, by word and act together, actuates the engagement of a mind with ideas, is perhaps the most effective means of diffusing knowledge from people who know much to those who know less.

But that teaching and research are combined in the same institutions has additional sources, additional justifications. In modern, open societies, access to knowledge has come to be seen as a right, one nowhere more widely cherished than in the United States, whose comparatively egalitarian system of higher education is the envy of most others. While that system may be exploited by too many students seeking simply to gain career benefits and a degree increasingly necessary for most employment, other students – the most satisfying kind – wish to learn the most up-to-date knowledge from the most expert teaching scholars and researchers. And rare are the experts who do not teach their new knowledge and fresh thinking to students before it finds its way into print. Teaching is often the most effective and speedy way to present new knowledge and to synthesize it with old, and for many students teaching provides them with historical knowledge much more vividly and with greater impact than written history. Thus, teaching is customarily the spouse of research.

Few academics have not experienced the transit of inspiration and insight between teaching and research. That their research often soon and always eventually finds its way into their instruction in the classroom is well known. But the reverse is often also true: that explaining knowledge to others often leads in the teacher's mind to questions or thoughts that might not have arisen in any other way. Historians often test their ideas first in graduate seminars, where students can be depended on to be critical and disputatious (which is one of the reasons that so many historians prefer to teach graduate than undergraduate students). Rare is the teacher who has not been provoked to speculation by a young student's innocent question, by the probing inquiry of a graduate student, or by a sudden realization that an uttered thought is incomplete, its substantiation weak, or its logic faulty. Teaching is integral to the academic enterprise because it supports scholars' reflection, is indeed a form of it.[11]

For students, teaching is even more essential. Though they may resist going to class or completing their assignments, the teaching of their instructors is at its best the enactment of learning. To see teachers bringing knowledge alive, working with it before a class, conceiving new ways to explain something: these are the means by which knowledge is often offered to students with more impact than any other. Particularly in this era, when the obstacles to reading are so numerous, lively, engaged teaching may be the only way to awaken in some students an interest in, to say nothing of a thirst for, knowledge about any subject.

Of course, the tension between the responsibilities of teaching and research cannot be overlooked. Teaching was the original formal, structured, institutionalized way, built on conversation, that ideas were conveyed to others. History teaching itself emerged from the tales told by rhapsodes, the bards, and the minstrels of ancient Greece, then by the poets of the Homeric era before the first written, prose histories of

---

[11] Much is made of academic historians' supposed neglect or dislike of teaching. Surveys reveal precisely the opposite. In the most recent survey, 44 percent of respondents (academic historians all) identified themselves as equally researchers and teachers, another 32 percent reporting themselves as more teacher than researcher. Robert B. Townsend, "A Profile of the History Profession, 2010," *Perspectives in History* 48 (October 2010): 36–39.

Herodotus and Thucydides. Since the days of ancient Greece, written and spoken words – writing and speech, literature and oratory – have vied for authority and precedence over the other, and each has had its champions. The enduring and competing claims of research and teaching are one residue of this conflict, as is the more actual tension between time spent on instruction and on research. In the modern academy, that tension is heightened, although it is not caused, by the greater professional weight and expectations placed on research and the greater compensation offered productive university research scholars than college teachers. The tension is also exacerbated by the market forces and administrative fiats increasingly bearing down on faculty members everywhere – increasing class sizes and teaching loads as budgets are cut, intensified performance standards, and the competition from adjunct teachers and even graduate teaching assistants. Yet because teaching while in residence on a faculty is almost inescapable, an academic has to learn to manage the sometimes-clashing responsibilities of teaching and research as part of the very nature of academic professional life. This is often difficult to do, because professional status depends more heavily on the widely known and reported results of research than on the more locally recognized fruits of instruction. And yet, especially for historians, teaching carries with it great cultural, educational, and humane purpose and significance.

History teaching's most venerable purpose is to substitute for the mythic tales and explanatory conventions that occupy young and other people's minds the more considered and closer-to-the-truth presentations of the past. Doing so is always an uphill fight, but the effort is all the more necessary for that reason. Many people, especially in our visual age, read too little; some learn best when hearing others speak or seeing the past presented in person. For these reasons alone, trying to counteract invalid notions of the past through instruction is essential to a free and informed society. Teaching also helps students see more directly and often more vividly than from books that everything they read in documents, texts, and other works is problematic, itself the product of the time and circumstances in which the documents and other texts were written or created, and thus open to independent reflection, criticism, and evaluation.

In our own age, when false analogy often passes for argument, tale telling by televised commentators substitutes for analytical history, and policy decisions are frequently arrived at without adequate knowledge of historical context, the give-and-take of face-to-face instruction also may well be the only way to heighten students' awareness of the utility, as well as the dangers of the misuse (often through weak analogies), of historical knowledge.[12] The works of history they are likely to read on their own will be narratives, often only modestly, if at all, critically distanced from their subjects. The conversations that use history into which they will enter are likely to be erroneous or formulaic. Classroom instruction may be the only time in their lives that students have the chance to become alert to the fundamentally problematic and contingent nature of all historical knowledge.

Moreover, because the subjects of the disciplines that constitute the humanities are taken to be more accessible to everyone than those of the natural and physical sciences, bad teaching in these subjects is less forgiven than in others. Proximity to the "great questions" of life, rather than to utilitarian ones, intensifies teachers' responsibilities to their students. That is to say, many of the charges that are leveled against academics for ignoring teaching in preference to recondite scholarship grow out of an abiding respect and recognition of the place of the humanities in human life. Teaching is a way, perhaps the best way, of awaking young people to issues of value, judgment, and complexity that they may encounter in serious form and formal circumstances at no other time in their lives.

In more recent decades, the teaching of history to undergraduates has also had to aim at overcoming poor secondary school history teaching. Many schoolteachers, lacking deep knowledge of their subjects, often pass along to their students as proven facts interpretations of the past long discarded by scholars and closer to myth than accurate knowledge. But equally problematic is the method by which history is taught in schools. What historian has not heard it said by adults – indeed, what historian has not experienced its truth directly? – that the teaching of history in school was for them nothing but the presentation of dry-as-dust facts and then the recitation back of lists of names and dates, as if history is constituted of nothing but those? Because of continuing failures of instruction at the secondary school level (combined with the political context of American schooling and the cultural deficits of students against which history teachers are relatively impotent), one of the most important duties of academic historians today is to resuscitate a love of historical knowledge that has been often seriously injured if not killed in school as

---

[12] The now classic works on the misapplication of analogies are Ernest R. May, *"Lessons" of the Past: The Use and Misuse of American Foreign Policy* (New York: Oxford University Press, 1973), and Ernest R. May and Richard Neustadt, *Thinking in Time: The Uses of History for Decision Makers* (New York: Free Press, 1987). See also Otis L. Graham, Jr., *Losing Time: The Industrial Policy Debate* (Cambridge, MA: Harvard University Press, 1972), chap. 11.

well as simply to create a love of history in students and teachers they never felt. If anything justifies teaching and makes it a worthy academic responsibility, this is it.

Yet correcting for poor secondary instruction cannot be academic teachers' only responsibility toward secondary schooling. Academic teaching of history must today also extend to increasing schoolteachers' historical knowledge, which is frequently much lower than it should be. Teachers share responsibility for this.[13] Too many of them fail to keep up (or at least to struggle to keep up) with their subjects. Rarely do they hold themselves out as participants in the world of learning, as part of a larger intellectual community of historians. Yet academic teachers of history have some responsibility for this state of affairs – and a considerable stake in its repair. To hold back from helping prepare schoolteachers to be well-informed generalists of their subject is to contribute to an old and dangerous division between schoolteachers and academics. Perhaps worse, it is to confirm the low status of history, long ago lost in the mush known as "social studies," in the school curriculum. Despite the efforts of some historians to prevent this decline, academics and their organizations contributed throughout much of the twentieth century to this state of affairs by inattention to the schools and arrogance toward schoolteachers.[14] If academics are concerned to see better-prepared students in their classroom, they must join with schoolteachers of history, as many have, to improve and maintain the latter's knowledge of history. And if academics are to become better prepared to teach history, they must also learn about effective teaching from their school-based

[13] I say this with due regard for the indefensible physical conditions under which secondary schoolteachers must often teach, the intensity of their schedules, the frequent absence of community support and funding for improved schooling, the poor training that many teachers have received, and the pall that bureaucracy, state licensing and testing requirements, and sheer public ignorance cast over school classrooms. Here, I focus on teachers' frequent deficiencies in knowledge simply to emphasize historians' particular responsibilities to them.

[14] So, of course, did the National Council for the Social Studies, the principal organization of teachers of history and related subjects in the school. For a single, telling example of the NCSS's stance, see *Handbook on Teaching Social Issues* (Washington, DC: National Council for the Social Studies, 1996). Academic historians have only recently rejoined their colleagues in the schools to seek higher standards for history teachers' certification and recertification, the improvement of teachers' professional development, and the design of national and state standards of knowledge against which schools are measured and their students are tested and promoted. In addition, academic teachers of history have contributed to, and greatly benefited from, many teacher education efforts. These include the *OAH Magazine of History*, the National Council for History Education, and National History Day.

colleagues, who are often more highly skilled in instructional techniques than academics.

Of the three elements of the Academic Trinity, the most problematic, least understood, and most infrequently discussed is the norm of service.[15] While the role of teaching in the preparation of graduate students and the adequacy of faculty members' commitment to undergraduate classroom instruction have in recent years received increased professional scrutiny and public attention (much of it polemical and ill-informed), the complementary ideal of service continues to attract comparatively little notice.[16]

[15] Telling evidence in support of this assertion is embodied in the exemplary fact that four of the most trenchant and robust, as well as widely differing, recent reflections on universities and the pursuits of history contain no mention of the service ideal. See Theodore S. Hamerow, *Reflections on History and Historians* (Madison: University of Wisconsin Press, 1987); Donald Kennedy, *Academic Duty* (Cambridge, MA: Harvard University Press, 1997); Jaroslav Pelikan, *The Idea of the University: A Reexamination* (New Haven: Yale University Press, 1992); and Henry Rosovsky, *The University: An Owner's Manual* (New York: W. W. Norton, 1990). A chapter promisingly titled "To Serve the University" in Kennedy's book has in fact little to do with the matter. Edward Shils, *The Academic Ethic* (Chicago: University of Chicago Press, 1984), 73–96, contains the most extended discussion of what constitutes academic service to the larger society, but that discussion is couched in ideal terms, does not concern the concrete services by which an academic is supposed to be evaluated, and, faithful to its title, is limited to the academic profession. Other recent and thoughtful evocations of academic life are Stuart Rojstaczer, *Gone for Good: Tales of University Life after the Golden Age* (New York: Oxford University Press, 1999), and Alvin Kernan, *In Plato's Cave* (New Haven: Yale University Press, 1999).

[16] Critiques of the academy and professoriate now amount to a small library in themselves, too much of its contents based upon ideology rather than knowledge. See, for example, Martin Anderson, *Imposters in the Temple: A Blueprint for Improving Higher Education in America* (Stanford: Hoover Institution Press, 1996); Lynne V. Cheney, *Telling the Truth: Why Our Culture and Our Country Have Stopped Making Sense* (New York: Simon & Schuster, 1995); Charles J. Sykes, *ProfScam: Professors and the Demise of Higher Education* (Washington, DC: Regnery Gateway, 1988); Alan Charles Kors and Harvey A. Silverglate, *The Shadow University: The Betrayal of Liberty on America's Campuses* (New York: Free Press, 1998); and Dinesh D'Souza, *Illiberal Education: The Politics of Race and Sex on Campus* (New York: Free Press, 1991). Page Smith, *Killing the Spirit: Higher Education in America* (New York: Viking Penguin, 1990) is more sober and informed than the others. All tend to be overwrought (the "shame" of universities, "professors' crimes against higher education"), ignorant ("the new vogue of specialization"), resentful, polemical, selective in their use of evidence, silly (can a country, rather than a person, make, or stop making, sense?), and proceeding by anecdote rather than by sustained argument. Their authors, like those who rush to observe fires with fiendish delight, savor the most foolish and egregious incidents and ways of some academics and some campuses and take them to characterize all the rest. These works do, however, reveal the continuing appeal of the old-time college – engaged teachers, generalists at the podium, small classes, instruction in values, robust expression – and the enduring tension

In fact, even the most serious recent evaluations of the professoriate and of collegiate and graduate education have uniformly neglected consideration of the meaning of academic public service and its estimation in the employment, advancement, compensation, and work of college and university faculty members. This is not to say that the issue of what constitutes service never arises on campus, that the obligations of service are not of concern to faculty members, or that academics fail to figure out their obligations to their larger professional community. On the contrary: particularly in times of political turmoil, academics engage in heated public debates and arraign each other over the nature and extent of their public involvement – either for not speaking out on issues of the day or, the reverse, for compromising the academic mission by dragging colleges and universities into the public arena and applying academic ideas to issues to which, it is argued, they are irrelevant. Occasionally, too, legislators join members of the public in debating whether their states' publicly supported universities are adequately contributing to the public good in return for annual appropriations or, conversely, whether their faculties are too involved in public affairs – which usually, although not always, means too involved in supporting liberal or leftist causes. Yet once such moments have passed, little residue of new understanding, new policies, or new expectations about public service can be found. The ideal of service remains as it long has been: an ideal whose existence academics and others acknowledge but to which they seem to owe no clear fealty and to which they bring no clear understanding. And well might that be, for on closer inspection, the norm of service has always been fundamentally confused.

The ideal of academic public service is deeply American in its origins. Arising coincident with the establishment of state and land-grant universities, public service joined the venerable Anglo-American collegiate ideal of cultural education and the more modern German university ideal of advanced research to create by the early twentieth century the tripartite mission of almost all American universities – what I call the

---

between the British collegiate and German research ideals in American education. But most of these books also lack any appreciation of such attributes of American universities as their flexibility and avoid any comparative perspective on other university traditions, such as the European, still often ossified in their nineteenth-century form. Francis Oakley has wickedly characterized these books' manner of argumentation as "disheveled anecdotalism" in "The Elusive Academic Profession: Complexity and Change," in Stephen R. Graubard (ed.), *The American Academic Profession* (New Brunswick, NJ: Transaction, 2001), 43–66. A more optimistic argument in a mistitled book is David Harlan, *The Degradation of American History* (Chicago: University of Chicago Press, 1997).

Academic Trinity – and, by the mid-twentieth century, of a large majority of collegiate institutions as well. From the creation of the great public universities of individual American states, a commitment to public service constituted one of their given missions. Receiving public funds, these universities were expected to contribute to the needs of the citizens of the jurisdictions whose legislatures had chartered them. The universities could and did legitimately claim that they discharged this responsibility through their teaching function (by conveying knowledge to, and enriching the lives of, their students) and through their research function (by contributing to the bodies of knowledge that undergirded the occupations that citizens of their states pursued). And it was under the herald of public service that universities established their extensive and often distinguished vocational programs – medical, law, business, engineering, agricultural, public affairs, and normal (or education) schools, as well as agricultural and other extension services. It was also in the name of service that universities sent forth their graduates and faculty members to benefit their communities, as the University of Wisconsin proudly did – for example, with John R. Commons as well as other early labor historians – in the era of Robert M. LaFollette under the pennant of the "Wisconsin Idea." So powerful did this ideal become that most universities, even private ones, could over time justly claim – much as Princeton University, although a private institution, still claims in Woodrow Wilson's formulation – that their teaching and research were "in the nation's service."[17]

As long as the German research ideal remained comparatively isolated in a few distinctive universities such as the Johns Hopkins University, Clark University, and the University of Chicago and as long as in most of the others it took second place to the Anglo-American collegiate tradition – or at least as long as both remained in some kind of equilibrium, as they more or less did until the Second World War – the service ideal could be taken for granted. It could be assumed, as often it still is, that teaching and research fully constituted a university's service to society.[18] But when,

---

[17] Recent attacks within Wisconsin itself on historian William J. Cronon for having criticized that state's governor suggests that that state's venerable ideal of academic public service, one embodied in the Wisconsin Idea, may now be under assault because of the nation's hyperpoliticized environment.

[18] See, for example, Catherine Gallagher, "The History of Literary Criticism," in Thomas Bender and Carl E. Schorske (eds.), *American Academic Culture in Transformation: Fifty Years, Four Disciplines* (Princeton: Princeton University Press, 1997), 151–171, where the author quite emphatically identifies the "'service' function" of "the profession" of literary criticism with responding, through teaching, to undergraduates' desire to understand their own lives.

under the spur of hot and cold wars and a vast inflow of federal funds, university faculties redirected their energies largely toward the production of new knowledge, legitimate fears arose about the subordination of teaching to research and about the sacrifice of undergraduate and graduate students' welfare to faculty members' scholarly contributions to their disciplines and society. As a result, how to define the meaning and nature of the third component of the Academic Trinity became newly problematic. Public service might become a cover for an even more intense focus on research. Not only were faculty members ignoring their students in preference to their scholarly endeavors, it was feared and charged; they were also turning inward, to their own careers and specialized academic interests and away from the communities that they were obligated to serve. Such charges continue to be lodged against American colleges and universities and their faculties.

Regardless of the validity of the charges, they imply a set of assumptions that have never been well thought out. The result is that academics – and, because of the distinctive role of history, academic historians especially – have been left to improvise their own understanding and practice of service without benefit of clear expectations, models of practice, or the confident guidance of others. Nor has it ever been clear what, in addition to teaching and research, might precisely constitute a contribution to society by historians or any other academics. Does the public service ideal refer to an institution's service to the community or to the particular social contributions of its individual faculty members? Is the "service" embodied by the ideal meant to be service to one's academic institution or to its warranting society and culture? Do the creation of knowledge through research and the transmission of knowledge through teaching not constitute service enough? Is "service" discharged when an academic historian temporarily steps outside the classroom to be a public historian as, say, curator of a museum exhibit? That is, is public history to be considered "service" instead of a contribution to the advance of knowledge and to teaching? And how does one measure service – by its frequency and duration, its quality, or its purpose? Who is to evaluate it, and for what ends?[19]

---

[19] Examples of the assumption that service means service to academic departments and institutions and not to the larger world are the works of Steven M. Cahn. See, for example, *Saints and Scamps: Ethics in Academia* (Totowa, NJ: Rowman & Littlefield, 1986), chap. 3, and *From Student to Scholar: A Candid Guide to Becoming a Professor* (New York: Columbia University Press, 2008), chap. 9.

The answers to these and related questions can have direct, though rarely acknowledged, impact on the professional lives of individual faculty members and, by extension, of nonacademic scholars as well. But then these questions are rarely asked and their answers rarely sought. If by contribution to the public good the service ideal concerns only an institution's posture toward its community, then academics would be justified in arguing (as few now do) that, as long as their colleges and universities are offering some benefit to society and increasing the stock of public good through the collective activities of their faculties, individual faculty members have no particular responsibility to make distinct and personal contributions themselves and ought not to be held accountable for ignoring public service. If, however, the norm of service obligates each faculty member to make a measurable contribution to institution, town, state, or nation, then each must be held responsible for doing so – and suffer the costs for not doing so. But, once again, it is not at all clear whether this obligation is part of the service ideal.

Similarly, if an institution decides that it serves the public good fully enough by teaching its students well and contributing, through faculty research and scholarship, to the community's stock of knowledge – no small contributions in and of themselves – then its faculty members may be under no obligation to apply their knowledge to specific public problems or offer their knowledge to nonacademic citizens.[20] On the other hand, if an institution defines public service to mean that each faculty

[20] For instance, in writing of service, Jaroslav Pelikan concerns himself only with institutions', not individuals', service to society; see *The Idea of the University*, chaps. 13, 14. The same thrust is found in Ernest L. Boyer and Fred M. Hechinger, *Higher Learning in the Nation's Service* (Washington, DC: Carnegie Foundation for the Advancement of Teaching, 1981), whose central argument, borrowed from Woodrow Wilson's phrasing, is an institution's obligation to serve society through educating the young, creating knowledge, and advancing civic learning. The authors say nothing of the service of individual faculty members. In *Scholarship Reconsidered: Priorities of the Professoriate* (Princeton: Carnegie Foundation for the Advancement of Teaching, 1990), a book devoted principally to the tensions between research and teaching, Boyer writes of "applied scholarship" and, on page 37, devotes a single paragraph to how it might be evaluated. Nor does he distinguish among fields (say, biomedicine and musicology) and how the service ideal might be implemented in each. The same inattention to service is found in Charles E. Glassick et al., *Scholarship Assessed: Evaluation of the Professoriate* (San Francisco: Jossey-Bass, 1997). It is worth noting that none of the principal scholarly and professional associations in history have tried to set forth concretely how historians might be obligated to public service and how institutions might evaluate it. An extended, fresh consideration of the academic public service ideal, as well as a fresh justification for academic public service itself, is greatly needed.

member must make a tangible contribution to institution, community, or nation, it becomes incumbent on the institution to spell out the nature and evaluation of that contribution and on each faculty member to implement it appropriately. Rarely is either done.

The result is that those historians who join college and university faculties are likely quickly to discover that they are without benefit of clear guidelines on matters relating to service, public or otherwise. Yes, local norms of service are usually absorbed easily enough, and a high percentage of historians adapt to the service norms of their institutions and engage in some kind of service without reward or excessive complaint; enough institutional citizens exist to keep historical institutions running reasonably well. But historians receive no formal training in public service or any kind of briefing about it when joining a faculty. While helping to administer a department or college cannot easily be identified with the public service ideal, often it is placed under the protean term simply of "service," thus seriously muddying a concept that, at its origins, had weightier civic and moral dimensions. Young academics also quickly learn that, despite what is often averred, consideration of service plays little role in assessments of faculty members' qualifications for advancement in rank and compensation. Membership on departmental committees – faculty search committees, for instance – or work as chief departmental adviser to undergraduates or director of a department's graduate program is expected of most academics at some point in their careers; but rarely is the quality of that work assessed or rewarded (or, as the case may be, penalized). Service at the institutional level on interdepartmental bodies – on admissions committees, deans' councils, and the like – falls almost entirely outside the ken of departmental colleagues and so, whatever its quality, is likely to make no difference to advancement and pay, which are largely determined at the departmental level or by rigid public scales that give little heed to scholarly productivity, quality of teaching, or the nature of public service to begin with. When service rises to the community, state, or national level, even when confined to activities seen as related to professional knowledge and skills – in-service assistance to local schools, membership on a governor's commission, contribution to boards constituted by federal agencies like the NEH or the National Academy of Sciences – evaluation of a faculty member's work is even more problematic. What should be surprising under such circumstances is not academics' unwillingness to offer their services but their widespread readiness, despite the confusions attending definitions of public service, to do so.

Professional consulting – providing expert advice to others for a fee – is sometimes held out as an example of service. But colleges and universities duly recognize work compensated by fees (rather than honoraria) as distinct from public service by setting limits, usually one day a week, to the amount of time faculty members can devote to it. Furthermore, the problems of evaluating the quality of consultative work as public service (if consulting can even be considered that) are the same as those pertaining to contributed community service, especially its uncertain importance within the academy and the difficulty of its assessment. As a result, few institutions weigh consulting in making decisions about appointment and promotion, certainly about the appointment and promotion of historians.[21]

None of these observations address the larger issues of the public service of colleges and universities themselves – issues beyond the scope of this book. But under the current conditions of institutional funding and outside pressure from ideological and other special interest groups, the danger of tilting public service to serve others' interests has increased sharply. No greater evidence of this is the rising imbalance between the influence on campus of the sciences and professional schools on the one hand and the humanities and related social sciences on the other. The temptation among historians and other humanists to serve masters other than the truth will only intensify as their segments of colleges and universities feel increasing pressure to justify their existence – their curricula, their faculty allotments, their proportion of distribution requirements – through bringing in more funds. On the other hand, the provision of service to the larger society will also be essential in meeting the doubts and aspersions of critics of higher education while justifying the classic mission and utility of knowledge.[22]

Although all academics find themselves involved at one time or another in puzzling out how they should distribute their time and attention to the three elements of the Academic Trinity, academic historians have a more than small stake in the way public service is defined and in the standards

[21] Efforts are currently under way to create evaluative standards for what is now called "public scholarship." That can only be to the good. But one should bear in mind that invigorating academics to carry their knowledge into extra-academic realms and to recognize and reward them for it does not address the larger issues of the service ideal in American higher education. For a brief report on one of these efforts, see Nancy Cantor and Steven D. Lavine, "Taking Public Scholarship Seriously," *Chronicle of Higher Education*, June 3, 2006, B20.

[22] On these and related matters, the incisive words of David A. Hollinger, "Money and Academic Freedom a Half-Century after McCarthyism: Universities amid the Force Fields of Capital," in Hollinger (ed.), *Cosmopolitanism and Solidarity: Studies in Ethnoracial, Religious, and Professional Affiliation in the United States* (Madison: University of Wisconsin Press, 2006), 77–105, are directly pertinent.

that guide its implementation. Since the days when James Harvey Robinson (in debt to nineteenth-century European historians who coined the term) proclaimed the existence of a "New History," historical knowledge has been taken to provide a service to the public in helping it orient itself in the world, and a diverse range of scholars – one need only name Charles A. Beard, Richard Hofstadter, Gordon Wright, Gerda Lerner, Fritz Stern, C. Vann Woodward, John Hope Franklin, Eric Foner, and William E. Leuchtenburg – have always devoted themselves in this sense to public enlightenment and orientation. But the emergence of public history as a distinct historical profession and the increasing public concern about the responsibilities of faculty members has given urgency to the task of defining what academic historians mean by public service. Suffice it to say here that, because an academic historian's engagement in those activities taken to constitute public rather than academic history can be defined as professional, rather than civic, service, even being a public historian does not offer exemption from the puzzles of professional public service.[23]

Until academic institutions, individually and collectively, devote their energies to addressing some of these confusions, the public service ideal will continue to be valued at a discount within academic walls. Because the ideal remains confused at a time when the discipline of history is rapidly increasing its utility and expanding its relevance within other professions and to many public issues and institutions, academic historians should justifiably feel particularly troubled by this continuing confusion. Should they write op-ed articles and serve on peer-review panels of the NEH or, instead, agree only to occasional, conventional service on departmental committees? Should they offer in-service courses for schoolteachers or concentrate solely on their scholarly research? It may well be that all historians must make up their own minds and act from their own dispositions and aspirations. But their having to do so without generally accepted guidelines makes that task no easier.

Despite the complexities and confusions of the academy, it is understandable that an academic professorship is the holy grail of so many aspiring historians. Nothing that I have written here should suggest that it ought

---

[23] This is an aspect of public historical work that deserves more attention. The public service ideal may simply be irrelevant, because so encompassing, for those who work, say, as historians in government, and it may be difficult to achieve for historians in business.

not to be or that the deficiencies of the academy – and there are others irrelevant to the purposes of this book – should be considered severe enough to deter historians from an academic career. On the contrary. For while much has been written in recent years of the iniquities and inanities of academics, on a scale of ideal institutional health and welfare colleges and universities are less ill-governed, their practices less questionable, the behavior of their employees less deceptive, and their practices less indefensible than those of most other modern institutions, especially institutions of business.

It is precisely by such comparisons that academic careers have long seemed attractive to those who have entered upon them.[24] For those whose principal aspiration is to create knowledge or to lead a comparatively reflective life, there are no other institutions that provide the atmosphere in which to do so to the same degree, as well as to enjoy relative freedom of schedule and hierarchy, than research universities. For those who choose to devote themselves as historians principally to teaching, collegiate institutions retain great appeal. But in no academic pursuit can the conventions of the Academic Trinity be escaped; and historians, whether working inside or outside academic walls, should not expect those conventions to diminish appreciably in number or kind or to lose their salience. Research will not soon be dethroned as the principal determinant of rank and pay at research universities. Land-grant colleges and universities will not soon give up their commitment to public service. Baccalaureate and many university colleges will not easily allow their cherished ethos of teaching to erode. And even those nonacademic institutions that employ historians will be found applying at least some of these conventions to those historians who carry out research and other functions. These are the "givens" of academic life in its different settings, and altering those realities will be as easy as changing the planets' transit of the sun.

Those who are thinking of entering the academy must therefore consider directly whether they wish to pursue academic or other careers in history – whether by temperament and commitment they are ready

---

[24] A sunny and bracing, and thus distinctive, evocation of an academic's life and a clear exposition of what gratifications as well as challenges that life can hold is James Axtell, *The Pleasures of Academe: A Celebration and Defense of Higher Education* (Lincoln: University of Nebraska Press, 1998). Two other robust and provocative reflections on academic life are David Damrosch et al., *Meetings of the Mind* (Princeton: Princeton University Press, 2000), and Marjorie B. Garber, *Academic Instincts* (Princeton: Princeton University Press, 2001).

to take on the responsibilities of the Academic Trinity. The matter of clear choice cannot be too heavily emphasized, for socialization into the expectations of academia is stealthy, unconscious, and quick. Instead of preparing graduate students for deliberate choices, advanced training in history rapidly accustoms students to thinking only in academic terms and to accepting almost without question that being a historian in a research university is the only worthy professional berth to seek. With every step forward into academia, aspiring historians find it increasingly difficult to stay clear of the forces acculturating them without much opposition solely to academic perspectives. They find it hard to assess clearly the many obstacles – a limit on opportunities for academic employment (as well as employment in a place of one's choosing) and the costs and length of graduate study being the chief among them – that face them, an assessment that might lead some, with their sense of self intact, to extricate themselves from the expectations of academic work and choose other careers as historians.[25]

Despite these difficulties, to embark with open eyes and full heart on an academic career is to enter upon a professional life full of intellectual and personal satisfactions. If the academy is the site of occasional acts and thoughts that seem preposterous, if academic conventions in some instances become pieties, if colleges and universities reveal some of the calcification that eventually overcomes all institutions, and if academic life is no longer, if it ever was, a sanctuary from a heartless world, all of these shortcomings pale beside those of most other institutions and professions. To be an academic is thus to be privileged. It is not, however, to be exempt from the obligations of privilege – to try with demonstrable effort to meet the obligations of research, teaching, and service for the general good.

---

[25] On these careers, see Chapter 5. A Committee on Graduate Education of the American Historical Association examined these and many other obstacles and tried to determine how to reduce their number and severity. Its report is the important work, Thomas Bender et al., *The Education of Historians for the Twenty-First Century* (Urbana: University of Illinois Press, 2004). While this overdue effort is welcome, it is difficult to see how historians, or departments of history, alone can address problems that in one way or another affect graduate preparation in all disciplines. These are issues that the American Council of Learned Societies, the Social Science Research Council, the Conference of Administrative Officers of the disciplinary associations (within the orbit of the ACLS), and the Council of Graduate Schools ought to take up together.

5

History outside the Academy

Those who enter upon graduate study in history are not preparing themselves simply to undertake research and produce scholarship that advances human knowledge. They are – or at least should be – also commencing their preparation to be historians in the full sense of that term, people whose aim it is to discover meaning in the past and to create meaning in the present for all who seek to find in historical knowledge an anchor in the world or a source of knowledge and pleasure. Such students ought to be seeking to gain not only the skills of research scholarship but also the ability to convey historical knowledge to others through whatever means are appropriate and the capacity to help their fellow citizens understand life by reference to its origins in times before their own. Yet most graduate history programs prepare their doctoral candidates only to become scholars – to undertake historical research and to produce written scholarship. Few graduate faculties in history encourage their students to consider as career choices all professional pursuits that are open to them, pursuits among which they should be prepared to make reasoned, rather than reflexive, choices.[1] Consequently, graduate students in history are

---

[1] Some universities, under the auspices of such organizations as the Association of American Colleges and Universities and the Council of Graduate Schools and with funding from the Pew Charitable Trusts, have undertaken welcome efforts to prepare their graduate students better for academic work, especially work as classroom teachers. In my estimation, however, these efforts fall short of what these and other universities should be offering their students, an increasingly large proportion of whom will pursue their scholarly and professional careers outside the academy, for they fail to prepare students for the full range of professional pursuits in their disciplines. While I share the view of many critics that scholarly associations and universities must not relent in creating full-time, tenure-track positions for doctorate holders and pressing colleges and universities to

usually left to learn of many, perhaps of most, components of their discipline on their own, and they have to struggle especially hard to learn of those professions of history and occupations for historians that are not academic.

That should not surprise us. The weight of inertial forces, especially those that can reasonably be said to have brought about more than serviceable results over time – great scholarship, for instance – are always due more than grudging respect. Perhaps, too, given the ever-increasing variety of historical subjects and practices, we should realistically expect graduate schools to select and then emphasize in their programs of instruction only a fraction of what might be offered in a curriculum that already requires many years to complete – providing that these emphases exhibit evidence of conscious deliberation, not inadvertence or convention, in their selection.[2] Nevertheless, to create research scholars is how most Ph.D.-granting history departments envisage their principal function. More, but still too few, prepare their students to teach, although teaching is, after all, what a majority of those entering academic employment will do and be paid to do on receipt of their degrees. Many, if not most, university faculty members believe (or at least act as if they believe) that, once aspiring historians gain experience in scholarly research, master the bibliography and basic knowledge of their fields, and complete

reduce their reliance on part-time faculty members, I see nothing inconsistent in matching those efforts with broader student preparation for the nonacademic professional careers that many will follow. In addition – and this is no small professional matter – those who are fully prepared for the many kinds of work in their disciplines in the way I have in mind, even though they may eventually enter upon academic work, will be far more conversant with the professional lives of their own future students who enter upon nonacademic careers as well as of their nonacademic colleagues than is now the case and will thus be better professionals. For reports of such programs in history, see David Rayson et al., "Preparing Future Faculty: Teaching the Academic Life," *Perspectives* 37 (January 1999): 1ff.; Jonathan Grant, "Preparing Future Faculty at Florida State University," *Perspectives* 41 (October 2003): 42–44; and Kevin Kenny, "Preparing Future Faculty at Boston College," *Perspectives* 41 (October 2003): 46–48. Unfortunately, these programs suffer from the shortcomings I suggest here. A 2001 survey of graduate students found that history graduate students gave their graduate programs a grade of only 72 percent, or B minus, for overall satisfaction and only 57 percent, or C plus, for preparation for a broad range of careers. See http://survey.nagps.org.

2 I say this with due regard for the costs involved in mounting public history instruction. But just as departments have slowly adjusted over recent decades to the proliferation of historical topics – let me mention simply the many subjects of non-Western and social history – they will have to similarly, even if gradually, recast their faculties to accommodate nonacademic history issues. One way to do so is to find historians who can offer instruction in both traditional fields and in those of public history and not segregate the two into distinct specialties.

their dissertations, they have achieved their formal education in history. In so preparing their students, these senior historians assume that they have discharged their responsibilities to their students, who can then "pick up" the remainder of their professional knowledge and education through on-the-job experience. Most university faculty members, it is safe to say, would maintain if asked that it is on preparation for the academic world, and not other professional pursuits, that graduate-level training principally should be focused.[3]

Yet it is questionable whether this single-minded approach to preparing professional historians is any longer justified or functional for aspiring historians – if it has ever been. Many people trained in the academy exclusively for academic work have never confined themselves exclusively to academic employment. In fact, J. Franklin Jameson, one of the nation's very first doctoral recipients in history and the scholar who, more than any other, stamped academic history in the United States with the force of his vision, spent much of his career outside academic walls. If one looks behind the raw statistics showing that the preponderance of historians earning their doctorates in the twentieth century has taken up academic employment, one discovers that some others have always followed Jameson's lead. Other career options related directly to historical studies besides academic work have always been open to those who selected them, just as, even for those holding academic positions, other career emphases than scholarship and teaching have been available to those

[3] These must of necessity be only sketchy remarks about a complex subject, one about which virtually no research has been undertaken. I refer to the sociology of the humanities in general and of the discipline of history in particular. That there exists no sociology of the humanities analogous to the powerful existing literature on the sociology of science remains one of the puzzles of the history and sociology of ideas and the professions. (For modest exceptions to this generalization, see Robert H. Knapp, *The Origins of American Humanistic Scholars* [Englewood Cliffs, NJ: Prentice-Hall, 1964], and Tony Becher, *Academic Tribes and Territories: Intellectual Enquiry and the Cultures of the Disciplines* [Milton Keyes: Open University Press, 1989].) In addition, historical studies would greatly benefit from research into the practices of history – how individual historians actually carry out their work of teaching, research, and other service. An exemplary study of scientific practices that might serve as a model is Steven Shapin, *The Scientific Life: A Moral History of a Late Modern Vocation* (Chicago: University of Chicago Press, 2008). Probes have of course been made into the psychological impulses to academic work and the psychological realities of graduate preparation. See, for example, Peter Loewenberg, *Decoding the Past: The Psychological Approach* (New York: Alfred A. Knopf, 1983), 43–95. One would no doubt start with the centrality of the text, of criticism, and of uncertainty and the lack of stable authority in interpretation and then consider the institutions and practices that reflect the humanities as well as the kinds of personality traits that might incline people to the humanities.

inclined to pursue them from their academic berths. In recent decades, these extra-academic choices have proliferated to the point that academic history, while still the center of gravity among the professions of history, is only one among many pursuits in which advances in historical knowledge, departures in the presentation of that knowledge, and significant, sometimes great, achievements in the historical arts occur.

Why most academic departments continue to prepare their students for professional lives principally, sometimes only, in the academy – why they fail to envisage their responsibilities in broader terms – is not difficult to explain. The force of tradition accounts for much. So, too, does the vindication of experience. Having seen their principal, often sole, function to be the preparation of college and university faculty members, graduate programs in the arts and sciences, especially those in the disciplines of the humanities, from their founding after the Civil War until the 1970s saw almost the full number of those completing their Ph.D. degrees absorbed by the need for faculty recruits in the nation's colleges and universities.[4] As a result, changes in traditional graduate instruction did not for decades seem needed, and even now most approaches to preparing aspiring professional historians, even after the improvements they have seen in recent years, remain tied to conventions that took their general shape early in the twentieth century.

In addition, many, possibly most, university faculty members themselves have had little experience in professional work outside the academy (except perhaps in activities closely related to their roles on campus, such as serving as public commentators about current events or as expert advisers to people in other occupations, such as filmmakers). Strange though it may be, many of them – experienced teachers all – consider it to be beyond their competence, and some outside their responsibilities, to help prepare their graduate students to gain the skills to teach. Even more so, they resist exposing their students to the ways and satisfactions of off-campus history in the roles of museum curators, documentary editors, government officials, or independent consultants that all aspiring historians can now choose to be. And many have given little thought to, and are often not competent to train others in, any of these extra-academic occupations.

Yet responsibility for the tendency of most graduate students to envisage their future professional lives in academic hues does not originate entirely with departmental inertia or professorial myopia. It arises also

---

4 With the exception of the Great Depression and briefly after the absorption of the large cohort of graduate students caused by the GI Bill of Rights.

from an overlooked aspect of the social psychology of graduate education: the overwhelming tendency of graduate students, because they can
become trained historians only by studying with academic scholars at the
sole institutions authorized to award them doctoral degrees, to imagine
themselves occupying the same positions as those who teach them. Acculturated almost from the first day of graduate school to the professorial
ideal, graduate students thereafter tend to consider any position other
than a professorship as unworthy of their aspirations even if it might be
more appropriate to their talents and more congenial to their temperaments. Therefore, those who resist the academic ideal or simply prefer
to practice history outside the academy too often must struggle on their
own, if they are aware of their predicament at all, to keep themselves free
of the forces working, against little competition, to assimilate them into
academic culture and into that culture alone.

Furthermore, such is the nature of graduate school preparation that
few, if any, doctoral programs encourage their degree candidates in history to think of their possible responsibilities – as writers, critics, and
engaged intellectuals – to public culture. That most doctorate-granting
history departments allow acculturation to the professoriate to occur
without undertaking any effort to explore its implications or to counteract its negative effects – inappropriate career choices, for instance; an
often misplaced, career-long sense of second-class professional status; and
narrow professionalism being the principal negative effects among them –
is one of the signal failings and major ethical shortcomings of graduate
education in history in the United States.[5]

Not that research universities' failure to prepare their students for the
full range of practices that now constitute professional work in history
deters doctorate holders (any more than it ever has) from entering non-
professorial work. On the contrary: as surveys by the late 1990s have

---

[5] This failure to prepare historians in the applied arts of their discipline is shared among
disciplines of the humanities generally and puts them at sharp odds with other learned
professions. In contrast with professional training for the legal, medical and dental, engineering, and scientific professions, where few conflicts between theory and application are
to be found, training in literature and philosophy, as well as in history, is confined largely
to academic preparation alone. "Here," as Otis L. Graham, Jr., has written, "teaching and
research have no sustained engagement with the application of the discipline's findings,
and there is no sense that this is remarkable, let alone questionable." *Public Historian*
12 (Spring 1990): 5–6. It should be added that, partly as a result of their professional
education, individual doctors, engineers, scientists, and attorneys frequently cross back
and forth between clinical and applied work and research. Professionals in the humanities
disciplines do not.

repeatedly shown, over 35 percent of the doctoral recipients in history, perhaps as many as two-thirds – one should pause to absorb that figure – have been taking up work outside the academy. While it is not clear whether they have done so by choice or necessity (most commentators assuming the latter without sufficient evidence), it is not far off the mark to charge most graduate programs with irresponsibility toward their students in that large cohort for not exposing them to the full range of extra-academic professional work, much if not most of it related directly to the creation and diffusion of historical knowledge, into which so many people, willy-nilly, are now taking their knowledge of history.[6] That

---

[6] See Thomas Bender et al., *The Education of Historians for the Twenty-First Century* (Urbana: University of Illinois Press, 2004), 6. A 2001 survey reports that only 46 percent of the 1999–2000 Ph.D. cohort (and only 54 percent of those from the twenty-five most prestigious graduate programs) had found full-time faculty positions. Robert B. Townsend, "Job Market Report 2001: Openings Booming . . . but for How Long?" *Perspectives* 39 (December 2001): 7–12. An even gloomier assessment is Townsend, "Job Market Report, 2004," *Perspectives* 43 (January 2005): 13–19. Yet until academic year 2007–2008, the picture was more favorable. Townsend, "A Good Year on the Job Market, but Troubles Loom," *Perspectives on History* 47 (January 2009): 4–6, and Townsend, "Job Market Sagged Further in 2009–10," *Perspectives on History* 49 (January 2011): 13–16. It remains unclear what proportion of those with recent Ph.D.s has sought academic positions and failed to find them and what proportion has decided to be historians outside the academy and has not sought academic posts in the first place. Nor are the motivations of the latter group well known. Whatever the case, the statistical information, largely from periodic studies undertaken by the National Research Council of the National Academy of Sciences on which most conclusions regarding the status of historians are based, is seriously deficient in not disaggregating the information embodied in gross categories of employed doctoral recipients. How, for instance, is one to consider a published historian, formerly a tenured member of the faculty of a distinguished college, who purposefully left its employ because of its geographical isolation to take up nonacademic work in a large city but who continues to teach occasionally, participate in seminars in her field, and publish her scholarship as much as she can? To ask that question and to be uncertain about its answer is to give evidence of the poverty of our thinking about the professional careers of historians. In addition, even general statistics about the employment of doctorates must be used with great caution. For instance, a 1998 study of postdoctoral employment found that only 3.3 percent of humanities doctoral recipients between 1991 and 1994 were unemployed in 1995, but its authors, blaming the lack of universities' efforts to track their former students, admitted their ignorance about the actual employment of the other 96.7 percent. Committee on Graduate Education, Association of American Universities, "Report and Recommendations," October 1998, http://www.tulane.edu/~aau.GradEdRept.html. Also, the American Historical Association's indefatigable Robert B. Townsend who strives to improve the statistical reportage of the NRC but to little effect, has told me that, according to the NRC's own data, at least eight thousand history doctorate holders, sometimes called "invisible historians," are not accounted for in its statistical reports and that even less is known about those who left graduate school before completing their dissertations but who may well be serving history's muse. The AHA's first report on the employment of historians may be found in Susan Socolow, "Assessing Trends in the Job Market," *Perspectives* 31 (May–June

irresponsibility also extends to their students who will become academics, for these programs are in effect reproducing as prospective university faculty members men and women who will be similarly uninformed about careers in the many nonacademic professions of history and incapable of exposing their own students, of yet another generation, to their pursuit.

The failure of most history graduate programs to prepare their students adequately, indeed the failure of academic professionals to take due cognizance of this major change in the composition of their discipline, has not, however, deterred many of those students from forging new kinds of professional careers in history. Simply by taking up employment as historians outside the academy, virtually all of these doctoral recipients have become participants in a comparatively young, institutionalized profession of history that organizes their self-perception, promotes their professional activities, and sets standards for their professional conduct. It is a profession of history that has gradually gained an intellectual tradition of its own – the profession of public, or applied, history.[7]

While public history may be a relatively new, self-conscious profession, it is decidedly not, nor has it ever been, outside the discipline of history itself. In ways not adequately recognized, from the earliest years of the twentieth century its pursuit has run parallel to academic history and never entirely separate from it. If it is to gain its deserved stature alongside academic history, its full history must be recaptured and become more widely understood.[8]

1993): 3ff. Since then, Robert Townsend has been regularly reporting and analyzing data relating to history in issues of the same publication. One of the most encouraging recent developments in measuring many dimensions of the humanities and their respective disciplines and taking up where the National Endowment for the Humanities left off, is the Humanities Indicators project of the American Academy of Arts and Sciences. See www.HumanitiesIndicators.org.

7 The literature about public history is already large and constantly expanding. In addition to the pages of the *Public Historian*, the best introductions to the varieties of public history work are to be found in the essays in Barbara J. Howe and Emory L. Kemp (eds.), *Public History: An Introduction* (Malabar, FL: R. E. Krieger, 1986), and in its successor volume, James B. Gardner and Peter S. LaPaglia (eds.), *Public History: Essays from the Field* (Malabar, FL: R. E. Krieger, 1999). It should be borne in mind that the emergence of public history into a distinct profession of history has been part of a more general development of the "public humanities" throughout all fields of the humanities, a subject worth more attention.

8 See Chapter 1. A full and authoritative history of public history, sorely needed, has yet to be written. But a superb recent addition to the literature about one dimension of public history's history is Ian Tyrrell, *Historians in Public: The Practice of American History, 1890–1970* (Chicago: University of Chicago Press, 2005).

The formal organization of public history, first as a subspecies of academic history and then as a full-blown profession of history on its own, dates from the mid-1970s.[9] Yet its informal practice long antedated that decade. In fact, one can lay responsibility both for the founding of public history and for the divorce of academic from public history to J. Franklin Jameson, the founding statesman of the modern structure and pursuit of historical studies in the United States. After earning his doctorate at Johns Hopkins in 1882 and then teaching successively there, at Brown, and at the University of Chicago, Jameson left the academy in 1905 at the age of forty-six to become director of the Department of Historical Research of the Carnegie Institution of Washington, from which he launched a grand series of enduring projects. He was also founding managing editor of the *American Historical Review*, chief of the manuscript division of the Library of Congress, a founder of the American Council of Learned Societies and the National Historical Publications Commission (now the National Historical Publications and Records Commission), the moving force behind the construction of the National Archives, and the original editor of the *Dictionary of American Biography*.

Because the many roles that Jameson occupied have since come to seem the normal professional responsibility of academic historians, we have lost sight both of how contingent on the circumstances of Jameson's era they were and of the fact that Jameson created many of those roles, as he created many institutions, from outside university walls. That Jameson spent a good part of his career in the academy, thought of his most enduring endeavors after he had resigned his last faculty appointment as academic endeavors, and conceived of them as essential to the academic professionalization of historical scholarship and related pursuits did not then, and does not now, make them inherently or by definition academic activities. They have come to be defined as that only through the subsequent history of historical practice. The conflation of "professional" with "academic" did not exist at the birth of modern history work, nor was the symbolic marriage of the two terms inevitable or necessary.

Instead, it was Jameson who took the lead in consecrating that link. The principal figure in the professionalization of history, the parent of many enduring institutions and the wet nurse of many others, he was

---

[9] It should be clear by now that I use the term "public history" as over against "academic history" only because of convention and for analytical purposes, not because I believe that each is a distinct universe of thought, view, and occupation or because I like the terms or the distinctions they connote. An increasing number of historians comfortably inhabit both professional worlds and move back and forth between them.

key to cementing the early marriage of the academy and the discipline of history and set in motion the eventual estrangement of most academic historians from people outside the academy – other historian-professionals, schoolteachers, and fellow citizens. Although Jameson was practicing his era's version of public history just as much as he was involved in academic history, there is no evidence that Jameson recognized the professionally fateful steps he was taking in absorbing many extra-academic professional pursuits, such as documentary editing, within the purview of academic work, even though he himself had left the academy. He made no distinction between academic and public history no doubt because, at a time when scholarship was becoming institutionalized and "scientific," when training in history was being regularized, and when historical practices and institutions were being inaugurated outside the academy, Jameson, like a few other historians, was moving easily back and forth between roles.

It is therefore not enough that public history be seen as the professional result of a recent struggle to distinguish one kind of history work from another or as the institutional consequence of public historians' efforts to free themselves from the thralldom of the academy. It must be seen also as an accepted and legitimate form of historical pursuit, existing during the birth years of the professionalization of history in the United States, that was submerged by stronger forces striving to remove historical research and writing from the hands of amateurs and to place them on a firmer foundation of scholarship in the academy. At the founding of modern American historical practices, those who were pursuing that day's kind of public history, even the founder of public history himself, had a choice to make, and he made that choice in such a way that he failed to protect public historical work, even though he was practicing it, from becoming defined as of secondary importance and professional standing to academic history.[10]

From that early injury public history has never fully recovered. It still struggles to gain clarity of definition and purpose as well as weight of

---

[10] Pertinent materials on Jameson's life and career are now available in the indispensable published edition of his selected work and correspondence: Morey Rothberg et al., *John Franklin Jameson and the Development of Humanistic Scholarship in America*, 3 vols. (Athens: University of Georgia Press, 1993–2001). I cite Jameson's role so prominently only because of his unparalleled influence on the institutionalization of history in the United States. But we should not lose sight of other nineteenth-century doctoral recipients, such as Henry Cabot Lodge and Woodrow Wilson, who, in their own distinctive ways, brought historical knowledge into public service.

authority and reputation within the discipline of history. Yet, despite this continuing struggle, the flow of historians back and forth between academic and public history work, exemplified by Jameson's career, has never ended and, in fact, never suffered interruption. For example, a near contemporary of Jameson, Benjamin Shambaugh, practiced public history and, probably as the first to employ the term "applied history," should be considered a parent of the profession. Pursuing a dual career as chairman of the political science department of the University of Iowa (1900–1940) and head of the State Historical Society of Iowa (1907–1940), Shambaugh worked to merge academic expertise with the service responsibilities of a public institution. His efforts yielded, among other products, the six-volume Iowa Applied History Series and a string of Commonwealth Conferences in the 1920s that focused on state and municipal governance.[11] Among hundreds of possible other examples of early public history performed by historians who did not recognize themselves as practicing it were the activities of historians in the Department of Agriculture, which, as early as 1916, established its history office. Among the many historians performing one kind or another of public history work were Arthur M. Schlesinger, Jr., and Eric Goldman in the White House; Gordon Wright in the Department of State and the American Embassy in Paris during and after World War II; Samuel Flagg Bemis and Thomas A. Bailey as advisers to the State Department; Robin Winks as a cultural attaché; William L. Langer in the Office of Strategic Services; Samuel Eliot Morison, W. Frank Craven, and James L. Cate as historians of the navy and air force during wartime in the 1940s; John Hope Franklin, C. Vann Woodward, Rayford Logan, Herbert G. Gutman, and Alfred H. Kelly in their profound contributions to the preparation of the legal testimony and arguments that eventuated in the landmark 1954 Supreme Court decision in *Brown v. Board of Education*; Oscar Handlin in his successful work to abolish country quotas in the Immigration Act of 1965; Richard G. Hewlett as longtime historian of the Atomic Energy Commission (whose present and broader incarnation is the Department of Energy); and Wayne D. Rasmussen in the federal Department of Agriculture, the last two of whom pioneered in the establishment of modern offices of history in the federal government.[12]

[11] See Rebecca Conard, *Benjamin Shambaugh and the Intellectual Foundations of Public History* (Iowa City: University of Iowa Press, 2002).
[12] For a frustratingly brief autobiographical sketch of Franklin's participation in the preparation of the case in *Brown v. Board of Education*, see John Hope Franklin, *Mirror to*

Much of this kind of work, except for work in government history offices and temporary wartime work, has been undertaken from faculty positions and largely from academic concerns. It should therefore be distinguished from more conventional academic, monographic history and be seen as what can best be termed "applied academic history." Probably the most venerable example of this variety of history is public policy history, which has taken the form both of research into the history of public policies and of direct participation in policy making.[13] Historians long have been and are still from time to time summoned as consultants to assist government officeholders and staff officials to draft legislation and formulate executive decisions through their knowledge of the actual workings of past policies. In addition, because the results of historical research and deeply consequential historical debates often escape the boundaries of the academy – one has only to mention the history of slavery or of the Holocaust – academic historians frequently find themselves involved in lively public controversies and increasingly often facing resistance and criticism for doing so. This is surely history being used for the public good, and it involves academic historians in the application of historical knowledge outside their studies. Yet despite its undoubted legitimacy as public history and the urgency with which many people have been encouraging historians to assume greater involvement in public affairs and make more active contributions to public debates, forms of applied academic history like these no longer constitute the central

---

America: The Autobiography of John Hope Franklin (New York: Farrar, Straus and Giroux, 2005), 156–159. The careers of some of the early practitioners of public history have been captured in the series of occasional interviews, under the general title, "Pioneers of Public History," in the pages of the *Public Historian*.

[13] Superb reviews of the history of policy history, as well as analyses of its recently reduced status within historical studies generally, are Hugh Davis Graham, "The Stunted Career of Policy History: A Critique and an Agenda," *Public Historian* 15 (Spring 1993): 15–37, and Julian E. Zelizer, "Clio's Lost Tribe: Public Policy History since 1978," *Journal of Policy History* 12 (2000): 369–394. See also Zelizer, "Introduction: New Directions in Policy History," *Journal of Policy History* 17 (2005): 1–11, and the entire issue that it opens. A discussion of Graham's essay is to be found in the *Public Historian* 15 (Fall 1993): 51–81. The appropriate terminology for nonacademic history has long been a matter of discussion. Recently, Jack Holl has proposed using "practicing professional historian" to distinguish a public historian from an academic historian. But are not academic historians also practicing professional historians? "Cultures in Conflict: An Argument against 'Common Ground' between Practicing Professional Historians and Academics," *Public Historian* 30 (May 2008): 29–50. While taking exception to Holl's argument as well as to his terms, I consider his essay to be a penetrating, muscular argument of its kind, one deserving attention from all historians.

component of public history.[14] That core of public historical work has now been taken over by activities that, rather than being simple extensions of academic pursuits, require a different order of skills and thus extensive and specialized preparation of their own.

It would require a discrete historical study to review the many foundations of public history.[15] Even before the emergence of academic history, historical and antiquarian societies as well as museums were introducing citizens through their collections and publications to historical knowledge and discussion and enlarging history's audiences, a trend that continued throughout the twentieth century. The national government more forthrightly than before began to discharge functions previously left in private and state hands when, in 1933, the National Park Service assumed responsibility for interpreting historical sites; and two years later Congress created the National Archives to preserve and present documents and artifacts in the nation's legal possession. Nor can one overlook the role of history-based and dramatic radio programs, such as those of Norman Corwin, of such costume dramas as *Gone With the Wind*, and of television documentaries such as *Victory at Sea* in awakening a large portion of the public to the pleasures, as well as the significance, of historical knowledge.[16]

Yet it was to prepare aspiring historians for participating more consciously and expertly in the growing number and kinds of such extra-academic activities that those who first conceived of public history as a distinct subdivision of historical work created separate graduate programs for them. The need for additional kinds of preparation for young historians had been recognized in some quarters in the 1960s, when computers first made possible the application of historical statistics to the analysis of current, as well as retrospective, events, when concern over the purported insularity of academic scholars began to mount, when

---

[14] I say this despite the assumptions, in my view erroneous, of some historians, such as William E. Leuchtenburg, who seem to believe that the service of historians as policy advisers or television commentators constitutes the principal thrust of public history and that public history is best understood as civic engagement. See his 1991 presidential address before the American Historical Association: "The Historian and the Public Realm," *American Historical Review* 97 (February 1992): 1–18. Leuchtenburg was confusing public history with what I term applied academic history.

[15] A useful, reflective overview of the profession's history is "The Emergence of the Modern Public History Movement," chapter 7 of Conard, *Benjamin Shambaugh*.

[16] It was some remarks of Michael Kammen at a 1999 Salzburg Seminar on Public History and National Identity that reminded me of the role in broadening public access to historical knowledge played by some of these productions conventionally considered to be "art." Many others could no doubt be adduced.

problems in the nation's public schools became increasingly manifest, when the "New Social History" focused fresh attention on the histories of ordinary people, when the civil rights and feminist movements put new emphasis on influencing one's own history, and when, simultaneously under the spur of the anti–Vietnam War movement and sharp changes in American culture, academics began to take a larger role in public affairs, usually as outspoken advocates of changes they supported and challengers of policies they did not. In addition, the emergence to public note of historical institutions such as Colonial Williamsburg, the adoption of tax policies encouraging the adaptive use of historic properties, fresh concerns about national, ethnic, and racial identities, and the creation of state humanities councils under the aegis of the National Endowment for the Humanities served, among other influences, as external stimuli to the application of historical knowledge outside academic walls. But it was the crisis in the employment of new doctoral recipients in the 1970s that precipitated the first formal steps to institute new forms of graduate instruction in history and to create the intellectual underpinnings and institutional structure of public history.[17]

What can be considered the single most formative act in the professionalization of public history occurred within the history department of the University of California at Santa Barbara when Robert Kelley and G. Wesley Johnson founded there in 1976 the Graduate Program in Public Historical Studies.[18] The inauguration of this program, authorized

---

[17] This fact should not be taken to suggest that once the supply of doctoral recipients comes into balance with the demand (if it ever does), the rationale and need for public history, as well as its appeal, will end. The case for public history rests on the value and legitimacy of history work outside the academy, not on the employment situation of historians.

[18] There has always been some dispute over precedence in inaugurating the academic pursuit of public history. Peter N. Stearns and Joel A. Tarr at Carnegie Mellon University initiated graduate training there in their Applied History and Social Science Program at roughly the same time that Kelley and Johnson did in Santa Barbara, and they should be credited with foresight and boldness equal to the Californians' in doing so. But that the principal credit for the formative acts of bringing an institutionalized professionalization of public history into being, especially in the form of a scholarly journal and professional association, belongs to the Santa Barbara faculty members there can be no doubt. It also bears emphasis in this regard that academic as well as public historians initiated and led many recent developments in public history. An appreciation of Kelley's central role in public history is Otis L. Graham, Jr., "Robert Kelley and the Pursuit of Useful History," *Journal of Policy History* 23 (2011): 1–9. For some information about the founding meeting of what became the National Council on Public History, see the special issue of the *Public Historian* 2 (Fall 1979) and, more particularly, 21 (Summer 1999). One of the striking features of the 1999 issue of the *Public Historian* is the evidence it provides of the strong role of government historians within the public history profession.

initially to grant master's degrees in public history and now offering a
doctorate, was soon followed in 1978 by another stage in the birth of this
new profession of history: publication of the first issue of the *Public Historian*, immediately and still the principal, indispensable quarterly journal
in its field, in whose volumes have been recorded the history, practices,
and intellectual substance of public history and from whose pages one can
learn, more than from any other single journal, of this profession of history. By 1979 Kelley and Johnson, with others, had imagined, organized,
and summoned enough interest in public history to justify the founding
of the National Council on Public History, the major general association
of public historians.[19] Within another year the council convened its first
open annual meeting, and by 1984 it became an organization of individual
members. Since then, history departments offering some kind of training
and degrees in public history, mostly, but by no means exclusively, at
the master's level and usually as a subspecialty of American history, have
come to number upward of eighty, and public history projects now find
no difficulty receiving that coveted stamp of approval: funding from the
National Endowment for the Humanities. A new profession of history
was born, or at least formally institutionalized.[20]

[19] The founding in 1976 of the National Coordinating Committee for the Promotion of
History under the joint auspices of the AHA and OAH has occasionally been seen as
the first step in the institutionalization of public history. However, while involved from
its inauguration in representing the public interests of the discipline – for example, in
seeking solutions to the crisis of employment among young historians – the NCCPH by
the early 1980s, during a crisis over NEH funding, began to turn more exclusively to
representational activities and did not take on the attributes of a professional organization of and for public historians. By the time, however, that the NCCPH had made this
shift, it had helped create the two organizations that now represent the interests of public
history and public historians: the Society for History in the Federal Government and the
National Council on Public History. Since then, the NCCPH, now under the name of the
National Coalition for History, a consortium of professional organizations in history,
has become the discipline's greatly respected and effective lobbying arm in Washington
whose original director, Arnita A. Jones, and her successor and long-serving executive
director, Page Putnam Miller, pioneered in the political representation and guardianship
of history's many interests. On the NCCPH, see Page Putnam Miller, "Advocacy on
Behalf of History: Reflections on the Past Twenty Years," *Public Historian* 22 (Spring
2000): 39–49, and Arnita A. Jones, "Bookends," *Perspectives on History* 48 (February
2010): 5–6.
[20] That public history as practiced in the United States is overwhelmingly a specialty of
historians of the United States should not be surprising. Calls for public historians'
expertise arise principally from individuals, organizations, agencies, and businesses that
seek answers to questions regarding the history of the nation and locales in which they
exist. The same is true of public historians in other countries, such as the United Kingdom
and Australia, where, especially, public history has emerged as a distinct profession.

No more than any other field of history, however, has public history been immune to subsequent specialization of expertise and fractionalization of institution. Public historians working within or in close association with various offices and agencies of the three branches of the federal government throughout the country have organized the Society for History in the Federal Government, which holds an annual meeting in Washington, D.C., publishes a newsletter, and has in recent years, distinctively among associations of professional historians, organized professional development seminars to broaden the knowledge and skills of aspiring and experienced government historians. Because public historians practice such a diversity of work, often through means different from those of academics and in interdisciplinary and interprofessional concert with others, they are as likely to be found in the institutional company of nonacademic professionals as in strictly historical organizations. For instance, many students and practitioners of oral history gather with folklorists, journalists, and genealogists in the Oral History Association. In fact, a list of organizations bearing the word "history" in their names would by no means exhaust the roster of groups that welcome and serve public historians and that compose the larger institutional structure of public history in the United States. These include the major professional membership associations in adjunct fields in which public historians often work, such as the American Association of Museums, the American Association for State and Local History, and the Society of American Archivists. And there are no doubt "caucuses" of historians within other occupational associations of which I am unaware.[21]

How does one account for the rapid growth and professionalization of public history and the achievements of its practitioners, as well as the increasing interchanges between them and their academic colleagues? The desire to remain professional historians on the part of those frustrated in their search for academic employment explains much of public history's growth. So, too, do the professional challenges, coincident with the birth of any profession, which many have found in public history.

---

[21] This diversity of institution and skill should make clear that public history, which I refer to as a profession, is in reality a congeries of many occupations and that its practitioners are to be found throughout many other professions. A brief introduction to the work of federal historians is Victoria A. Harden, "What Do Federal Historians Do?" *Perspectives* 37 (May 1999): 19–24. See also Holl, "Cultures in Conflict," and, for a description of the uses of history within a single federal department, see Kristin L. Ahlberg, "Building a Model Public History Program: The Office of the Historian at the U.S. Department of State," *Public Historian* 30 (May 2008): 9–28.

Nor ought one to discount the sheer satisfaction of public history work to those who have taken up its practices; accumulated experience has shown that much is to be gained in personal gratification as well as public enlightenment from bringing historical knowledge to those who choose to go to, see, and do, as well as to read, history. Perhaps also the relative insulation of public historical pursuits from the ideological battles swirling throughout the discipline of history after 1960 made those pursuits attractive to some people.[22] In addition, such legislation as the National Historic Preservation Act of 1966, the National Environmental Protection Act of 1970, and much state legislation gave historians a role in research aimed at protecting the nation's natural and physical heritage and made funds available to them to do so.[23] Also, some people have been actuated to become public historians out of concern that only by engaging new audiences, only by broadening the definition of practicing historian, can history begin to regain its former hold on the civic imagination and its role in civic culture.

But perhaps more important in its list of achievements, public history has taken the lead in creating entirely new subfields of historical research and in using and refining particular methods of historical inquiry. That is to say, unrecognized as this may be, public historians have been at the intellectual and methodological frontiers in many subjects and fields. At least one subdivision of public historical inquiry, the exploration of historical memory and national identity, has exploded with activity and in many respects permeated research into historical topics previously considered to be "purely" academic. In fact, it would be hard to

[22] Although one should not push this argument too far. The impulses for some kinds of public history (such as oral history, community history, and in many cases film history) surely originated on the Left among those concerned to use historical knowledge to "empower" people, while some practices (such as corporate and government history) exhibited a less reformist thrust and may have appealed to more centrist and conservative historians.

[23] For the general, early history of the preservation movement in the United States, see Charles B. Hosmer, Jr., *Presence of the Past: A History of the Preservation Movement in the United States before Williamsburg* (New York: Putnam, 1965) and *Preservation Comes of Age: From Williamsburg to the National Trust, 1926–1949* (Charlottesville: University Press of Virginia, 1981). Other works include William J. Murtagh, *Keeping Time: The History and Theory of Preservation in America* (New York: Sterling Publishing, 1993); Diane Barthel, *Historic Preservation: Collective Memory and Historical Identity* (New Brunswick, NJ: Rutgers University Press, 1996); and James M. Lindgren, *Preserving Historic New England: Preservation, Progressivism, and the Remaking of Memory* (New York: Oxford University Press, 1995) and *Preserving the Old Dominion: Historic Preservation and Virginia Traditionalism* (Charlottesville: University Press of Virginia 1993).

determine whether public or academic historians have taken the lead in, or contributed most to, the growth of memory studies. Many public historians possess special research and analytical skills for interpreting public and private memories that academic historians often lack, and the former are also better prepared to take seriously (and perhaps to tolerate) unwelcome interpretations of the past held by members of the public at large but no less significant as historical memory for their lack of academic sophistication.[24] As for methodological and critical innovations, it has been public historians who have made leading advances in cultural resources management and oral history and in broadening the range of historical criticism through reviews of museum exhibits and, perhaps most distinctively, of significant, unpublished historical research (now known as "gray literature").[25]

To attribute the emergence of public history into a full-fledged profession to employment needs, legislative mandates, and methodological

[24] The literature concerned with historical memory has mushroomed in recent years. A useful introduction to these works can be found in David Glassberg, "Public History and the Study of Memory," *Public Historian* 18 (Spring 1996): 7–23. While Glassberg, writing for public historians, argues that they must become acquainted with the more academic works in this genre of scholarship, I believe that the reverse is also emphatically true – that academics must know of the contributions to memory studies of public historians. A discussion of Glassberg's arguments is to be found in the *Public Historian* 19 (Spring 1997): 31–72. A revealing work about general public attitudes toward historical knowledge is Roy Rosenzweig and David Thelen, *The Presence of the Past: Popular Uses of History in American Life* (New York: Columbia University Press, 1998). While the authors correctly argue that the public must be asked to work as hard to engage historical knowledge and interpretations created by scholarship as scholars must recognize and credit the existence of nonscholarly views of the past, they overlook the fact that the public attitudes that their survey has uncovered are characteristic of a particular historical era and probably not invariable or permanent. This point is also overlooked by commentators on the book and its findings in the roundtable discussion printed in the *Public Historian* 22 (Winter 2000): 13–44. Historians should not, however, lose sight of the fact that one of the central purposes of history is to correct memory – if necessary, to tell members of the public that they are wrong when they are.

[25] A word about "gray literature" is in order. The term itself has been coined to identify historical literature that has not been formally published – for instance, assessments of historical sites by government historians, in-house corporate histories, and consulting reports. Even though often not having been subjected to peer review by other historians, many such documents result from wide and deep research, qualify as historical texts in every sense, and contribute to historical understanding. The *Public Historian* when under the editorship of Otis L. Graham, Jr., was the first publication to recognize the significance of this body of literature and the need to bring it under critical evaluation. The older journals of historical scholarship have yet to recognize the existence of "gray literature" or its legitimate claim to (and need of) critical assessment. Since the conclusion of Graham's editorship of the *Public Historian*, even that journal has discontinued its reviews of these kinds of documents.

advances is, however, to lend weight to the assumption that public history's principal contributions lie in its having broadened the occupational options of historians and the applicability of historical knowledge. While both of these assessments are valid, the result is, as David Glassberg has commented, that "we think of public history as a collection of career paths, not a coherent subject of study."[26] Yet it is beyond dispute that, after almost a century of intellectual achievement and a third of a century of institutional development, public history now deserves to be considered a ripened, independent subfield of historical inquiry and a distinct profession of history, coequal in status and importance to any others that can be named and not simply tributary to academic history.

Surely as much as a result of its expansion of subject matter and technique as of its intellectual challenges and achievements and the pleasure it provides both its practitioners and the consumers of the knowledge it conveys, public history has been able to absorb an increasing proportion of young historians and has greatly outpaced the ability of the academic profession to do so. The increased call on historical knowledge in other professions and occupations – a call largely created by historians skilled enough to make known convincingly the applicability of their knowledge to human affairs – has created not just new historical practices and new opportunities for historians' employment but also a fresh way of conceiving the significance of historical knowledge and distinctive perspectives on the past.

One should not, however, conclude that, any more than within academic history, the maturity of public history has meant the absence of intellectual and professional challenges of the first order. For example, the very term "public history," as well as its less widely used cognate "applied history," reveals the difficulties that historians, even public historians themselves, have had in defining the position and status of this new profession within the larger discipline of history and the large and varied universe of its practitioners.[27] No doubt the youth and comparative novelty of public history as a distinct arena of historical endeavor has

---

[26] Glassberg, "Public History and the Study of Memory," 7.

[27] Terminological distinctions seem to be common in regard to public history. None other than Jameson involved himself in this endeavor. He once tried to distinguish "historians," among whom he placed "any historical writers or investigators of recognized standing" and "those who have written histories," from "historical investigators," the latter being "writers of monographs." Significantly, Jameson put himself in the second category. Jameson to Henry Pinckney McCain, March 21, 1912, in Rothberg et al. (eds.), *Jameson*, 3:97–98.

something to do with that. So, too, does the status of academic history as the conventional standard against which the legitimacy and worthiness of all historical pursuits are measured. (Witness the formerly widespread use of the negative term, "nonacademic" history, to denominate public history work.)[28] Yet one is surely justified in asking whether the terms "public" and "applied" history are meant to imply that academic history, from which public history means to distinguish itself, is "private" or "inapplicable" history – as if the value of historical knowledge gained from academic research lies intrinsically in the exquisite intellectual and aesthetic pleasures it may provide rather than in its civic or public significance.

Robert Kelley implied as much in 1978 in his otherwise sound founding prospectus for the profession of public history. He argued there that public history refers to "the employment of historians and the historical method outside of academia" and is to be distinguished from academic history, through which "we minister to humanity's generalized need to comprehend its past and to diffuse that comprehension, by means of formal schooling, within each generation." But Kelley's distinction begged the definitional question. One of the principal issues with which all historians must grapple is precisely whether public and academic history can or should be distinguished at all and, if so, whether the two professions should be distinguished by the locations in which historical work takes place, by the intentions and self-definition of the historians who pursue one or another kind of historical activity, by the products of their labors, by the audiences to which they address their work, or by the kind of historical knowledge they apply to whatever may be their tasks.[29]

Part of the difficulty in defining the contents of public history stems from the reluctance of many academic historians to conceive of their

---

28 Another term, "alternative career," was employed at the height of the crisis of employment for young historians in the 1970s and 1980s to signify occupations in which they might apply their knowledge outside the academy. As the strength and contributions of public history grew and the pejorative implications of the term "alternative career" became manifest, it came to be recognized that academic history could also be seen as an "alternative career" to public history. As a result, the term has almost completely dropped from use. But for a residual anachronism, see the use of the term in a session of the 1999 annual meeting of the AHA: "Roundtable: Alternative Careers for Historians," *Program of the American Historical Association's 113th Annual Meeting* (Washington, DC: American Historical Association, 1998), 129.

29 "Public History: Its Origins, Nature, and Prospects," *Public Historian* 1 (Fall 1978): 16–28, quotation on p. 18. My taking issue with Kelley here should not be taken to imply any fundamental criticism of his extraordinary, enduring efforts on behalf of public history.

work as possessing any public import at all; they find it difficult to see their scholarship as having application to the world simply through its enrichment and strengthening of thought and its contribution to public enlightenment and moral engagement – as if these were not useful and public applications. One would think that the diffusion of knowledge through "formal schooling, within each generation," in Kelley's terms, is a public service of the most weighty sort. Surely, too, the postures occasionally assumed by both academic and public historians toward each other – by public historians dismissive of the comparatively hermetic work of academics and by academics prideful of what they assume to be the superior significance of their labors – does nothing to ease the integration of public and academic history into each other. A change in such attitudes will be necessary to bring about the desirable fusion on respectable terms of the two professions, one old, the other younger – or at least less developed.

One consequence of public history's comparative youth as an organized, institutionalized profession is its comparative intellectual underdevelopment. Public history suffers from not yet having what one of its leading practitioners calls a "sustained intellectual discourse." It has "failed to yield a literature" commensurate with its significance within the discipline, writes another. One should not, of course, indict it too severely for not having the kind of intellectual framework and elements that come with full maturity. Also, public history remains too segregated from academic history, a situation surely not entirely of its own making; and public historians have necessarily been engaged principally in these early years in defining public history's professional ways and developing its practices. In fact, it is around issues of practice that signs of public historians' greater engagement with matters of theory and historiography are now to be seen. Michael Frisch and Noel Stowe, for instance, have written with penetration how "shared inquiry" and "reflective practice" distinguish public from academic history.[30]

---

[30] The quotations are from Rebecca Conard, "Public History as Reflective Practice: An Introduction," *Public Historian* 28 (Winter 2006): 9–13, and Noel J. Stowe, "Public History Curriculum: Illustrating Reflective Practice," *Public Historian* 28 (Winter 2006): 39–65. See also Michael Frisch, *A Shared Authority: Essays on the Craft and Meaning of Oral and Public History* (Albany: State University of New York Press, 1990). The appearance of Stowe's valuable essay in the house organ of public history is an example of the still-too-internalistic attitude of public historians. Had his essay appeared in, say, the *Journal of American History*, it would undoubtedly have been read by a wider circle of historians – in the United States and elsewhere – and been recognized for its theoretical and professional value to all history.

Yet to maintain an emphasis on what distinguishes these two forms of history only perpetuates their separation. Rather than taking place in the pages of the *Public Historian*, too little read by academics, such contributions and debates about public history would better appear, say, in the *American Historical Review*. Furthermore, just as academics increasingly incur costs by ignoring public history, public history itself should be showing more signs by now that it is open to the larger intellectual winds blowing through the discipline. For example, public history has yet to be significantly affected by the already deep permeation of theoretical issues into the more purely scholarly dimensions of history. How the profound questions raised by linguistic theory and epistemology, as well as by deconstruction and postmodernism (to cite only a few of these developments and the terms under which they are known), might affect the perspectives and work of public historians has scarcely been in evidence as a subject of concern among them. One might also wonder whether it is not a major responsibility of public, rather than academic, historians to examine more intently the structure of contemporary, rather than past, public discourse, with which it claims to be so intimately involved. After all, it is not inconceivable that public history might have something significant of its own to add to all of these subjects (and those that will surely displace them in historians' eyes) if only public historians would take them up with the seriousness and depth of thought they have elsewhere received.[31]

By raising these issues here, I mean less to criticize academic and public historians than to suggest that, as in definitions, concerns, and practices as in everything else, the boundaries between the many varieties of historical activities, just as they were in Jameson's day, are unclear, fluid, and permeable and that efforts to maintain them are misguided. The implication, embodied in their very names, that public history and academic history are residual categories of the other – that public history is everything that is not carried on in the academy, and that academic history is what remains when every other kind of historical pursuit is taken out – in fact denies how most historians, whether on or off academic faculties, pursue their professional lives and use their knowledge. An increasing proportion of them practice both public and academic history and move

[31] A muscular review of some of the challenges still facing public history and a plea for more attention to its practice, is Rebecca Conard, "Facepaint History in the Season of Introspection," *Public Historian* 25 (Fall 2003): 9–24. It may be that academic interest in theoretical and epistemological questions is now passing, but my larger point still holds: that public history does not seem adequately to respond to larger intellectual currents.

back and forth between research and the public application of historical knowledge, even if many do not think of their professional lives in such segmented terms.[32] Academic historians engage in formally conceived public history projects, and public historians produce examples of the most rigorously academic historical research. Thus, to distinguish public from academic history in abstract terms is to ignore the realities of historical practices, as well as the ways in which both overlap. Just as the public understanding of history can be advanced from an academic berth, so significant knowledge can be created from outside academic walls. In fact, human nature being rather more seamless than professional categorizations suggest, it would probably be difficult for many historians to say when they are acting as public and when as academic historians. Public history and academic history are professions and roles rather than essentialist qualities.

Nor do their basic methods allow us to differentiate the two kinds of work in sharp terms. Training in public history has in general been as deeply grounded in conventional research methods, bibliographical knowledge, and clear writing as training for academic employment, so that in much of their work public historians pursue their research in precisely the same way that academic research scholars pursue theirs. Surely the same basic standards of accuracy and fidelity to evidence ought to govern the activities of both, just as conventional critical canons should direct the evaluation of public as well as academic history work. By the same token, the production of scholarship is no longer coextensive with publication in book form, and the occupational locations of historians do not always allow us to distinguish academic from public historians. Academic historians who serve as curators of museum exhibits, who help produce or appear in historical films, and who write corporate histories are engaging, albeit in its applied academic form, in public history – that is, applying their knowledge to issues and forms of presentation in which different audiences and an often larger public than classroom students are interested.

Therefore, there is no justification for valuing one pursuit of history over another, for extending to academic history the presumption of greater weightiness, seriousness, and difficulty than public history. Just as

[32] Phyllis K. Leffler and Joseph Brent, *Public and Academic History: A Philosophy and Paradigm* (Malabar, FL: R. E. Krieger, 1990), examines the similarities and differences, in theory and practice, between public and academic history.

there exist many examples of superb and path-breaking scholarship, so instances of superb and distinctive public history abound (as, of course, workmanlike and failed examples of both exist, too). All varieties of history must be evaluated against the same generally accepted standards of accuracy, explanatory power, and clear presentation. All must strive to achieve the same high level of intellectual authority. If the products of public history seem not yet to reach that level as often as works of academic history do, if public history has yet to demonstrate its entire intellectual endowment, it is no doubt because of the youth of public historical practices and the lower esteem in which they are held, a level of esteem that no doubt affects the recruitment to its ranks of some of the best young minds. Nevertheless, the growing quality of public history is as undeniable as the mounting influence of its increasingly numerous practitioners and the back-and-forth shifting between public and academic historical pursuits of more and more historians. The future will no doubt see the further evolution of this new profession of history.

Yet whatever boundary blurring may exist between public and academic history (and surely the more the better), these two major varieties of historical practice can be distinguished from each other, at least in a general sense. Because many public historians occupy academic berths and many academics engage in public history, the distinction cannot be based upon the location of history's practitioners alone (although it would be foolish to overlook the fact that the majority of public historians hold positions outside the academy). Nor, it seems, can the distinction be based upon particular fields of history, such as American history or social history. While most public historians practicing in the United States are historians of their nation, public history as a separate profession exists elsewhere, and public historians are called on to apply their knowledge to a great variety of subjects in addition to social history – from the changing technology of missile launches to the history of neighborhoods – in which members of the nonacademic public take an intense interest. Similarly, during their professional lifetimes, academic and public historians are likely to convey the results of their researches in roughly the same forms – books, articles, and reports – and to have appropriate recourse to the same variety of research methods – for example, documentary analysis, oral history, or historical and marine archaeology. And so it will not do to distinguish them by the kinds of texts they write, by the variety of audiences they serve, or by the research means they employ. Instead, the basic distinction between public and academic history must be grounded upon their different stances and intentions regarding utility and purpose. What are these?

In the first place, it is a rough, but strong, approximation to say that public history emphasizes the direct utility, rather than the diffuse applicability, of historical knowledge to human affairs. Public history is the response to calls from members of the nonacademic public for answers to questions about the past in which they have a specific interest, answers that will affect their understanding of the world and that may also affect their well-being. Public historians' responses to these questions differ widely in their consequences, purpose, and concreteness. For instance, one public history project may concern research into tribal water rights, whose outcome may directly affect the economic future of Native Americans under existing treaties, while another project may concern the reorganization of a government agency's files so that elements of the agency's history may be more easily accessible to the public as well as to future scholars. While academic scholarship usually relies on the gradual permeation and interpenetration of new knowledge and understanding into old, public history is expected to have a more rapid and direct impact on human affairs.

Second, whereas academic history seeks principally to advance human knowledge and to integrate new with older knowledge, largely for the benefit of scholars and formally enrolled students, public history's central tendency is to advance understanding of knowledge about the past among nonstudent audiences. In this sense, public history belongs in some direct way to the public at large, to its members' sense of possessing some stake in the past and in how it is interpreted. It is historical study and reflection undertaken outside the classroom. It encourages people to form their own interpretations of the past, although it is not faithful to its mission unless it emphasizes everyone's responsibility to come to their views out of existing authoritative knowledge and with regard to existing known evidence. It responds to citizens' concerns to understand particular issues, artifacts, and events through their historical contextualization, and it works to deepen the public's living consciousness of its past in ways that members of the public request, not because of the current trajectories of historiography.

This being the case, genuine public history work must be distinguished, as sometimes it is not, from work that historians may do in the course of their occupational lives, as well as from "applied academic history," about which I have already commented. Because public history represents the application of historical knowledge to perceived public needs, it will not do to argue, as for instance did Robert Kelley, that because historians manage information, historians who manage information as the employees of corporations are serving as public historians.[33] Surely, the practice of history is more than information management, which has little to do with the creation and evaluation of knowledge or the application of knowledge to felt public needs. If justification for the pursuit of public history must still be advanced, it must be advanced on grounds other than the usefulness of historians; it must be advanced on the grounds of the usefulness of historical knowledge, which is the special province of historians.

But what do these general differences between academic and public history mean in practice? What kind of challenges can public historians anticipate that may be foreign to academic historians? In what different ways do public historians have to orient themselves professionally?

First, public history work is almost always mission-oriented rather than governed by discipline-driven questions about the past. Public historians are those who step in when others believe they need some particular knowledge of the past for some concrete purpose – knowledge of, say, the history of a building to determine its historic value for preservation or demolition, of a corporation's history to help its leaders understand how it reached its current stage of development, or of a community's history in order to commemorate its founding accurately. In the process of providing that knowledge, public historians frequently have to unearth or create new knowledge, but their principal aim is to meet, with immediacy and specificity, the felt needs of their clients who are looking for directly useful knowledge.[34]

In the second place, public historians serve clients rather than students and are often involved in clientage relationships. Clientage is a contractual arrangement, in which a public historian is expected to fulfill an agreement to provide certain services to an individual, an employer, or an organization or corporation in return for compensation. As in all

---

[33] "Public History: Its Origins, Nature, and Prospects."

[34] As this chapter should make clear, most public historians respond to others' need or desire for knowledge or its particular presentation. But in addition to earning salaries and fees for doing so, some public historians make profits in the endeavor. A number of business firms, some of them from time to time enjoying annual earnings above $1 million and owned, administered, and staffed by historians, now dot the national landscape. Among them, but by no means exhausting the category, are History Associates (Rockville, MD), the Winthrop Group (Cambridge, MA), the Business History Group (Columbia, MD), and the History Factory (Chantilly, VA).

professional client arrangements, the public historian is responsible for providing expert services – in this case, accurate knowledge. The client, like a medical patient, is free to accept or reject the knowledge; and both parties can terminate their relationship with the other.

In the eyes of some critics, clientage implies that public historians are freed from – that is, that they do not benefit from – peer review, a bedrock principle of the academic profession. Originally, this was sometimes so. The extent and nature of the professional review of public historians' work differed from the evaluation of academic scholarship; and public history sometimes lacked exposure to, and the discipline of, assessment by professional peers. Increasingly, however, this is no longer the case. For while, unlike academic scholars, public historians must often first satisfy those who employ their knowledge, their reputation within the community of historians is always at stake. Moreover, their work is usually available for the use of other historians and, even in the case of somewhat fugitive "gray literature," is increasingly reviewed in professional journals by peers. In addition, save for the exceptional cases of classified work (and often not even then), public historians are usually in a position to seek and gain on request the evaluation of their work by colleagues. Nothing intrinsic to public history work renders it immune from evaluation, and most public historians seek and welcome such evaluation at every turn.

Also in some contrast with academic history, the work agendas of public historians are usually established by nonhistorians – by officers of the corporations that employ historians as staff members, the agencies that hire them as consultants, or the museums that invite them to be curators – and sometimes these clients are committees composed of people of diverse interests, expertise, and knowledge. Thus, public historians are at least as apt to address questions posed by others as to answer those they pose themselves (although surely they can – and indeed are professionally obliged to – suggest to their employers or clients lines of inquiry that ought to be followed). As a consequence, public history is less driven than academic history by the sheer curiosity of its practitioners to learn about subjects that engage their interest or by the internal developments of a particular field.

This is not, however, to say that public historians do or ought to consign themselves to inquiries for which they have no concern, or that they do not or cannot bring to bear on their researches the very latest methods, questions, and knowledge in their fields. Far from it. They must be as up-to-date as their academic colleagues in the elements, intellectual and methodological, of their profession. Yet to point to the comparative freedoms of academic and public historians is to indicate the relative difference in historians' independence in the two professions and to suggest that public historians normally have to work to deadlines, within budgets, and toward particular goals – constraints not often imposed on, or easily accepted by, academics. This does not, however, mean that they exercise no influence over their clients. In fact, as often as not, they are able to modify the questions, alter the focus, enrich the inquiry, and therefore be of greater use to their clients than their clients originally anticipated.

Public historians are often employees of agencies or firms and thus, to some modest degree at least, responsible to the institutions that employ them. While concern continues to be expressed regarding the degree to which public historians who are employed by governments and large organizations are "court historians" under restraint against "telling truth to power," there is no more reason to think that they are under any more pressure to shade the truth to please their employers than to think that academic historians slant their written histories to satisfy ideological or political predispositions or that public historians bend to the expectations of their audiences more than do academics. To the degree that both kinds of historians accommodate themselves to others (sometimes voluntarily, sometimes out of necessity), they do so out of individual inclination rather than out of differing standards of their professions. In fact, whether serving as expert witnesses in adversarial court proceedings or employees of large government agencies, public historians best – most professionally, most ethically, and most usefully – discharge their obligations to their clients or employers by providing them with the truth, or as close to the truth as can be gotten, whether it be palatable truth or otherwise, so that their clients know all they must know of what they seek to learn. Of what good are historians to clients if, for example, they do not fully apprise them of the strength of legal cases against them or make them fully knowledgeable about the weaknesses or errors in their agencies' pasts?[35]

Public historians are somewhat less independent than academic historians in another way. In contrast to the usually solitary work of academic

---

[35] On "court historians," see Ernest R. May, "A Case for Court Historians," *Perspectives in American History* 3 (1969): 413–432. Useful reflections by an experienced historian of corporations about the maintenance of scholarly independence while working for hire are to be found in Joseph A. Pratt, "Warts and All? An Elusive Balance in Contracted Corporate Histories about Energy and Environment," *Public Historian* 26 (Winter 2004): 21–39.

researchers, public historians frequently work as members of groups seeking common ends. Unlike academic departments, which may be said without sacrifice of either charity or accuracy often to be fissionable groups of ungovernable individualists, members of the groups within which public historians work are often composed of people from diverse disciplines and occupations who have as their goal the satisfaction of the same mission. Their work is pointed in the same direction and toward discharge of the same obligation toward the same client, and so they must work closely together. Nevertheless, it remains the case that salaried public historians are always free outside their salaried work hours to involve themselves solitarily in professional activities of their choice – research and professional service on their own – and that many of them do so.

Yet, by way of making clear the variety of public historical pursuits, it should be pointed out that, in contrast to the many public historians who are staff members of agencies and organizations or members of working groups, many other public historians are less institution bound even than their academic colleagues. While obliged to honor and meet conventional disciplinary standards, they pursue their work on their own, holding themselves out as "sole practitioners" of the historian's arts. Working from their homes and offices as independent contractors and consultants, they meet the terms of their contracts, pursue their scholarship, teach their courses, and make their other contributions to historical understanding without formal ties to any institutions. They remain free to act as opportunities arise and without the inhibitions of the academy. In this way, public history exhibits a much larger range of occupational roles and possibilities than does academic history and often allows its practitioners a fuller range of congenial gratifications than for many people may be gotten from academic work.

Another distinction between public and academic history lies in the materials and means of research in which each is likely to be most rooted. While anchored to evidence and judged, as is all research scholarship, by its fidelity to evidence and strength of argument, public historical research often goes beyond the confines of the books and manuscripts housed in libraries and extends itself instead into the community – to the evidence of its buildings, neighborhoods, industrial products, and other dimensions of its past. Public historical research is characteristically community oriented, not library centered, and public historians often have an affinity for research into material culture, the arts, and music as well as into the political, institutional, and intellectual past. In this regard, surely, public history, taking up the histories of people whose past may not be found in documentary records, is in a position to lead academic history into new realms of research, evidence, and knowledge.

Yet it is frequently difficult to distinguish the two professions by virtue of either their evidentiary bases or their methods. Take, for instance, oral history. It originated as a method of capturing the texture of current events in the 1930s and 1940s through the activities of the Works Progress Administration and within the military services as a means of gathering information about armed engagements. But as a means of recording the experiences and views of major historical figures, oral history gained an academic foothold at Columbia University through the initiatives of Allan Nevins, who founded that institution's oral history office in 1948. Since then, however, oral history – for no reason intrinsic to its method – has come to be seen as a province of public history. While increasingly used, especially by historians of contemporary affairs, to create and capture a record for future use and scholarly analysis, oral history is also now employed by amateurs and professionals alike to record such varied evidence as family and community histories and linguistic traditions and styles. Through oral history, some of the most compelling and inventive academic and public history is being produced. By the same method, two professions of history are being enriched.[36]

Public and academic history can also be distinguished to some extent by the different natures of their likely audiences. When compared by the audiences to which they address their work, public historians, in keeping with their name, tend to speak to audiences that are broader, more diverse, and frequently more engaged in learning about a particular subject than

---

[36] Of course, oral history, like all kinds of history, is practiced widely by amateurs. Increasingly often, no doubt because of the popularity of biographies and memoirs, people are paying large sums to have their stories recorded, transcribed, published, and sometimes documented on film or a Web site by "personal historians," much as other people are paying to have their bodies shaped by "personal trainers" and their wardrobes fashioned by "personal consultants." It is worth observing that in this and other instances of historical practice, the boundaries between professional and amateur work are porous and indistinct and perhaps increasingly so – which may be one reason academic historians wrongly take public history at a discount. Furthermore, what has come to be called "critical oral history" – the recording of conversations between living survivors of events, such as the Cuban Missile Crisis, the Vietnam War, and the September 11th attacks for the purpose of creating new as well as evaluating old evidence, much of it carried on by academic historians – is just one example of the permeable boundaries between academic and public history and the mounting conflation of the two. See Danny Postel, "Revisiting the Brink: The Architect of 'Critical Oral History' Sheds New Light on the Cold War," *Chronicle of Higher Education*, October 18, 2002, A16–A18.

those which their academic colleagues encounter in undergraduate and graduate classrooms. In their professional lifetimes, most public historians, more than most academics, will surely direct the products of their work to a greater variety of demanding "consumers" of history than the captive students and scholar-colleagues to whom so much academic history is directed, and they are more likely to gain the satisfaction of the direct and candid inquiries and encouraging responses that are sometimes in short supply in undergraduate classrooms. Where college students are often the unwilling, passive subjects of social expectations and curricular requirements (however just those requirements may be), public consumers of – the audiences for – history outside the classroom tend to be active and eager recipients of knowledge and participants in its diffusion. They seek their own authority over knowledge of the past; they seek interactive relations with, not lectures from, those more knowledgeable than they; they want to find their own, often personal connections to the past.

In fact, the engagement of opinionated, increasingly well-educated citizens is turning out to be at once the most demanding and most satisfying challenge of public history. One has only to cite the furor surrounding (among many other similar museum offerings) the widespread commentary and ideological disputes over the art exhibit, "The West as America," at the National Museum of American Art in 1991, the original plans for the *Enola Gay* exhibit at the National Air and Space Museum in 1994 and 1995, the exhibits "Back of the Big House" (canceled) and "Sigmund Freud" (first canceled, then reinstituted) at the Library of Congress respectively in 1995 and 1998, and the exhibit on sweatshops, "Between a Rock and a Hard Place" at the National Museum of American History in 1998 to drive home the point that public history often exposes historical knowledge to unexpected considerations and unanticipated uses.[37]

---

[37] On these and other museum controversies, see Steven C. Dunn, *Displays of Power: Memory and Amnesia in the American Museum* (New York: New York University Press, 1999). On the *Enola Gay* exhibit, the best source is Edward T. Linenthal and Tom Englehardt (eds.), *The Enola Gay and Other Battles for the American Past* (New York: Metropolitan Books, 1996); Robert P. Newman, *Enola Gay and the Court of History* (New York: P. Lang, 2004); and the forum in the *Journal of American History* 82 (December 1995): 1029–1144, especially Richard H. Kohn, "History and the Culture Wars: The Case of the Smithsonian Institution's Enola Gay Exhibition," 1036–1063. On Williamsburg, see the penetrating reflections of Cary Carson, "Colonial Williamsburg and the Practice of Interpretive Planning in American History Museums," *Public Historian* 20 (Summer 1998): 11–51. The Freud exhibit has not to my knowledge been subjected to critical evaluation by historians; but see Margaret Talbot, "The Museum Show Has an Ego Disorder," *New York Times Magazine*, October 11, 1998, 56–59. Industrial museums are the subject of the major part of the issue of the *Public Historian* 22 (Summer 2000). See especially Harold Skramstad, "The Mission of the Industrial

Recently, too, the public has been invited to participate in developing effective interpretations of sites and practices. Two signal examples of such openness are Colonial Williamsburg's skillful adaptation throughout the 1990s to engaged public concerns over its depiction of slavery and the more recent involvement of special collections curators, academics, journalists, and members of the public in creating the National Park

Museum in the Postindustrial Age," 25–32. These exhibits and the controversies and scholarship that have arisen from them draw on an increasingly large body of literature on the history of tradition and memory – the creation of both historical tradition and memory, like modern historiography itself, linked to the need to create usable pasts for the people of modern nation-states. Only a few examples of this literature can be indicated here. In American history they include Warren Leon and Roy Rozensweig (eds.), *History Museums in the United States: A Critical Assessment* (Urbana: University of Illinois Press, 1989); Michael Kammen, *Mystic Chords of Memory: The Transformation of Tradition in American Culture* (New York: Alfred A. Knopf, 1991); George Lipsitz, *Time Passages: Collective Memory and American Popular Culture* (Minneapolis: University of Minnesota Press, 1990); Edward T. Linenthal, *Sacred Ground: Americans and Their Battlefields* (Urbana: University of Illinois Press, 1991); John Bodnar, *Remaking America: Public Memory, Commemoration, and Patriotism in the Twentieth Century* (Princeton: Princeton University Press, 1991); and Mike Wallace, *Mickey Mouse History and Other Essays in American Memory* (Philadelphia: Temple University Press, 1996). Other notable works include the father of them all, Pierre Nora (ed.), *Les Lieux de mémoire*, 7 vols. (Paris: Gallimard, 1981–1992), published in the United States as *Realms of Memory*, trans. Arthur Goldhammer, 3 vols. (New York: Columbia University Press, 1996–1998), as well as Nora's synoptic presentation in "Between Memory and History: *Les Lieux de memoire*," in Jacques Revel and Lynn Hunt (eds.), *Histories: French Constructions of the Past* (New York: New Press, 1995), 631–643; the penetrating, wide-ranging work of David I. Lowenthal, *The Past Is a Foreign Country* (Cambridge: Cambridge University Press, 1985) and *Possessed by the Past: The Heritage Crusade and the Spoils of History* (New York: Free Press, 1996); Benedict Anderson, *Imagined Communities: Reflections on the Origin and Spread of Nationalism* (London: Routledge, Verso, 1983); Paul Fussell, *The Great War and Modern Memory* (Oxford: Oxford University Press, 1975); John R. Gillis (ed.), *Commemoration: The Politics of National Identity* (Princeton: Princeton University Press, 1993); George L. Mosse, *Fallen Soldiers: Reshaping the Memory of the World Wars* (Oxford: Oxford University Press, 1990); Jay Winter, *Sites of Memory, Sites of Mourning* (Cambridge: Cambridge University Press, 1995); and Jonathan D. Spence, *The Memory Palace of Matteo Ricci* (New York: Viking Penguin, 1984). Two wide-ranging and penetrating reviews of Nora's work, with implications for the entire subject of memory studies, are John Bodnar, "Pierre Nora, National Memory, and Democracy: A Review," *Journal of American History* 87 (December 2000): 951–963, and Hue-Tam Ho Tai, "Remembered Realms: Pierre Nora and French National Memoir," *American Historical Review* 106 (June 2001): 906–922. More acerbic and hard-hitting reflections on recent historical analyses of the portrayal of the recalled past in film is Jay Winter, "Film and the Matrix of Memory," 857–864, a commentary on three preceding articles in the same issue. A superb guide to all these matters and the entire range of issues related to museums and their history is Randolph Starn, "A Historian's Brief Guide to New Museum Studies," *American Historical Review* 110 (February 2005): 68–98. A distinctive reflection on the future of history museums is Cary Carson, "The End of History Museums: What's Plan B?" *Public Historian* 30 (November 2008): 9–27.

Service's interpretation of Washington's slave quarters on Philadelphia's Independence Mall. While public responses to professional historians' considered and evidence-based interpretations may often chagrin and sometimes embitter them, such responses should be seen as witness both to the public's intense interest in the past and, more important, to its keen sense of having a valid stake in that past. Furthermore, precisely because history, both mythic and valid, is one means by which people "empower" themselves, the effort to develop ways to criticize citizens' erroneous knowledge while not cutting themselves off from those very citizens remains one of the severest challenges facing historians today. But better it is by far to enjoy absorbed, rather than to suffer inert, audiences.[38]

Finally, public historians are likely over a lifetime's career to present their work in a variety of forms that differ from the forms of academics – often in the media of museum exhibits, consulting reports, site assays, and verbal testimony. While academic historians, undertaking applied academic history, often serve as commentators in, say, television film series, public historians are more likely to write consultant reports, produce corporate histories, and otherwise serve a wide and varied clientage of consumers of historical knowledge.

None of these many distinctions between academic and public history should be taken to be hard and fast. They are not so, and in the best of all possible professional worlds they will have disappeared. Fortunately, there are some indications that the distinctions are beginning to wane. The National Council on Public History and the Organization of American Historians (OAH), for instance, have held a number of their respective annual meetings together, and recent programs of American Historical Association (AHA) annual meetings have begun to contain sessions devoted to public history. More independent public historians are being asked to teach college and university courses, and more faculty-based historians are venturing to undertake public history projects.

---

[38] The way in which popular and deeply culturally embedded conceptions of the past have enduringly affected entire fields of historiography is the leitmotif of many of the essays in Anthony Molho and Gordon S. Wood (eds.), *Imagined Histories: American Historians Interpret the Past* (Princeton: Princeton University Press, 1998). See especially the essays by Molho, "The Italian Renaissance, Made in the USA," 263–294, and Richard L. Kagan, "Prescott's Paradigm: American Historical Scholarship and the Decline of Spain," 324–348. Academic historians have no doubt weakened the role of historical knowledge in the general culture by too long overlooking the fact that historical writing can be inspirational while empirical and speculative while factual. The best historians, never forgetting this, reap the benefits of readers and renown.

It should not be expected, however, that either academic or public history – or, for that matter, all aspects of each – will prove equally agreeable and attractive to each historian. Ideally, one should be in a position both to make knowledgeable choices of professional work, to move back and forth freely between different kinds of history work throughout a career, and, most important, to make lasting contributions to historical knowledge and understanding in all its forms and for all varieties of audiences.

But through what kinds of public history work have historians already made these contributions? A conventional answer would be that they have done so in every kind of history work save academic teaching. Yet that answer once again makes academic and public history nothing but the residuals of each other, when in fact their pursuits have instead become inextricably intermixed. Many public historians, although not members of history faculties on full-time employment, teach part time at schools, colleges, and universities, and many academic historians pursue history work, such as documentary editing or oral history, that has come to be considered the province of public history. In addition, to define public history occupations as all those that are extra-academic is also, in its undiscriminating inclusiveness, of no help in indicating the principal occupations of professional public historians.

Even so, to even begin to define public history by the activities in which public historians engage professionally or by the sites of their work requires a small encyclopedia.[39] What links these activities, of course, is that they are performed by trained historians who are compensated for creating, applying, and conveying historical knowledge. What distinguishes these activities from academic history is that, although all are associated with each other through the same discipline, they fall into different professions and occupations. Given their variety, however, few people would agree about how to group these occupations. But it is reasonable (if by no means entirely satisfactory) to see them as falling into the general principal categories of administration; scholarly editing and publishing; film and other media making; manuscript, archival, and records management; historical and cultural resources preservation; museum education, curatorship, and interpretation; bibliographic and archival work; legal and litigation research; oral history; research librarianship; professional

---

[39] And encyclopedic is what the two most inclusive guides to public history – Howe and Kemp, *Public History: An Introduction*, and Gardner and LaPaglia, *Public History: Essays from the Field* – are. Much about the diverse occupations of public historians can also be gleaned from the cumulative volumes of the *Public Historian*.

genealogical research; community and policy studies and planning; historical archaeology; and independent consulting and contracting (the last of which almost defies definition by its possible applications). Reflecting this variety of work, a selective register of the places where public historians carry out their work would have to include museums of all sorts, historic houses and buildings, natural parks and other sites, libraries, historical societies, historical agencies and historical offices at every level of government, business corporations and law firms, and of course the offices, at home and elsewhere, of self-employed historians.[40]

These are long and seemingly promiscuous lists, and their contents do not exhaust the possibilities. Some will protest the groupings as not inclusive enough, while others argue that some activities do not constitute history work at all. For instance, are not bibliographic endeavors the province of librarianship, and are not bibliographers nothing more than organizers of information? No doubt in some cases yes. Yet surely two such diverse works of bibliographic art as Charles Evans's masterful guide to American imprints or *The American Historical Association's Guide to Historical Literature* are indispensable and profound embodiments of historical research;[41] and many bibliographers produce authoritative scholarship. Does not historical archaeology fall outside Clio's discipline into the precincts of archaeology? In some cases, no doubt also yes. But once ancient artifacts and sites are unearthed and their composition, age, and use are established, historical methods, whether employed by historians or archaeologists, must be used to determine the meaning and significance of what has been dug up.

---

[40] This is probably the place to note the unusual, and unsung, offices of military history, especially those of the army and air force, both of them probably the largest history programs in the world. Hundreds of people, ranging from academically trained, doctorate-holding research scholars to field and wing unit members (who, while not professionally trained, are prepared for their work) collect, digest, report, and interpret information that, it is intended, will help military personnel better perform their combat and other duties. In these branches, history is a staff function performed from the smallest units to the offices of the chiefs of staff. Historians serve in every major command, and well-staffed historical offices are maintained in Washington and elsewhere in the country. It can justifiably be argued that American military forces take historical knowledge and its potential utility more seriously than any other institutions in the United States.

[41] Charles Evans (ed.), *American Bibliography: A Chronological Dictionary of All Books, Pamphlets and Periodical Publications Printed in the United States . . . 1639 . . . 1820*, 12 vols. (Chicago: Blakely Press, 1903–1934); Mary Beth Norton et al. (eds.), *The American Historical Association's Guide to Historical Literature*, 2 vols. (New York: Oxford University Press, 1995).

As this list of occupations suggests, historical knowledge has proved itself applicable to an extraordinary broad range of subjects and in a surprisingly broad range of fields. In their intellectual and occupational diaspora, public historians have helped diffuse historical research far beyond its older focus on elites. But even more important, their achievement has been to bring every subject, as well as every historical actor, within the compass of historical investigation and method and to historicize issues that, excluded from academic consideration, had previously been without historical context and understanding. What often began as a well-intentioned effort to find employment for doctoral recipients disappointed in their search for academic positions has resulted in the awakening of millions of people far beyond academic walls, task-oriented professionals and simply interested citizens alike, to the utility and satisfactions of historical knowledge.

Despite these achievements of public history in recent decades, it would be misguided to believe that public history will easily gain coequal status with academic history in academics' minds in coming decades or that the needs and attainments of its practitioners will readily receive due note. Even as public history gains strength, respect, and practitioners, public historians are unfortunately likely to remain suspect among at least some academics for their choice of professional career (were they unqualified to secure academic posts?), for their academic seriousness (is not published scholarship the sole "good" among historical pursuits?), and even for the value of their work (how can answering the needs or desires of nonstudent and nonscholar consumers of historical knowledge be creditable?). Yet such doubts are no longer warranted, if they ever were, and the remaining condescension of some academic practitioners toward their colleagues beyond college and university walls can only lead to a loss of the confidence of aspiring public historians and, more fatefully, to the weakening of the historical enterprise generally. Public historians are as much scholars skilled in their own pursuits and serious about the diffusion of historical understanding, as are their academic colleagues. History being among the most democratic of the human arts – after all, are not all humans acting as historians when chronicling and understanding their own biographies, evaluating the meaning of the pasts they think relevant to their lives, and trying to construct a life out of what the past has given them? – any act that makes historical knowledge available to others is intrinsically a humane and civic act. Moreover, any attitudes that insulate historical knowledge and debates about the past from public view are therefore by their nature undemocratic and uncivic. There should be no need for academic or public historians to have to justify their pursuits to each other or to anyone else.

Nevertheless, converting academic historians fully to this view will be as difficult as it will be naïve to think that many can be converted to it quickly. It is one thing to recognize the existence of new careers in history, quite another to recast the discipline, its programs of training, and the views of its leading figures to reflect these changes. Instead, those who wish to become public historians will be well advised to steel themselves in advance for inertial resistance. They should also be prepared to accept the fact that the perceived divide between public and academic history will continue for some time to make it difficult for those prepared in public history doctoral programs (few in number, most offering only M.A. degrees) to gain academic appointments should they seek to do so. Accordingly, each aspiring public historian should assess the risks of choosing between a conventional graduate program and the newer variety of public history program that does not yet possess the same legitimacy. The status of public historians will probably for some time continue to be taken at a discount to their academic colleagues, and it is likely to be years before the AHA and OAH adapt fully to the changes that have overtaken the discipline or before a public historian has been elected president of each of them.[42]

A more serious danger for public historians is that their preparation in specialized public history programs may start them down the road toward separation, if not isolation, from the intellectual currents of academic history. Just as academic historians must become more deeply versed in public history, so public historians must be as fully knowledgeable of the venerable and important subjects of conventional, academic historical inquiry – with the ancient and rich historiography of their discipline, with a wide range of national histories, and with newly inaugurated

---

[42] All the early presidents of the Mississippi Valley Historical Association occupied professional positions outside the academy. In 2008 Pete Daniel became the first public historian to be president of the modern OAH, as the MVHA was renamed in 1964. William D. Aeschbacher, "The Mississippi Valley Historical Association, 1907–1965," *Journal of American History* 54 (September 1967): 339–353. In response to the changing demographic and occupational profile of historians, both the AHA and OAH have begun to address the professional needs and issues facing public history, and we can reasonably expect them to adapt even more to changes in the discipline in the future. However, it is likely to be longer before the more prestigious graduate programs include public historians among their senior faculty members and offer full-fledged introductions to applied history to their graduate students.

lines of inquiry – as those who devote themselves to research scholarship alone. To be widely conversant with such subjects and deeply engaged in history's intellectual currents is as incumbent on public historians as knowledge of public history is increasingly incumbent on academic historians. For the latter, this will also require acknowledgment, contrary to their inclinations, that their ignorance of public history risks cutting them off from participation in the fastest-growing and possibly most innovative profession of history, as well as from the careers and trust of many of their students.[43] Furthermore, given the growing and intense concern among historians with issues of language, knowledge, objectivity, and meaning, wider knowledge of public history among academic historians can only deepen their understanding of the utility of historical knowledge – indeed, of the significance of history as a naturally human and profoundly humane endeavor.

The consequences of these realities for aspiring public historians are likely to make themselves felt most directly in graduate education. Those historians-to-be who matriculate in departments that offer courses or programs in public history will be assured of early support and encouragement in their professional endeavors, to say nothing of the benefits of the expertise of those who teach them. But what of those who enter graduate programs that offer no specialization in public history – those who, initially intent on academic careers, instead decide that careers as public historians are more congenial to them yet find few opportunities to pursue their interests in their uniformly "academic" departments?

In the end and for the foreseeable future, such aspiring public historians will have to assume much more of the improvisational responsibility for preparing themselves and establishing themselves in their careers than will aspiring academic historians or those who entered public history programs at the start of their graduate education. Fortunately, as many have found out through experience, one can become a skilled public historian

---

43 But danger lurks even in any genuine acknowledgment on the part of academic historians that public history is a fully legitimate form of intellectual and professional enterprise. That danger is that academics will then be able to assume that because public history exists as the part of history's discipline that faces outward, they can rely on public historians to undertake "public work" for them and go about isolated academic business as usual. A commensurate danger for public historians lurks in the wings. Because they respond to others' desires and needs, they may become even more specialized in their knowledge and practices than academics and cut themselves off from research and knowledge about national, international, and comparative history. That this is already so in some cases it has been my sad experience to observe.

without having been trained by others specifically to be one.[44] In most respects, after all, a historian is a historian, and what one learns of history in the most conventionally academic graduate program will do no harm to – indeed, it can only benefit – the most determined aspiring public historian. The same rules of evidence, argument, and presentation must be observed in public history work as in the preparation of the most erudite monograph; the same puzzles of language, evidence, logic, and perspective bedevil public historians as much as the most devoted library-bound scholars. Public historians serve their discipline and exemplify fidelity to its exacting aims and standards as much as do their academic colleagues. Nevertheless, until the day – and it will surely come – when public and academic history have joined themselves again into the common enterprise from which they first emerged to go their separate ways, public historians will have to remind other historians of the sometimes professionally unpopular truth that the past is a public possession. They will have to maintain the courage of their conviction that, while always demanding, Clio's art in any way practiced is at its foundations a public and civic art.

A Note on "Public Intellectuals"

Much ink has been spilled in recent years decrying the purported disappearance from the American scene of those whom we now call public intellectuals, thinkers and people of letters whose principal intellectual engagements are with the great public issues of their day and with the content and texture of public culture. Public intellectuals are said to distinguish themselves, by virtue of the range of their interests and the independence of their stances, from other thinkers and writers who also locate themselves in the world of ideas – from academic intellectuals, whose work is often driven by issues internal to their disciplines; from critics and historians of recent and contemporary events, whose knowledge is frequently in high demand by journalists desirous of getting the facts out; and from pundits, columnists, and press commentators, who are

---

[44] In fact, most training for academic history concerns the pursuit of research scholarship, not preparation for those activities, especially teaching, for which, after all, one is paid by an employing academic institution. In fact, it can be identified as a distinct feature of academic work that, in general, one is paid for what one is not trained to do – to teach – and comparatively uncompensated for what one's training has emphasized and for what one's professional status most depends on – the production of research scholarship. From this fact, little studied by sociologists or historians, much follows.

called on to give their opinions but who too rarely, in the spirit of Walter Lippmann or Edward R. Murrow, can offer extended reflections on the compelling challenges of their times.[45] By contrast to these academics, critics, and journalists, as well as to those who write popular nonfiction and history and steer clear of contemporary issues, public intellectuals are found both standing back from immediate partisan and political debate and weighing deep into current issues. All of them of course are trying in one way or another to influence general, often political, thinking. But some reflect from a distance on one or more dimensions of society and culture, be it the state of literature (the subject of Alfred Kazin's and Edmund Wilson's enduring works), the structure of society and the economy (C. Wright Mills's, James Q. Wilson's, and John Kenneth Galbraith's concerns), profound issues of morality and philosophy (to which Hannah Arendt turned her mind), the quality of the built environment and urban

---

[45] To this list should also be added those who have been called policy intellectuals. They differ from public intellectuals, who occupy positions in culture as critical outsiders, in being insiders, often serving on boards and commissions and occasionally in higher office and striving directly to influence public policy. Among these, the quintessential modern American figure is Woodrow Wilson. Others are Walt W. Rostow, George F. Kennan, Henry Kissinger, and Daniel Patrick Moynihan. Yet like public intellectuals, policy intellectuals, as these very people's careers indicate, can move back and forth between academic and public positions. And some, like Theodore Roosevelt, historian, and Woodrow Wilson, historian–political scientist, can occupy the nation's highest office without in a strict sense being a policy intellectual. Therefore, no intellectuals – academic, public, policy – should be thought of as bearing essential characteristics but, like an increasing proportion of historians, rather as occupying roles, which may alter over time and which may, like hats, be donned and doffed somewhat at will. Much of this is put into broad, historical, and international context in Helen Small (ed.), *The Public Intellectual* (Oxford: Blackwell Publishers, 2002). See especially Stefan Collini, "'Every Fruit-Juice Drinker, Nudist, Sandal-Wearer...': Intellectuals as Other People," 203–223, in which he remarks (209) that "to speak of 'the public role of intellectuals' risks being as pleonastic as speaking of 'the military role of soldiers.'" An extended effort at defining public intellectuals and distinguishing genres of them is chapter 1 of Richard A. Posner, *Public Intellectuals: A Study of Decline* (Cambridge, MA: Harvard University Press, 2001), a strong, if in the end unruly and unconvincing, attack on public intellectuals. Surely Posner is correct in arguing that the triumph of university-based thinkers has lessened the social significance of public intellectuals, that the peer-review system forces academics to be more responsible in their arguments and use of evidence than public intellectuals, and that academics often surrender breadth of view for depth of knowledge. However, his claims about the relevance of economics to the issue of public intellectual work are unconvincing, and his arguments are often internally inconsistent. It should quickly, however, be said that Posner's book is measured and worthy of attention compared with two other books, both unbridled diatribes against intellectuals in general: Paul Johnson, *Intellectuals* (New York: Harper & Row, 1988), and Thomas Sowell, *Intellectuals and Society* (New York: Basic Books, 2010).

life (on which Lewis Mumford and Jane Jacobs concentrated their writings), the nature of ethnic and race relations (about which Daniel Patrick Moynihan and Nathan Glazer wrote so extensively), or the large themes of history (of which Richard Hofstadter was a master). Others, like Cornell West, Abigail Thernstrom, and Eric Michael Dyson take more overtly partisan stands. While occasionally members of academic faculties, these intellectuals rarely consider themselves to be academic scholars alone – Hofstadter once characterized himself as an essayist – and all are by inclination outsiders, disinclined by temperament to pursue public service and normally taking adversarial, contrarian, or critical positions on matters of public concern. Their eyes are focused outside university walls, they do not write only or even primarily for academic audiences, and they think of themselves as offering ideas and arguments that will help intellectually engaged citizens to understand their world and policy makers to produce sounder programs.[46]

Yet a definition of public intellectuals like this one, which stresses their intentions and dispositions, begs many questions. Why not define them by their influence on the public (however that might be measured) or, more in keeping with their being intellectuals, by the depth and power of their thinking, whatever its influence, or even by their being intellectuals, rather than, say, polemicists or ideologues? Must public intellectuals be original scholars, or is their better role rather to diffuse and, by debating them, to insert ideas into public consideration with perhaps greater force and flair than most academics can? In recognition of the increasing diversity of professional history-related pursuits, we must also recognize that someone need not be a public intellectual full time. Cannot a historian or anyone else, whether business executive or academic, occupy the role occasionally but not always? Can a historian not be an eremitic scholar one moment, an outreaching public commentator, critic, and popularizer another? These questions make clear that no discussion of publicly engaged intellectuals can remain "pure" – that is, focused on them alone. Neither their existence nor their work would be an issue at all but for the alternative example of academic intellectuals, against whom public intellectuals are often favorably compared.[47]

---

[46] Hofstadter's self-characterization is to be found in David Hawke, "Interview: Richard Hofstadter," *History* 3 (New York: Meridian Books, 1960), 135–141.

[47] The antiacademic literature is cited in n. 106, Chapter 4, "The Academic Trinity." An exception to these assaults is Posner, *Public Intellectuals*. See also the disheveled exchange of views ("Do You Need a License to Practice History?") some of them cogent, about writing for the public in *Historically Speaking* 9 (March–April 2008): 2–23.

Disregarding such complexities, much opinion now has it that public intellectuals are little more to be seen.[48] Those who might in earlier days have taken up their pens as independent thinkers – as did their American precursors John Adams, Thomas Jefferson, George Bancroft, Theodore Roosevelt, and Woodrow Wilson – are said to have retreated to the cloistered fastness of college and university faculties where the courage of one's convictions is taken at a discount, where ideological homogeneity rules the day, and where jargon-ridden discourse takes the place of the language of normal conversation. In surely the most powerful elegy for the allegedly long-gone public intellectual, Russell Jacoby, himself writing in the manner and with the intent of a public intellectual, one very much in the spirit of Julian Benda's *La Trahison des clercs*, rues the "the impoverishment of public culture" because of the absence from it of the voices of learned men and women, especially of younger ones.[49] To explain their absence, he acknowledges the changing economics of intellectual life, the growth in power and reach of the electronic press, the siphoning off of

---

[48] Apparently, they have been disappearing for decades. "Where are our intellectuals?" Harold Stearns asked in his book, *America and the Young Intellectual* (New York, 1921). Some participants in a more recent discussion about public intellectuals dispute their retreat from the scene. See the forum on "The Future of the Public Intellectual," *Nation*, February 2, 2001. Good examples of historians who are serving as public intellectuals outside the celebrity circuit as I write (2011) are academics Nelson N. Lichtenstein and Joseph A. McCartin, who have offered their views on public-sector unionism when it is under attack. The difficulty facing historians, like so many academics who seek to influence public discussions, is gaining access to the public stage.

[49] *The Last Intellectuals: American Culture in the Age of Academe* (New York: Basic Books, 1987; repr. 2000 with a new introduction). A reconsideration twenty years later, only modest in scope, is Jacoby, "Big Brains, Small Impact," *Chronicle Review*, January 11, 2008, B5–B6. Jacoby appears to have coined the term "public intellectual." Two subsequent, less polemical, and more nuanced studies of public intellectuals focused on those in New York in the thirty-five years after 1910 are Steven Biel, *Independent Intellectuals in the United States, 1910–1945* (New York: New York University Press, 1992), and Joan Shelley Rubin, "The Scholar and the World: Academic Humanists and General Readers in Postwar America," in David A. Hollinger (ed.), *The Humanities and the Dynamics of Inclusion since World War II* (Baltimore: Johns Hopkins University Press, 2006), 73–103. Also apposite is Jeremy Jennings and Anthony Kemp-Welch (eds.), *Intellectuals in Politics from the Dreyfus Affairs to Salmon Rushdie* (New York: Routledge, 1997). There is reason to believe that many more public intellectuals exist than thinkers whom the public recognizes as major figures, who are likely, in any case, to be older and for that reason alone more widely known than younger intellectuals. For an argument, by no means far-fetched, that what we now term "public intellectuals" can be said to have existed as early as the fourteenth century (and what about Socrates?), see Daniel Hobbins, "The Schoolman as Public Intellectual: Jean Gerson and the Late Medieval Tract," *American Historical Review* 108 (December 2003): 1308–1335.

intellectual talent into films and television (where the impact of ideas, or at least of impressions, can be so much more powerful and immediate than in print), and the substitution of journalistic, adversarial punditry for extended and deep commentary and reflection.

Although he holds such changes in culture and society in part responsible for the decline in the number and impact of public intellectuals, Jacoby arraigns academics for contributing to public intellectuals' disappearance by their insouciant neglect of the large public and joins others, like Edmund Wilson and Lewis Mumford earlier, in decrying many characteristics of scholarly work (such as overspecialization, jargon-ridden prose, and, more recently, a romance with theory). He also blames academics for losing their audiences – not (in an omission tellingly indicative of critical stances on his matter) audiences for abandoning the hard work of understanding what academics write. Jacoby challenges academic scholars (and, by extension, public historians) to reconsider their responsibilities to society, to cast off the many inhibitions of academic culture, and to respond to the public's keen desire to know and understand the world in ways free of jargon, fashionable ideology, and narrow specialty. The problem, he implies, lies in intellectuals' aspirations, not in the general culture.

In an analogous but less polemical commentary, this one on academics' concern about lowering their standards if they reach out to the public, Alexander Nehamas, usefully distinguishing between "public" and "popular" writing, has noted that philosophers – and by extension many academics – confuse the two.[50] He implies that popularization runs real dangers in trying to affect the thinking of the least informed members of the public, and he fairly points to the unfortunate impatience of many people with ideas that cannot be presented in the simplest garb. Nevertheless, he also insists that scholars need to write for those people – the "public" – who devote serious effort to understanding ideas that require careful thought and "serious and sometimes relatively long preparation."

Jacoby's and Nehamas's are worthy ideals and worthy goals, and the application of fresh will toward creating new audiences, speaking

---

[50] "Trends in Recent American Philosophy," in Thomas Bender and Carl E. Schorske (eds.), *American Academic Culture in Transformation: Fifty Years, Four Disciplines* (Princeton: Princeton University Press, 1997), 227–241, at 238. An astute criticism from within the discipline of literature of the many issues involved in public intellectual debate is John Michael, *Anxious Intellects: Academic Professionals, Public Intellectuals, and Enlightenment Values* (Durham: Duke University Press, 2000).

and writing in colloquial terms, and satisfying people's wide, sometimes passionate, interest in the past cannot be without extensive benefit to historians, to say nothing of the general public. Surely something has been lost in the long journey from belletristic history to history-in-the-monograph, from the cadences of Gibbon to the dry prose of the research scholar. And surely engagement with one's fellow citizens is a high responsibility, one too often shirked by historians. Yet it is not precisely clear how Jacoby's complaints apply to historians and precisely what historians might do specifically to address those complaints.

Professional responsibility does not and cannot mean that all historians should choose their fields of expertise in order to be useful to the public. After all, historians must be free to study what they wish to study, to address the central issues of their discipline, and to apply (or not to apply) their knowledge to public questions as they choose. As long as they can earn a living doing so, historians should be as free as everyone else to pursue the work of their lives unmolested by public concerns. Nor can every historical topic pursued by every historian have a bearing on public issues. In this regard, students of modern history will typically have an advantage over historians of the more distant past, and Americanists will often have an advantage over scholars of other cultures, at least in the United States. But there are nothing like events, such as the Vietnam War or terrorism, to transform obscure historians beavering away on obscure topics into scholars whose knowledge is suddenly found to be directly relevant to world affairs and who thereby become, if only briefly, "public intellectuals" – in high demand and of great utility.

Furthermore, historians – albeit not all of them – have, and always have had, public audiences, sometimes large ones. Witness, for example, the public's insatiable appetite for works, including works of high scholarship, on the history of the American Revolution, the "Founding Fathers," the Civil War, and the Holocaust. And while it is difficult to see how important theoretical works on "subaltern" studies or controversies over such subjects as "court" and "country" ideologies in the eighteenth century and the "objectivity question" in historiography can gain large general audiences, such works, often read by more people than book sales indicate, bring about a deepened understanding of the past. And eventually that understanding makes its way into the work of critics and commentators who are conversant with academic scholarship and then into public discourse. Such, at least, has been the career of much recent historical work on such topics as race relations, women's lives, ethnicity, and foreign affairs. By making their academic contributions, academic historians contribute in more ways than is often acknowledged to public knowledge and understanding.[51]

It is also the case that historians possess a kind of knowledge whose use in ways deemed desirable by critics of academic culture is not always possible. Much of it is retrospective social science (if it is social science at all) rather than the forward-looking, reformist, and speculative thinking of many, perhaps most, public intellectuals. Being concerned with the past, works of history can only imply, they cannot as history propose, courses of action; they can evaluate, sometimes magisterially, the conditions of society and culture, but they cannot as history directly help society out of its predicaments. The historians of greatest weight and influence tell stories of times gone by rather than analyze current affairs. They charge the present with meaning by locating it in the past; they do not, and cannot, convey us into the future. Historians may become well known and influential; their works may enjoy brisk and enduring sales; people may seek their advice. But their work must stand or fall, not on the temperament or ideology their authors bring to it, not on their works' arguments for change, but instead on their foundations in knowledge and the power of their presentation. Reform may arise from historical knowledge, but bringing about reform is the province of others – or at least of historians on their days off.

All this being said, surely there is much in Jacoby's and Nehamas's critiques that is valid. Public debate has always been enriched by the participation of men and women, widely read and deeply versed in their particular subjects, who have been willing to speak to their fellow citizens in words they can understand and with confidence in citizens' ability to understand them. A society without the likes of W. E. B. Du Bois, Carter G. Woodson, Hannah Arendt, Angie Debo, Malcolm Cowley, Paul Goodman, David Riesman, Russell Kirk, Dwight MacDonald, and Irving Howe – and without Charles A. and Mary Beard, Samuel Eliot Morison, Henry Steele Commager, and Richard Hofstadter – is an impoverished

---

[51] On this point, Jacoby's arguments reveal a certain obtuseness. One has only to cite such works as C. Vann Woodward, *The Strange Career of Jim Crow* (New York: Oxford University Press, 1955), and William H. McNeill, *Plagues and Peoples* (Garden City, NY: Anchor Press, 1976), both of which reached wide audiences, to recognize the deficiencies in his claims. Furthermore, Jacoby does not, because one cannot, make a case that public intellectuals cannot reemerge from within the academy. An exemplary study that suggests strongly that the academy is not by its nature inimical to public intellectual endeavor is Thomas Bender, *Intellect and Public Life: Essays on the Social History of Academic Intellectuals in the United States* (Baltimore: Johns Hopkins University Press, 1993).

society indeed.[52] But the days of independent belletristic historians, many of whom were amateurs of private means who, while laboring hard to base their works on research, were not held to the standards of research and presentation that have developed since the time of their greatest influence, have probably passed forever. Instead, if history is to speak to a large public (as it does when written by historians like James M. McPherson, Laurel Thatcher Ulrich, Joseph J. Ellis, Patricia Nelson Limerick, and Tony Judt), and if historians are once again to have the audiences that Jacoby and Nehamas assume they can have, then history will have to stay connected to the public largely from within the academy and the community of public historians – that is, through the writings of historians who, while not amateurs, take one of their gravest responsibilities to be engaging their fellow citizens in serious conversations. This ought to be considered the grandest sort of public history.[53]

Yet how, and in what frame of mind, are historians to do so? And what can sustain their work? These questions are important because it is not altogether clear, any more with historical studies than with twentieth-century concert music, whether, as charged, historians have lost the public or whether the public will no longer make the serious effort to approach historical knowledge on its own terms – that is, whether the social and cultural conditions that sustain public intellectual work have atrophied to the point that they cannot be reconstituted. One of these was a relatively homogeneous audience (or at least one assumed to be homogeneous), which has now fractured into diverse audiences, each of which is addressed in its own terms and rarely as part of a larger civic whole. We must also take into account the fact that many historians are crowded out of public debate by the prominence of a few people (like ill-named "presidential historians," many of them better at telling tales than at analysis) denominated by the media as historians who are public intellectuals. As a result, other historians who aspire to have their voices heard are frustrated in reaching wider audiences.[54]

---

[52] I note only historians here. Public intellectuals are to be found in many disciplines. On the academic and public intellectual crossover of a literary scholar, the University of Chicago's Robert Morss Lovett, see Anthony Grafton, "The Public Intellectual and the American University: Robert Morss Lovett Revisited," *American Scholar* 70 (Autumn 2001): 41–54.

[53] A superb study of the life of one activist intellectual is Neil Jumonville, *Henry Steele Commager: Midcentury Liberalism and the History of the Present* (Chapel Hill: University of North Carolina Press, 1999).

[54] Some wags have taken to calling these pundits "publicity intellectuals." Immediate-response punditry is fundamentally antipathetical to the reflective thoughtfulness, offered

To the question, What are historians to do about these challenges? some ready and compelling answers immediately present themselves. As many are already doing, they must – that is, if they wish to disseminate historical knowledge more widely to more and broader audiences – write lively prose, tell stories, avoid abstruse debates with other scholars, limn the histories of individuals, groups, institutions, and policies rather than of abstract forces, and treat their readers as their fellow citizens, not just their scholar-colleagues. Some, of course, are doing so. Less obvious but no less important is the need to discover new evidence and create new understanding – in other words, to undertake fresh research. Nonacademic readers are not always captivated by yet another overstuffed biography of a "Founding Father" (although many are) but by books about those parts of the past that are still being unearthed – of the lives of hitherto unknown or unremarked figures, of hitherto secret or undiscovered documents, of communities or people lacking a modern telling of their histories. But surely even retelling old stories in fresh ways and from distinctive perspectives has potentially great appeal. After all, many of the great works of history gain their lasting excitement from their authors' quest for new knowledge and understanding, always the most supreme of intellectual challenges. Thus, too, histories written on a broad canvas – of eras, wars, nations, and peoples – always have their readers.

But public intellectual work is more than writing for the public, more than transforming dryasdust monographs into riveting stories and prose. It is also contextualizing the present by revealing its roots in the past. To do so requires casting off some of the inhibitions of academic codes, risking committing the Whig fallacy of presentism and progress, and perhaps most of all having a strong "take" on a subject – embodying in historical writing and presentation robust arguments and clear points of view. It also often requires donning the critic's mantle: of evaluating the general culture from a historical perspective, and often of calling to account others' misuse of the past.[55]

As to whether there exists a public audience large and serious enough to engage in the difficult work of thinking about history critically, the answer must surely be yes – at least if by that is meant an audience for

in a distinctive authorial voice, characteristic of the writings of the great public intellectuals of all ages and places.
[55] I once proposed a way to undertake the latter in "The History Watch: A Proposal," *Public Historian* 15 (Winter 1993): 47–54. No one has taken up my suggestion.

the enduring and dramatic themes and moments of history: wars, revolutions, individuals, and eras. There can be little doubt that a large public for history, and not just for history as a chronicle of contemporary or recent events, exists, as attested, for instance, by the growing television viewership of the History Channel and by the presentation of historical knowledge elsewhere. A smaller, harder-working audience exists among those who also read the various kinds of general journals and magazines of criticism, such as the *Atlantic* and the *New Republic*. Yet the challenge for historians who aspire to be public intellectuals, as it is for all artists, whether they be playwrights or actors, composers or musicians, choreographers or dancers, is to create their own audiences for their particular works. Contrary to much criticism leveled at the dry monograph and the purported particularistic researches of many historians today, there is no intrinsic reason why any historical subject cannot be presented both in captivating form and with powerful impact.

Above all, a historian who means to assume the role of public intellectual must neither overestimate the public's knowledge nor underestimate its intelligence. One must be neither patronizing, obscure, nor dull. Writing effectively for a large public may for a few be a gift. But for most, like writing monographs or op-ed articles, it is an art learned through hard, often unremitting, practice. It also calls for risks – those of imagination, gesture, voice, and style. These are different risks than those entailed in writing for a scholarly audience only. And they are risks that occasionally defy academic convention and the opinion of one's academic colleagues.

Not all historians need try to be public intellectuals, and of those who try not all will succeed. It may be enough that more of them strive simply to write for larger audiences than their colleagues and to contribute to general understanding. But succeeding in reaching nonhistorians with historical reflection, however difficult it may be, should be among historians' greatest aspirations.

A Note on Advocacy and Expert Testimony

Many historians believe that advocacy is antipathetic to objectivity – at least to the degree that objectivity can be approached. If historians, using the same facts, disagree as to their interpretation, oppose each other in debate or in court, or employ the same evidence for different or opposite purposes, then, it is often asked, what are we to make of historians' vaunted commitment to the ideal of objectivity? Does not such use of history – in effect, historians trying to cancel out each other's arguments – vitiate history's authority as ascertainable and sustainable knowledge?

Those very questions, often put cynically, enshrine a serious misapprehension about the relationship between conviction and evidence and between interpretation and fact. They overlook the deeply problematic character of "facticity" and objectivity, around which great advances in understanding have taken place in recent decades. They also overlook an expanding body of commentary on the ways in which objectivity may house itself comfortably with advocacy and advocacy sometimes serve the interests of objectivity, or at least the gradual approach to truth.[56]

Advocacy of one sort or another is never far below the surface in all historical scholarship and writing, whether it be the almost unconsciously embodied transmission of a general view of history (say, nineteenth-century Liberalism or Marxism) or the more open assertion of a more particular perspective (say, modern-day feminism or neoconservatism). Advocacy also takes many forms, from the argument of specific positions based on historical knowledge (in op-ed newspaper articles), to the presentation of material artifacts from a particular perspective (in museum exhibits), to the use of historians' knowledge to prepare legal arguments. The last was the case in the celebrated 1954 instance of *Brown v. Board of Education*; in the 2003 Supreme Court decision in *Lawrence v. Texas*, in which some historians' amicus curia brief was critical to the outcome; and most recently, in 2010, in the federal trial court decision in *Perry v. Schwarzenegger*, in which the direct and influential testimony of Nancy F. Cott and George Chauncey provided an exemplary use of historical knowledge for the public good.[57] No less than scholarship, point-of-view and political advocacy have always been subject to public scrutiny and to retrospective critical evaluation and response. Yet because of the spreading use of historical information and knowledge beyond the scholar's page and because of the efforts of historians themselves to discover new

---

[56] For general observations about expert testimony by historians, see the following articles in the *Public Historian*: Carl M. Becker, "Professor for the Plaintiff: Classroom to Courtroom," 4 (Summer 1982): 69–77; Leland R. Johnson, "Public Historian for the Defendant," 5 (Summer 1983): 65–76; J. Morgan Kousser, "Are Expert Witnesses Whores? Reflections on Objectivity in Scholarship and Expert Witnessing," 6 (Winter 1984): 5–19; and Hal K. Rothman, "*Historian v. Historian*: Interpreting the Past in the Courtroom," 15 (Spring 1993): 39–53.

[57] For a brief, yet important, introduction to some of the issues surrounding amicus curiae briefs, see Michael Grossberg, "Friends of the Court: A New Role for Historians," *Perspectives on History* 48 (November 2010): 27–30. Grossberg has himself helped prepare and been a signatory of amicus briefs, as have an increasing number of historians.

applications for historical knowledge, new and comparatively untried varieties of advocacy, many of them producing more tangible consequential results than scholarly argument and raising fresh issues of objectivity and criticism, have come into being and been the subject of bitter dissension and condemnation.

Perhaps the most heated disputes among historians over advocacy have come to bear on the challenges of expert legal testimony, or "expert witnessing," as it is sometimes termed. While much expert testimony tries quite directly to establish facts, some takes on the coloration of advocacy. And in no legal case were the problems of such advocacy brought home more clearly than in the 1980s case of *Equal Employment Opportunity Commission v. Sears, Roebuck & Co.* Usually evaluated as a critical moment in women's history (which it surely was), the case must also be seen for the light it throws on the challenges of expert legal testimony and thus of historians' ventures beyond the classroom and the printed page.[58]

The case, whose full history must be put aside here, raised most historians' worst fears about the use (to some, the misuse) of knowledge, to say nothing of such other considerations as participants' reputations

---

[58] A dispassionate history of this celebrated case has yet to be written. The general context of the case is set forth in Katherine Turk, "Out of the Revolution, into the Mainstream: Employment Activism in the NOW Sears Campaign and the Growing Pains of Liberal Feminism," *Journal of American History* 97 (September 2010): 399–423. On the case itself, see Alice Kessler-Harris (who testified in the case), "Equal Employment Opportunity Commission v. Sears, Roebuck and Company: A Personal Account," *Radical History Review* 35 (1986): 57–79; "Women's History and EEOC v. Sears, Roebuck and Co.: Interviews with Rosalind Rosenberg and Alice Kessler-Harris," *New Perspectives* 18 (Summer 1986): 21–34; Ruth Milkman, "Women's History and the Sears Case," *Feminist Studies* 12 (Summer 1986): 375–400; Sandi E. Cooper and Jacquelyn Dowd Hall, "Women's History Goes to Trial: *EEOC v. Sears Roebuck, and Company*," *Signs* 11 (Summer 1986): 751–759; Katherine Jellison, "History in the Courtroom: The Sears Case in Perspective," *Public Historian* 9 (Fall 1987): 9–19; Thomas Haskell and Sanford Levinson, "Academic Freedom and Expert Witnessing: Historians and the *Sears* Case," *Texas Law Review* 66 (1988): 1629–1659; Kessler-Harris, "Academic Freedom and Expert Witnessing: A Response to Haskell and Levinson," *Texas Law Review* 67 (December 1988): 429–440; Haskell and Levinson, "On Academic Freedom and Hypothetical Pools: A Reply to Alice Kessler-Harris," *Texas Law Review* 67 (June 1989): 1591–1604; and the reflections in Peter Novick, *That Noble Dream: The "Objectivity Question" and the American Historical Profession* (Cambridge: Cambridge University Press, 1988), 502–510. One must not however assume that adversarial scholarly testimony remains restricted either to history among the disciplines of the humanities or to American history within the discipline of history. See the brief discussion of a major court case that pitted philosophers against each other in Richard Saller, "American Classical Historiography," in Anthony Molho and Gordon S. Wood (eds.), *Imagined Histories: American Historians Interpret the Past* (Princeton: Princeton University Press, 1998), 222–237.

and the advance of feminist goals. Although it should have surprised neither the two historians who testified on the stand for the opposing parties in the case nor anyone else accustomed to the ways in which facts and knowledge take on their own lives and do not exist free of context, the scholarship adduced by the testifying parties was put to uses that the scholars who had produced it had scarcely intended, indeed in ways abhorrent to them. In fact, the earlier research of one testifying historian was cited against her own courtroom arguments. Furthermore, the very format of the judicial proceeding – codified rules of procedure; presentation, rebuttal, and surrebuttal; attorneys' aggressive interrogations during discovery proceedings and in open court; decisions by the judge – constricted the manner in which evidence could be adduced and applied. The court proceedings made historical knowledge seem static and fact ridden when it is always dynamic and interpretive. Once entered on the record, the historians' knowledge, however partial, was open for use by all other participants in the case, none of them historians, and one could have predicted with confidence that subtlety, qualification, and nuance would be lost in the resulting contest. The historians, although free initially to submit what evidence and arguments they wished, in effect were at the mercy of the strategies adopted by attorneys for each party to the case and were not at liberty to change the grounds of debate. Although they had agreed voluntarily to be expert witnesses, both found that instead of serving the Truth, they had taken sides freighted with political and ideological baggage as well as with enduring consequences for the parties at trial – to say nothing of all women in addition to the plaintiffs and all corporations in addition to Sears. And in the end, it was not the typical product of scholarship – oft-delayed consensus arrived at through the filtration of criticism and the accumulation of additional research – that either served or emerged from the case. Rather, what resulted was a dispositive legal decision – a decision that, unlike scholarship, could not be altered by further scholarship.

While the outcome of this particular case was a profound disappointment to many, the use of history during its proceedings was not a particularly unusual employment of historical knowledge, nor was that single case characteristic of all legal cases that rely on historical testimony for their resolution. More typical expert testimony has been offered since the 1970s in voting rights and occupational health and disease cases, as well as in those concerning abortion, the internment of Japanese Americans during World War II, civil rights, the Holocaust, Indian affairs, tobacco, immigration, and gay and lesbian rights. In voting rights cases, for instance, historians have been employed to present in court the history of racial discrimination, of discriminatory laws and ordinances, and of the effects of discrimination on African Americans in the South; in occupational and health cases, they have been called on to present the history of chemical poisonings and industrial accidents and of companies' failure to protect their workers and the public. Historians' testimony has helped correct egregious past errors and injustices in notorious cases of the miscarriages of law. In all these instances, historians have been subjected to intense questioning, much of it strongly factual, some unnerving. While the cases have raised issues as politically charged and momentous as those in the *Sears* lawsuit, the historical knowledge presented during them has not attracted the widespread controversy of *Sears* or spilled far beyond the confines of the courtroom. In fact, if one seeks ideal instances of both applied academic history and the direct utility of historical knowledge, these cases provide it.[59]

---

[59] A history of historians' participation, and thus of history's role, in the ending of legal discrimination in the South has yet to be written. But for historians and voting rights cases, see in particular J. Morgan Kousser, *Colorblind Injustice: Minority Voting Rights and the Undoing of the Second Reconstruction* (Chapel Hill: University of North Carolina Press, 1999); Peyton McCrary, "History in the Courts: The Significance of The City of Mobile v. Bolden," in Chandler Davidson (ed.), *Minority Vote Dilution* (Washington, DC: Howard University Press, 1984), 47–63; McCrary, "Discriminatory Intent: The Continuing Relevance of 'Purpose' Evidence in Vote-Dilution Lawsuits," *Howard Law Journal* 28 (1985): 463–493; McCrary and J. Gerald Herbert, "Keeping the Courts Honest: The Role of Historians as Expert Witnesses in Southern Voting Rights Cases," *Southern University Law Review* 16 (Spring 1989): 101–128; McCrary, "Racially Polarized Voting in the South: Quantitative Evidence from the Courtroom," *Social Science History* 14 (Winter 1990): 507–531; and McCrary, "Yes but What Have They Done to Black People Lately? The Role of Historical Evidence in the Virginia School Board Case," *Chicago-Kent Law Review* 70 (1995): 1275–1305. On public health litigation, see, for example, Gerald Markowitz and David Rosner, *Deceit and Denial: The Deadly Politics of Industrial Pollution* (Berkeley: University of California Press, 2002). Rosner offers additional reflections in "Toxic Torts: Historians in the Courtroom," in Jim Downs and Jennifer Manion (eds.), *Taking Back the Academy! History of Activism, History as Activism* (New York: Routledge, 2004), 103–112. The work of a direct historian-participant in cases involving the internment of Japanese Americans in the 1940s is reflected in Peter H. Irons, *Justice at War* (New York: Oxford University Press, 1983), and Irons (ed.), *Justice Delayed: The Record of the Japanese American Internment Cases* (Middletown: Wesleyan University Press, 1989). Paul Finkelman has also undertaken signally important work intervening as historian to reverse grievous errors of justice in past cases of racial prejudice. Direct and personal testimony to the perils, demands, and dangers of expert testimony, as well as to the misuse of historical facts for legal purposes, is provided by Allan M. Brandt, *The Cigarette Century: The Rise, Fall, and Deadly Persistence of the Product That Defined America* (New York: Perseus Book Group, 2007), 493–505.

One should therefore be cautious in drawing the wrong lessons – such as the conclusion that adversarial court proceedings are "lesser" applications of historical knowledge than academic scholarship – from expert testimony. Most scholarship is surrounded by analogous ambitions and limitations. When they seek knowledge about the past, historians, like attorneys and judges, try to determine fact, intention, and responsibility. Through the evidence they adduce and the force of argument they bring to their work, they seek to establish in their readers' minds a case "beyond a reasonable doubt." No strangers to controversy, historians expect their own work to undergo testing and challenge just as they anticipate testing and challenging others. Like opposing witnesses and counselors, historians often agree about evidence but disagree about its meaning, as well as about the significance of evidence that may be missing. No less than attorneys, historians argue about which evidence to credit and which to question and reject. Frequently, as in opposing court testimony, historians sharply disagree about facts. And it requires no cynicism to insist that historians in their scholars' studies are as good as expert witnesses and op-ed essayists at making advocacy seem objective. Much expert witnessing is "normal history."[60]

It would be easy to conclude from the *Sears* case (and from others that have followed it) that historians' participation in court proceedings as expert witnesses is likely to be nothing but a kind of prostitution of their knowledge for particularistic purposes. But it would be an unwarranted conclusion. While the outcome of the *Sears* case deeply disturbed many people, including those who hoped to vindicate the utility of historical knowledge beyond academic realms, it is difficult to see how, in general terms, historical knowledge was any more "misused" in this setting than it is "misused" elsewhere. For is it not true that in scholarly as well as public debate historical scholarship takes on an independent life, free from its authors' control? Have not individual historians been forced to admit the existence of meanings in their work that not they but their readers and critics have discovered? If knowledge is valid only to the degree that it is impelled into existence by the most celestial motives and without an inkling of its possible implications or use, then surely much of the scholarship of the past quarter century – scholarship pertaining not only to

---

[60] A brilliant example of the adaptation of evidentiary norms drawn from legal procedures for conventional historical argumentation is Annette Gordon-Reed, *Thomas Jefferson and Sally Hemings: An American Controversy* (Charlottesville: University Press of Virginia, 1997).

women, African Americans, and gay people but also to the market economy, the Cold War, the "Columbian encounter," and the United States Constitution, scholarship that has brought such extraordinary advances in historical knowledge – is inadmissible as scholarship, too.

All, most of all the greatest, scholarship is engaged scholarship, driven by deeply personal impulses to understand, possibly defend, and often vindicate a truth. Surely much of it has been created by people desirous of providing a written past for people previously denied one, moved to strengthen the foundations and appeal of particular ideological or belief systems, or gripped by the most personal questions that may be answered only with historical knowledge – all deeply committed and political impulses. While such scholarship must be, and always is, subjected to rigorous testing and evaluation, it is rejected not because of its authors' intentions or commitments but only when the scholarship itself is defective.

Because many judgments in life, not merely judicial ones, hinge on a shrewd assessment of facts from the past, how can history's utility be doubted? If historians deny others the use of their knowledge because of their fear of its misuse, then why do they practice history in the first place? When called on to testify in court proceedings, historians are obliged to present research that addresses questions, however much directed to issues under litigation in court, that are ipso facto historical questions and that cry out for historical address. The evidence they produce is not assumed to be superior to others' evidence, only different because it is the evidence of an expert. Courts, for instance, have been concerned to establish the intent of lawmakers in crafting and adopting civil rights legislation – without question an established and valid subject of historical inquiry – in order to render decisions about the constitutionality of civil rights laws. Similarly, courts have asked historians to determine past patterns of water use, also without doubt a valid subject of historical interest, in order to adjudicate riparian cases whose outcome may affect millions of people. While it is surely the case that the questions put to historians from the bench or by attorneys deeply affect the nature and content of historians' court testimony, it remains possible, as well as essential, that historians providing testimony offer thorough and balanced reviews of the empirical evidence they are asked to evaluate – which is no more than is asked of historians writing published scholarship. If knowledgeable historians fail to do so, who will?

To be sure, critical ethical and professional issues are at stake in adversarial proceedings. While it is a principle of law that each person and entity has the right of legal defense, it remains the case that some defendants have committed actions so blatantly contrary to the public good (or to the public good as particular historians might define it) that they may not deserve historians' assistance. Before joining any particular legal defense teams, historians ought to ask themselves whether they will end up defending lesser truths (such as the availability to average citizens of bits of information that might have inclined them to be more careful in using tobacco) at the expense of larger ones (such as the damage of all tobacco products to health). No historian, at any rate, should feel professionally obligated to serve as expert in defense of ethically indefensible clients, and surely all must guard against taking up expert witness roles simply for the income they may generate. And yet all expert witnesses are bound to make known to those who employ them the most unfavorable as well as favorable facts so that they can best defend themselves; to suppress unfavorable facts may be as harmful to a client (to say nothing of being unprofessional, unethical, and illegal) as to present only favorable ones.[61]

In many respects, adversarial proceedings speed, even if they do not always sharpen, the search for truth; surely they speed that search when compared with academic dispute. In addition, because documents examined during discovery proceedings and in court usually therefore become public documents, open to all, one can argue that adversarial proceedings are invaluable for making available to historians and the public alike information that would otherwise forever be closed in corporate or other archives.[62] Adversarial proceedings, whether in court or in head-to-head debate, also have as their aim the narrowing of factual and interpretive

---

[61] To my knowledge, no extended discussion by historians, no single work or collection of essays, has yet addressed the difficult, often troubling, ethical issues facing historians who present expert testimony. Such discussion is sorely needed. Nor has any historian yet written a "how to" guide for those who are approaching expert witnessing for the first time. Such a guide would also be a significant contribution. On developments in the law since 1994 that determine the admissibility and presentation of expert testimony in trials, see the brief discussion in Conard, "Facepaint History in the Season of Introspection," 19–21, and the citations there. An essay that lays out some of the complexities of expert historical testimony is Fredric L. Quivik, "Of Tailings, Superfund Litigation, and Historians as Experts: *U.S. v. Asarco, et al.* (the Bunker Hill Case in Idaho)," *Public Historian* 26 (Winter 2004): 81–104. For a report of one dispute illustrating the ethical issues that can arise from historians' serving as expert witnesses, see Peter Schmidt, "Big Tobacco Strikes Back at Historian in Court," *Chronicle of Higher Education*, November 13, 2009, A1, A8.

[62] I am indebted for this point, as I am for other observations about the subject of this note, to David Rosner.

differences, and the very form of such debates, as well as the rules by which they are governed, lend a kind of assurance of possible objectivity, if not apodictic certainty, to their findings. Believing that the approach to truth is asymptotic, historians aim through the exchange, even the combat, of ideas to more closely approach that truth, to rid their interpretations of bias, and to gain distance on their own interpretations.

Thus, if historical knowledge is going to be used in public for the purposes of advocacy despite the views of historians about the use of that knowledge – if it is going to be cited by courts or adduced as the basis of analogy by policy makers – should not historians try to influence its use or, in the event, use it themselves? Advocacy will never be to the taste or meet the approval of all historians. But it is now a part of the world of historians that some must employ.

6

Teaching and Writing History

Teaching, writing, and reading are the universal undertakings of historians. Of the three, teaching and writing require a concentration of will, a summoning of imagination, and an extension of self unimaginable to those who have attempted neither. Moreover, to be pursued well, teaching and writing require preparation and, above all, practice. Yet despite the innate difficulties associated with teaching and writing and the centrality of both to the professional lives of historians, they are activities for which aspiring professional historians are still too little schooled.[1] Teaching and writing are also activities to which historians-in-training are asked to give too little formal or concentrated thought, except perhaps when they struggle to prepare their first classes or push ahead with their dissertations (although there is evidence that this neglect is gradually being addressed in graduate programs). It may be, as some allege, that skilled teaching and writing, if not already possessed as a natural gift, cannot be taught, that one can become skilled in each solely through solitary practice. Even if so (and the validity of the claim is doubtful), these basic components of professional history work warrant more serious attention than they are typically given.

One is not a historian, academic or public, unless one teaches – in front of a class; through books, articles, museum exhibits, or films; or by the

---

[1] One cannot receive a doctoral degree in history without proven ability to conduct research and present it in decent prose. By contrast, although most historians formally instruct others at one time or another during their careers, the proven ability to teach has never been a requirement for the Ph.D.

very example, visible to others, of pursuing historical knowledge. In fact, a nonteaching historian is a contradiction in terms. Nevertheless, historians rarely think of their vocation as teaching or announce themselves by using the term that defines what all of them are – teachers. They are, they prefer instead to say, "professors," "scholars," "curators," or "editors"; they are "members of the history faculty," "National Parks historians," or "producers of history films." One cause of this terminological quickstep is historians' frequent desire to elevate themselves above the "mere" status of schoolteacher – a distinction that reflects ill on those who dance it, especially since a fair number of schoolteachers are also scholars and writers of note and as knowledgeable about the past as their colleagues on college and university faculties. Another reason historians avoid applying the term "teacher" to themselves is that many of them are originally drawn, by interest or temperament, to a particular nonclassroom pursuit of history, be it research scholarship or museum curatorship, rather than to teaching itself, only to have to resign themselves to teaching simply as a required activity entailed by the terms of their employment and necessitated by their need for pay.[2] So, too, historians are not exempt from the vast dissatisfaction with American schooling, which has the effect of deterring them from seeking careers as teachers of history in public or private schools. But many historians also avoid using the honorable title "teacher" out of a miscomprehension of the very concept of teaching.

Since the eras of classical Egyptian and Greek civilizations, teaching has been understood in the Western world as conversation and direct instruction – the exchange of ideas through spoken words – between people in public forums, religious congregations, and classrooms. It has also meant the diffusion of knowledge through writing – on papyrus, tablets, and scrolls, then in codices, and finally in bound books whose wide dissemination became possible through the invention of movable type. But in more capacious and modern terms, teaching can be viewed as any means by which ideas are conveyed to others – not simply by voice and written word but also through such media as films, museum exhibits, and works of art. Conceived broadly in this manner, most historians who

---

[2] Serious study of some of the elements embedded in this statement – especially the relationship of temperament, personality, intellectual bent, social origins, and economic status to career choice – would surely yield insights into many dimensions of the knowledge that historians produce. Until such study is undertaken, whether by historians, sociologists, or psychologists, our understanding of the history and achievements of the discipline of history will remain incomplete.

pursue work in their discipline outside school and academic walls have every obligation to think of themselves, and every right to be considered, as teachers. Whether as scholars leading their few graduate students in seminars and informing their specialist colleagues through monographs, or as museum curators creating exhibits that inform and please many thousands of people, historians transmit knowledge from themselves to others. And thus all who enter on a life of history work ought to conceive of themselves as, seek preparation to be, and school themselves to become teachers, not just scholars, of history.[3]

A principal reason for most historians' not doing so has been the absence of adequate incentives and rewards for good history teaching, although both are gradually increasing. In part, inadequate compensation arises from the nature of teaching itself. A reputation for fine teaching, unlike that for superb scholarship, usually remains local, and it usually depends on the evaluations of younger people. Fame for historians rarely originates in the classroom; and when it does, recognition for brilliant classroom instruction, recognition that spreads beyond a single institution to become more general knowledge, like the renown of such animating classroom presences as Henry Steele Commager and George L. Mosse, is unusual.[4] In addition, schoolteachers' and academics' compensation is rarely measured by the quality of their instruction, however that may be measured. Instead, published scholarship, as well as tenure rules and pay scales linked to seniority or graduate degrees, are the principal

---

[3] A powerfully suggestive introduction to the problematic position of pedagogy, education, and teaching in the United States since the early nineteenth century is Mariolina Rizzi Salvatori (ed.), *Pedagogy: Disturbing History, 1819–1929* (Pittsburgh: University of Pittsburgh Press, 1996), in which the editor's penetrating notes suggest what has been lost by the transmogrification of pedagogy into "education" and by the resulting decline in useful research on pedagogy. It is worth noting, however, that Salvatori traces the estrangement of pedagogy from the arts and sciences curriculum to earlier strains within the discipline of literature alone. It remains to be seen, and ought to prove a promising subject of further historical research, whether historians also had something to do with pushing the study of pedagogy out of the liberal arts into schools of education, where it experienced a sharp fall in status and legitimacy.

[4] The fact that a reputation for teaching travels only a short distance protects the poor teacher from far-flung bad notice. Take an exemplary case: Leopold von Ranke is celebrated for laying the foundations of the modern discipline of history, while no one recalls that he was a poor instructor of students. Television has occasionally brought celebrity or fame to scholars who have had leading on-camera roles in sweeping television narratives, which are varieties of popular courses in particular subjects. However, such renown is unusual. The limitation on classroom fame may loosen should courses by video, such as those offered increasingly by colleges and universities or commercially by the Teaching Company, take hold.

determinants of professors' and schoolteachers' salaries. Nor should it be overlooked that the sociology of the academy inverts the normal relationship between compensation and reputation. Academics are paid to perform a task – teaching – whose repute is limited, but they gain wider reputation through an undertaking for which they are not much compensated – namely, research scholarship. The satisfactions of teaching history must thus often be quiet satisfactions – those of knowing a job well done, one recognized by students and colleagues, sometimes honored nearby, but seldom recognized far and wide – rather than the more seductive satisfactions of the wider repute that may come from scholarly publication or other professional work. Fortunately, despite the disincentives involved, most historians care deeply about their teaching and go about it responsibly.

Lacking the incentives of professional recognition for teaching, especially in those professions in which classroom teaching is not a central activity, historians have to learn to motivate and prepare themselves to teach. On their own they must inure themselves to the hard facts of most instruction – among them that students can be taught but not often changed and that many students will ignore their teachers, however skilled those teachers may be, if their own assumptions and ways are ignored. Conventional academic training does little to help teachers-in-training learn such lessons.[5] Some universities provide laboratories and other opportunities by which aspiring academics can practice teaching, learn of their own strengths and weaknesses as instructors, and seek guidance to improve their instructional skills. Yet many universities either do not do

---

[5] A large proportion of history graduate students report not being prepared as they wish for the many instructional and advisory roles of academic positions. See Chris M. Golde, "The Career Goals of History Doctoral Students: Data from the Survey on Doctoral Education and Career Preparation," *Perspectives* 39 (October 2001): 21–26. No more recent such survey of historians in a wide range of careers has been taken. An assay of young history faculty members' satisfaction with their academic work published seven years later is Karla Sclater et al., *After the Degree: Recent History PhDs Weigh In on Careers and Graduate School*, June 21, 2008, available at http://depts.washington.edu/cirgeweb/c/wp-content/uploads/2008/07/history-report-july-17.pdf. Respondents found only modest limitations in their graduate preparation, but because they were academic historians, this survey of their views cannot be taken to represent the thinking of all historians at roughly the same point in their careers; and their responses reflected their felt academic needs, not those of all historians. Two books that can help young academics enter the classroom with some confidence are Alan Brinkley et al. (eds.), *The Chicago Handbook for Teachers: A Practical Guide to the College Classroom* (Chicago: University of Chicago Press, 1999), and Peter Filene, *The Joy of Teaching: A Practical Guide for New College Instructors* (Chapel Hill: University of North Carolina Press, 2005).

so or do so without adequate resources and conviction.[6] Preparation for secondary school teaching, in which active classroom instruction makes up the bulk of a professional's work, is even more defective. Required courses about teaching offered by schools and departments of education are typically of such quality as to make a mockery of the fundamental realities that experienced teachers face each day. While some skills and techniques of teaching can be gained through courses and practice, much of the ability to teach must instead be fashioned out of a combination of personality, character, spirit, and grit.

Like every art, teaching is an act of individual expression. Just as all teachers are unique in their combination of manner, attitude, voice, gesture, and knowledge, so all acts of teaching are unique. Effective teaching arises from within. Teachers bring their selves as well as their knowledge of subjects and techniques of craft to each of their acts of instruction. As everyone who has ever been a student well knows, innate qualities of character and personality – such as authority, energy, enthusiasm, and bearing – determine teachers' effectiveness as much as what teachers know or with what skills they present it. We recall the characters who taught us far more readily than we recall what they taught us or by what methods they did so. Therefore, to teach well – whether teaching students in classrooms or members of the public in other settings, whether teaching children or adults – requires that one be self-aware and knowledgeable of one's strengths and limitations as a teacher. Equally important, to teach well requires one to summon from within the qualities to instruct others. It is this very extension of self, called for by every kind of instruction, that makes teaching so demanding and often physically depleting.[7]

Moreover, it remains something of a mystery as to what precisely constitutes good, what bad, teaching. The greatest teachers often fail to reach a small percentage of their students, and the least effective are

---

[6] Graduate students who hold teaching assistantships or who are required to teach as a condition of receiving financial aid have not normally been offered preparation or orientation for their classroom responsibilities. Fortunately, in part because of pressures exerted in recent years by graduate students themselves, this situation has begun to change.

[7] On the human qualities of teaching, including the exactions and responsibilities of instruction, see James M. Banner, Jr., and Harold C. Cannon, *The Elements of Teaching* (New Haven: Yale University Press, 1997). An enduring, sage classic is Gilbert Highet, *The Art of Teaching* (New York: Alfred A. Knopf, 1950). A work of sharply different intent – both directly useful and wise – and concerned with college teaching alone is Kenneth E. Eble, *The Craft of Teaching: A Guide to Mastering the Professor's Art*, 2nd ed. (San Francisco: Jossey-Bass, 1988).

likely to be recalled with affection and admiration by a small proportion of theirs. Students frequently learn from teachers, not because of teachers' skills or knowledge but because of the particular fit between students and those who instruct them. Conversely, what students may recall as poor teaching is often due to some mismatch between teacher and student rather than to any particular failing of the instructor.[8]

Making the art of teaching even more mysterious is the fact that some people can be extraordinary teachers yet quite deficient human beings. Two well-recorded examples drawn from the world of dance – it would be out of place here to mention historians – are the cases of Martha Graham and Jerome Robbins, the great choreographers and dance instructors, who were notoriously difficult, arrogant, and often abusive. Yet both had a genius for eliciting from each of their students what was already within them and thus revolutionizing the art of choreography and the nature of dance itself.[9] By contrast, some teachers possess those unsung qualities, like patience, kindness, and the ability to instill aspiration in others, that constitute their particular gift of helping students learn. Surely this combination of qualities was the case with Albert Camus's beloved schoolteacher, Louis Germain, whom Camus cited on being named Nobel Laureate for Literature in 1957 for the qualities – "the loving hand you extended to the poor little child that I was" and "the generous heart that you offered me" – that only a teacher's young pupil would have known.[10] Germain's genius was to awaken his young student's inherent qualities, to take the raw material of Camus's inner nature and help him become the novelist and *philosophe* of his mature years. Such should be the aim and hope of all teachers.

How each teacher discharges this responsibility – and a weighty responsibility it is – each one has to discover alone. There are as many

---

[8] Poor teaching is also unethical teaching. Applicable to secondary school as well as collegiate and graduate instruction is John M. Braxton and Alan E. Bayer, *Faculty Misconduct in Collegiate Teaching* (Baltimore: Johns Hopkins University Press, 1999). Braxton and Bayer attribute much misconduct to universities' failure to teach aspiring academics how to teach. Among intolerable instructional behavior they list "condescending negativism," "inattentive planning," "moral turpitude," "uncommunicated course details," "particularistic grading," "personal disregard," and "uncooperative cynicism." A more recent study in the same vein is John M. Braxton, Eve M. Proper, and Alan E. Bayer, *Professors Behaving Badly: Faculty Misconduct in Graduate Education* (Baltimore: Johns Hopkins University Press, 2011).

[9] See Agnes de Mille, *Martha: The Life and Work of Martha Graham* (New York: Random House, 1991), and Greg Lawrence, *Dance with Demons: The Life of Jerome Robbins* (New York: Putnam, 2001).

[10] Albert Camus, *Le Premier Homme* (Paris: Gallimard, 1994), 327.

ways to do so as there are teachers and as many responsibilities as there are students. How often, however, do aspiring historians talk among themselves about such matters, and how often are they encouraged to do so? Most cooperate and learn from each other when studying in their fields; some form study groups to review a body of literature in preparation for their examinations; and most learn to ask fellow students and colleagues to read drafts of their written work. But rarely do more experienced historians form peer groups to discuss difficult cases of instruction or to puzzle out solutions to particular problems of personality or approach in their teaching as do psychotherapists, who typically meet to help colleagues solve refractory clinical problems concerning their clients. Not often are matters of instruction discussed around mailboxes in academic faculty lounges or over lunch. Aspiring historians are steadfastly encouraged to share their scholarship but rarely to examine the challenges of working with their individual students.

The reasons for their resistance should be no mystery. The exposure of self that is intrinsic to most school, college, and university instruction makes the discussion and practice of teaching before peers inherently difficult, even threatening, and the examination of self has never been an inherent part of historians' preparation, as it must be for psychotherapists. Not only are historians' knowledge and skills made visible when they teach; so are their quirks and mannerisms, their weaknesses and inadequacies. For many, perhaps most, historians, especially those early in their careers, appearing before classes of students – often captive in particular courses, frequently inattentive, occasionally scornful – is difficult enough. But to appear as an instructor before peers and colleagues is likely to be even harder. Yet since students are likely to be of little assistance in helping a historian become a better teacher, there are few alternatives, when seeking knowledge of one's own teaching abilities, to throwing oneself on the kindness of colleagues.[11]

---

[11] This is as suitable a place as any to mention another little remarked aspect of teaching that requires greater attention – namely, teachers' skills as speakers. If teachers are to exemplify the abilities that students should gain, they need to speak accurately and not in the colloquial manner typical of young people, whose accuracy in the spoken word teachers should expect as much as they should students' accuracy in the written. But when is this ever discussed? When are teachers themselves held accountable for their use of English (at least in the United States)? Because speaking ability is so personal, working with teachers (as with students) to improve their spoken language is sensitive and difficult in the extreme. But the matter should at least be liberated from its hiding place and discussed more openly and directly as the critical professional matter it is.

Nevertheless, the current state of the many professions in which historians work is hardly conducive to nourishing the circumstances in which the perfection of historians' teaching, especially the teaching of experienced historians, can take place as a conventional – and safe – part of preparation and work. A serious charge against the entire discipline is that the challenge of creating these circumstances has been neglected and long delayed – by history's professional associations, by graduate programs in universities, and by the institutions in which historians work. Thus it is not too much to say that finding the ways and means by which historians can safely learn and practice teaching stands as one of the most demanding and necessary that face history's many professions today.[12]

In the meantime, historians as teachers will have to continue to compose and sing their own songs, as they long have done. Some have an almost desperate need to teach and perform in front of others in classrooms and lecture halls; others tremble at the mere thought of appearing before students and colleagues. The strength of some is lucidity, of others organization; some shine through wit, others through passion; a few are marked by their eloquence, others by their gravitas. But all historians have a deep responsibility to themselves and to their students to figure out what their particular songs are and how best to sing them. And because that is never easily achieved, they also have an obligation never to cease practicing and trying to improve their teaching so that they can reduce their weaknesses and enlarge their given strengths.

But what are historians' particular responsibilities *as teachers* to students of history? What, if anything, is distinctive to teaching history that differentiates it from teaching other subjects? Just as until recent years most historians spent little time investigating and gaining from what had been learned about teaching by those who had studied it professionally, historians have been inattentive to these questions. Answers to them can be ventured only as invitations to further consideration. Surely what I say

---

[12] I say this in full cognizance of the efforts, and thus the progress, of the American Historical Association and the Organization of American Historians in recent years to move a commitment to the improvement of the teaching of history at all levels to the top of their agendas. I take issue not with these efforts, which ought to be applauded by everyone, but rather with their limitations. Too many of them concern content and approach (or method), too few the search for changes in the preparation of aspiring historians in graduate schools that would include a fuller, richer, and more humane introduction to the arts of teaching.

here is likely to be – indeed, deserves to be – challenged, modified, and expanded.[13]

History teaching, of course, differs in content from the teaching of other subjects. Teachers of history, as distinct from teachers in other disciplines, are obliged to instruct their students in the fundamental elements that distinguish historical knowledge from other kinds of knowledge. They must, for example, be true to history's essential intellectual components – that it concern the past and the consequences of the passage of time in the past, that it examine changes in human existence and in the consequences of human agency in the world over time, and that it offer explanations and interpretations of those changes. Teachers of history must emphasize history's evidentiary attributes – that the sources of written history have to be pertinently and accurately used in order to constitute valid historical knowledge, that those sources have to be cited, and that all known sources must be used and made available for examination and evaluation. And teachers of history must help students to understand history's qualities as a craft and an art – that it always arises from and reveals its particular teachers' and authors' (and, today, its exhibitors' and producers') convictions and temperaments; that it must pass a kind of basic test of plausibility (by conforming to generally accepted understandings of the way human nature and societies function); that it lead to greater understanding of human life; that it be clearly (better yet, winningly) written, filmed, and exhibited; and that it be aesthetically pleasing.

In addition, because of the moral content of historical knowledge, teachers of history must be true to the integrity of the past itself and, perhaps more important, to the integrity (however ugly it may in fact have been) of the lives of those who lived earlier. They must not represent

---

[13] Intimations of what distinguishes the teaching of history from the teaching of other disciplines, as well as materials useful to schoolteachers and students, can be gained from the *OAH Magazine of History*, a magazine published since 1985 under the auspices of the Organization of American Historians; from the *History Teacher*, published since 1967 by the Society for History Education; from the biannual *Teaching History: A Journal of Methodology*; and from a series of short articles about different teaching approaches published annually in the *Journal of American History*. A literature about historical cognition and its relationship to teaching and learning history is just coming into being. A tantalizing introduction to its promise is Sam Wineburg, *Historical Thinking and Other Unnatural Acts: Charting the Future of Teaching the Past* (Philadelphia: Temple University Press, 2001). See also Peter N. Stearns et al. (eds.), *Knowing, Teaching, and Learning History: National and International Perspectives* (New York: New York University Press, 2000).

the past for mere ideological or partisan purposes or present part of it to stand in for the whole. What distinguishes the discipline of history from all others is its insistence – indeed, its demonstration – of the historicity and particularity of everything. This requires that those teaching others about the past emphasize the contingency of all events, acts, thoughts, and institutions and that they make special efforts to bring alive the strangeness and sheer differentness of what has gone before – in other times, among other people and cultures, and in places and situations other than students' own. The awakening of students' consciousness to lives entirely different from theirs is one of the signal achievements of the best history teaching – as well, one hastens to add, one of its greatest challenges before the inertia of conventional wisdom and ingrained habitual ideas. That challenge is in no way lessened by the intellectual solipsism of today, when emphasis often falls on understanding one's own self, family, tribe, and nation to the exclusion of understanding others.

One can legitimately argue that these attributes must be those of historical scholarly research and writing as well as of teaching. And well they must be. But the teaching of history differs from its written presentation through the way teachers can bring visibly to life the significance, relevance, and effects of knowledge about the past. To do that, teachers of history must somehow appear to embody the qualities of curiosity, wonder, and seriousness – the very qualities they themselves feel toward the past – when teaching their subject to others; they must try to bear in on their students the significance for their own lives of knowledge about the past. Rather than committing the grave error of the title character of Muriel Spark's *The Prime of Miss Jean Brodie*, the error of projecting oneself onto one's students, historians must try instead to lead their students to find individuals worthy of emulation as the students themselves go about examining and interpreting the past and giving it meaning.[14] Teachers of history must also remain constantly aware that, like potters at their wheel, they are shaping the past in their students' minds and for that reason bear a profound fiduciary responsibility toward them.[15] To accomplish this deeply responsible – indeed, ethical – task, teachers of history must imagine the particular states of mind of those whom they

[14] It is telling that the ancient collective noun for teachers is "an example" – that is, "an example of schoolmasters," analogous to "a pride of lions."

[15] An important investigation into aspects of Americans' views of the past and of history that teachers are always struggling against as well as working with is Roy Rosenzweig and David Thelen, *The Presence of the Past: Popular Uses of History in American Life* (New York: Columbia University Press, 1998).

seek to teach, states of mind profoundly affected by their students' age and generation, preparation, knowledge, location, attitude, and culture – that is, by their own history.

Nevertheless, the sobering fact remains that, however well any teachers of history achieve these goals, they swim in a dark sea of ignorance regarding history teaching itself. Not until recently was any research devoted to that subject; even now little knowledge exists of the cognitive processes involved in teaching and learning history and thus about what are the best, and worst, methods for offering and gaining instruction about the past. Historians follow tradition, improvise, implement hunches, emulate those who seem to succeed best as teachers; but still they have little solid empirical ground upon which to situate themselves as they struggle to become effective history teachers.

Fortunately, however, this situation has begun to change. From now on, no historian can afford to remain uninformed about what is being learned, on scientific and other grounds, about the communication and reception of knowledge about the past. Practitioners in disciplines as diverse as epistemology, the cognitive sciences, psychology, anthropology, ethnography, education, and history itself (with its interest in myth, memory, texts, and consciousness) have begun to create an entirely new multidisciplinary field: the teaching of history – how people become historically minded and "what it means to learn and to teach history in classrooms and university seminars, in museums, and in society at large."[16] That field, slowly revealing how the teaching of history is a subject distinct from, say, the teaching of literature or of chemistry, is emerging

---

[16] Stearns et al., *Knowing, Teaching, and Learning History*, 2. This work, plus Wineburg's, *Historical Thinking and Other Unnatural Acts*, are currently the principal works in this infant field. But see also Lendol Calder, William W. Cutler III, and T. Mills Kelly, "History Lessons: Historians and the Scholarship of Teaching and Learning," in Mary Taylor Huber and Sherwyn F. Morreale (eds.), *Disciplinary Styles in the Scholarship of Teaching and Learning: Exploring Common Ground* ([Stanford]: Carnegie Foundation for the Advancement of Teaching, 2002), 45–67. Much of this work unfortunately appears in journals little known to historians, a situation that, however, is beginning to change. In this regard, see Lendol Calder, "Uncoverage: Toward a Signature Pedagogy for the History Survey," *Journal of American History* 92 (March 2006): 1358–1370. This compelling article is distinctive in providing a rare insight into the application of new research about historical knowledge being undertaken by Calder, Wineburg, and others. Historians are likely to grow impatient to have other such examples of how they can implement this new knowledge into their instruction. A critical challenge to those undertaking research into historical cognition and history teaching, a challenge not yet met, is, first, distinguishing and, then, integrating into teaching what is known about historical learning at different ages and levels of instruction and about how history instruction must adopt to each stage of students' development and education.

from research into the nature of historical knowledge, learning, and communication, and it aspires to create an empirical foundation upon which teachers of history at all levels can base their instruction. It is not too much to say that gains in knowledge of the subject hold promise of profoundly altering our understanding of what historians do, as well as what they must do to teach more effectively, not just to provide knowledge about the past but to lead students to think historically. While no scholar in the new field is yet prepared to tell historians on the basis of new knowledge how to teach, what in more general terms is called "the scholarship of teaching" is nevertheless likely to have a major and increasing impact on how historians present what they know to others.

As this growing body of research reveals, understanding the ways in which historical knowledge is and can be imparted is of no benefit unless matched with equal understanding about how the human mind, at its many stages, receives that knowledge. Whether standing before their students or presenting an exhibit of historical artifacts, history teachers make their way into a Sargasso of cognitive, developmental, and cultural complexity. Until now, most have been like the blind flyer, getting from takeoff to landing as much by luck as by skill. In the absence of a firm and accepted body of knowledge about history teaching, such approaches as emulating one's own teachers, learning various tricks of the trade from others, and attending an occasional workshop on teaching methods have had to stand in for applied knowledge of the specific cognitive realities of instructing others about the past. What have been called "historical habits of mind"[17] are, as new knowledge slowly reveals, both much harder to create and, when necessary, much harder to dislodge than was previously known. If historians can learn from the understanding being accumulated by research into history teaching how to apply this new knowledge in their day-to-day professional work and add that knowledge to the content of their historical learning and their teaching skills, the gains to their students, as well as to the discipline as a whole, ought to be substantial.

This is not by any means, however, to depreciate attention to methods and media of instruction. Until recently, lectures and discussions in small groups or seminars that relied for evidence and knowledge on printed or photocopied primary and secondary sources, supplemented by occasional museum or site visits, constituted the principal means of presenting historical knowledge in the classroom. Teachers themselves

[17] Stearns et al., *Knowing, Teaching, and Learning History*, 473.

composed the medium through which history was taught. Their performances, like those of actors and musicians, bore the full weight of interpretation. Their classroom presentations, growing from each "performer's" knowledge and personality, were immediate, and each teacher monopolized students' attention for the duration of any class. However, with the advent and refinement of new media such as photography, films, and, most recently, the World Wide Web, and with the advent of Web sites dedicated to teaching, to say nothing of significant developments in museum curatorship and the management and presentation of historic sites and buildings, teachers of history have begun to lose their centrality to the teaching of their subject.

At the same time, the challenges to instructors of history because of the changing mentality of students raised in the visual and aural world of television and the Internet have increased. As demanding as teaching from texts and by *viva voce* instruction has always been, the broadening of the sources from which instruction can now derive to include visual and aural sources, as well as a vastly widened collection of printed material now found in electronic form and the spread of informative and authoritative "blogging," has only intensified the difficulties, as well as opportunities, teachers face in selecting the subjects, evidence, and form by which they may instruct their students. It is too soon to predict that the availability of new materials will free many schoolteachers of history from the use of required texts, some mandated by public authorities, and give to them and their students new freedom to select the subjects and means of study. But it is certain that professional independence will not reduce the professional responsibility for academic historians as well as schoolteachers to be fully conversant with available sources and fully practiced in their use. Teachers are thus likely to find that instruction becomes more, rather than less, difficult.

By this I mean that the wealth, interactivity, and variety of new media opportunities will place upon instructors the need to make choices far more numerous than in the days of lectures, books, journal articles, and assigned papers. Students are now able to access remnants of the past in ways unimaginable until recently – through primary documents, photos of artifacts online, and mapping technologies to mention only a few. For instructional purposes, teachers and students can utilize such sites as Google Books and Google eBooks, the Republic of Letters, the Valley of the Shadow, and Common-place. The documentary records increasingly available through both public and proprietary sites – those, for instance, of the Library of Congress, Readex's Historical Newspapers, and Alexander Street Press's manuscript collection – greatly magnify the resources (and not just those about social and cultural history) available for research and teaching. Teachers themselves can offer guidance through electronic discussion groups, and students can complete assignments online and in new media. The challenge will not be to utilize these newly available means but rather to select wisely and consciously among them to gain particular curricular and learning objectives. While opening new possibilities, the availability of new media and new opportunities will not guarantee better instruction or improved outcomes. They will, however, offer a wider field for experimentation and for instruction tailored to every specific end.[18]

It is also too early to tell how far the loss of teachers' centrality in the classroom will proceed or what it will signify for them or for the subjects they teach. It seems certain, however, that history instruction will have to adapt (as it has already started to do) to new technological realities, that all historians (however much they resist or find fault with developing technology) will have to learn to use new media both as means of instruction and as sources of historical information and knowledge, and that they will have to alter their sometimes negative attitudes toward ongoing advances in technology.[19] Some will no doubt become adept at creating instructional materials for themselves and others through the new outlets that are becoming available to them and thus at bending the media to their particular purposes. Others will instead choose to, and an increasing proportion will no doubt simply have to, exploit the new media for instructional purposes and alter their teaching accordingly. In all cases, teachers of history are going to be pressed to deepen their understanding of the advantages, as well as the limitations, of the new media available for instruction.

As a new and bewildering professional world whose outlines may long remain unclear and whose consequences for history and its practitioners will make themselves felt over some decades opens before us, a realistic view of onrushing technological changes would seem to be that there is no way to reverse them, only to try to understand their prospective effects

---

[18] Fortunately, academic journals have significantly increased their reviews of history Web sites, Web-based exhibitions, and commercial documentary collections. Listservs, like those of H-Net, frequently carry discussions about the value of these new resources.

[19] Some historians, in addition to exploiting Web resources for teaching, will choose to offer instruction, often simultaneously, over the Internet. To do this will require special skills, if not special historical knowledge. The literature about Web resources in history is already vast, complex, and beyond summary here. One sampling of the many resources and opportunities becoming available, some necessary, for teaching, research, and communication, can be found in the issue of *Perspectives* 45 (May 2007).

on instruction, adapt to them, learn to put them to use, and try to shape their influence on Clio's discipline and her students.[20] Nevertheless, it is unlikely that any changes in teaching because of advances in the "digital humanities" will be either so injurious to historical studies as some fear or the savior of the discipline of history that others anticipate. It is hard to foresee young students becoming any less resistant to high school history instruction than they are now or to imagine the trajectories of research scholarship being altered simply because of novel technology. Some initial speculations about the changed role of history teaching in an era of overwhelming advances in the content and application of electronic media can, however, be ventured.

First, as to some of the gains.[21] The growth of the World Wide Web is making possible an accessibility to sources – for research no less than for teaching – that is limited only by the ability (and finances) of individual repositories to place their materials on their Web sites. Here, historians, disproportionately reliant on written sources that can easily be displayed on the Web, will have some advantages over, say, archaeologists, who ideally teach their discipline through fieldwork, or physical scientists, who have need of equipment. As time goes on, of course, the sheer magnitude of such Web resources in the public domain will themselves pose challenges of selection that printed textbooks and published supplementary materials have heretofore more or less obviated, and both teachers and students may be overwhelmed. Moreover, the multitude of sources added to the Web without peer review will tax the ability of individual historians, whether desirous of using these sources for research or for teaching, to evaluate their accuracy and completeness. In fact, developing agreed-on standards of evaluation of history-related Web sites, perhaps even some kind of certification system for them, ought to be a matter of high priority.

Whatever the dangers of Web sites, with them teachers will now have available an extraordinary variety of illustrative original source material – not only documents relating to social realities as well as to political and

---

[20] This is the strong message of Roy Rosenzweig, *Clio Wired: The Future of the Past in the Digital Age* (New York: Columbia University Press, 2011).

[21] Here I deal only with the substance of instruction. It should go without saying that computer programs are already making possible many changes in the administration of instruction through placing lesson plans, syllabi, tests and examinations, grades, transcripts, and many materials related to teaching on the World Wide Web in electronic form.

diplomatic events but also documents that are not text based, such as scanned photographs, artifacts, and works of art. Many such diverse archives of sources are already available through the American Memory Project of the Library of Congress and such venturesome university-based projects as the Valley of the Shadow and History Matters.[22] Consequently, teachers' ability to tailor their illustrations (aural as well as textual and pictorial) to their purposes will vastly increase. So, too, they will be more easily able to broaden the topics with which they deal. As a result, one can foresee a further decline in the place of the political, institutional, military, and diplomatic past as well as increased emphasis, because of the availability of bewitchingly attractive audio and filmed evidence, on recent, at the expense of more distant, times in the past. Similarly, paper-based documents will no doubt yield some ground to other kinds of evidence – another challenge to conventional archival and document-based history. Consequently, it will become essential to make a more conscious and concerted effort to retain for periodically less fashionable subjects and for eras in the more distant past the curricular place they ought to have.

In addition, the availability of sources on the Web will bring the documentation by which historians create knowledge and meaning closer in – into classrooms and the places where students study and prepare their own work. Teachers will therefore be able to demonstrate how they build knowledge and interpretations from evidence, processes that are typically hidden from students in lecture halls and seminar rooms. And because of the storage capacity of the Web, and the resulting flexibility, expansibility, and adjustability of Web-based sources, teachers will eventually be able to choose for instruction among the entire universe of historical documentation – if they have the knowledge and ability to organize discrete portions of it.

Another advantage of the availability of Web resources will be a comparative new freedom from textbooks. Instructors are already able to create their own, customized texts out of materials available in hypertext form in the public domain – that is, no longer protected by copyright.

---

[22] The American Memory site can be found at http://memory.loc.gov, the site of the Valley of the Shadow: Two Communities in the American Civil War at http://jefferson.village .virginia.edu/vshadow2, and that of History Matters at http://historymatters.gmu.edu. The first two are sites principally of source materials. History Matters more explicitly concerns itself with the teaching of U.S. history. See also the innovative "tools" page on the site of the Center for History and New Media at George Mason University at http://chnm.gmu.edu/index1.html.

Yet the sheer availability of such sources will require the expenditure of much time and energy, to say nothing of the development of the skills needed to create these electronic texts. Alternatively, publishers, who are already endeavoring to prevent the spread of customized texts and hold on to their markets with proprietary fee-based sites that provide materials companion to their published books, will be creating Web sites that allow history teachers much greater flexibility in the choice and use of instructional materials than is possible when students and teachers are tethered to overweight printed books. The choices that teachers face may thus be increasingly daunting.

Another benefit of the Web is that students will be better able to learn on their own. Teachers will remain their guides, but students will now have access, without the intermediation of their instructors, to resources unimaginable before – as long as they can be gotten to understand that even if something is not found on the Web it may still exist, as well as the reverse: the assumption that only what is found on the Web is authentic and real. No trips to distant libraries or to other countries will be necessary to view documents and other evidence of the past. In this regard, students will be better able to become independent of, even to get ahead of, their instructors. While challenging to teachers, who will have to devote more of their work to teaching students how to assess and use sources, greater student independence is likely to be a boon to inventive and fresh thinking. We are likely to see contributions to historical knowledge emerging earlier and from a wider range of people than in the past.

In assuming their role as guides through the new digital world (as they long have been through the world of print), historians will also find themselves able to exploit that world to reach new audiences, which ought to be considered a liberation of sorts from the confinements of classrooms. Colleges and universities are increasingly filming their faculty members in action and making those films available to alumni and others. Commercial vendors are also exploiting historians' desire to benefit from the availability of new, and new kinds of, students while disseminating historical knowledge. Such opportunities should be seen as yet another way in which historians can occupy many roles and find many professional embodiments in a world that is changing rapidly around them.

Yet if the new media offer gains for history instruction, they also create many dangers. Because the resources of the Internet will allow individual instructors to fashion their own courses in little consonance with others, even the frail power of textbooks or works of scholarship to maintain general and conventional historical narratives that all may share will be attenuated even further. Instruction directly on the Web or based upon assignments posted there is also likely to present tempting opportunities for instructors to teach from their own inclinations and ideologies; the natural egotism, sometimes the ignorance, of instruction will be checked on the Web even less than it now is by the naturally inhibiting forces of published texts and community norms. And what some champions of Web resources see as the democratization of access and information may instead yield, because of an absence of adequate peer review, a torrent of unevaluated materials that endangers, rather than promotes, the advance of knowledge.

Another danger of Web instruction will be the lock-in effect. While the opportunity to teach free of textbooks may increase the egotism of instruction, so the broadened reach of the Web, its near universality, increases the difficulty of altering what may come to prevail there. Previously, while particular interpretations of the past might become conventional until replaced by new ones, all teachers of history brought individual affect and mind to each instructional period, each of which differed from all others. Their interpretations of the past seemed to be their own, and they were repeatedly challenged to justify their views, just as they required their students to do so. Now, just as it has with music because of the spread, first of records, then of audio tapes and compact discs, and just as it has in the genre of filmed novels, so the power of a particular medium to create strong and abiding interpretations of works that then become both widespread and standard is increasingly likely to be felt in the teaching of history. Books read by thousands of people may spread a particular interpretation, and teachers may follow or dissent from that interpretation as they please. But a Web-based presentation or a particular film may be seen by tens and hundreds of thousands of people and imprint on more minds views of the past that are hard to dislodge. There should be no confidence that these views will be any easier to alter or remove than conventional, filiopietistic, patriotic, and nationalistic views gained from text and other books have been easy to dislodge in the past. Here, too, the need to equip students with the means to evaluate all sources of information and knowledge will increase sharply.[23]

---

[23] A useful presentation of the gains and challenges of using visual materials and confronting views of the past already embedded in students' minds is Michael Coventry et al., "Ways of Seeing: Evidence and Learning in the History Classroom," *Journal of American History* 92 (March 2006): 1371–1402.

The encroachments of new media will also force teachers to guard against inadvertently hastening the loss of their place and authority in the larger universe of learning. To substitute the resources of the World Wide Web for classroom instruction, rather than using electronic means to supplement and enrich more traditional methods of teaching, will be a grave error. Teachers will have to resist the temptation to post all of what they have traditionally offered directly – their lectures and examinations especially – on their Web sites and thus to reduce their vital presence in class. They will have to find ways to remain at the interpretive center of their courses; bring immediacy, mind, disposition, and self to their classrooms; and continue to instruct their students about how to create meaning out of the remains of the past.

Because the Web and films are also further weakening the previous near monopoly of written texts as historical evidence, teachers of history will have to become more adept at interpreting pictorial sources of knowledge, especially of moving or still film.[24] The grammar of artistic and photographic images differs from that of written expression. The conditions under which visual artifacts are produced – both the originals and the Web versions – differ from those leading to the creation of written and published documents. Teachers venturing to use Web-based images as instructional sources, just as scholars using them, will have to assess why they were put there, by whom, and with what fidelity to the original. None of this will be new to those who have always asked those questions of written documents. What will be new, however, is the fresh knowledge that may be required to answer these questions regarding new sources of evidence.

An entirely different and still little recognized opportunity for teachers of history, as well as a novel professional challenge, is the growth of Internet instruction, or what in the desiccated lingo of educationese has become known as "distance learning" – instruction offered to students not sitting in conventional classrooms or conventionally enrolled in the institutions offering it. Roughly four-fifths of existing U.S. institutions of higher education provide this kind of instruction in one form or another. They seek to attract new, and new kinds of, students to secondary and higher education. But the institutions themselves are attracted

---

[24] Because historical scholarship and films about history or using historical footage are different genres, different measures of validity, provenance, and evaluation must be brought to bear on them. This point is made repeatedly by Robert Rosenstone in "Reel History with Missing Reels," *Perspectives* 37 (November 1999): 19–22.

to Internet offerings by the huge number of people in information- and knowledge-based societies throughout the world who are not formally enrolled in degree programs – and who are seen as prospectively paying customers for learning. If even a fraction of these people were to take history courses offered on the World Wide Web, the spread of historical knowledge, to say nothing of the income available to those offering it, would be significant. The chance to offer courses reaching people in all corners of the globe, coupled with the potentially large sums that may accrue to them as well as to corporations, is therefore beginning to beguile teachers into venturing into these uncharted waters. In fact, were the prospects of the compensation to be gained from "distance learning" respectable, there might be some scholars and teachers willing to cut themselves off altogether from institutional affiliation to seek greater income through Internet teaching. But this is unlikely. Under present circumstances, this kind of instruction is likely to put additional downward pressures on faculty compensation and lead to the further exploitation of low-paid "content providers" paid hourly wages and not professional salaries.

Such developments suggest the new costs and complications of the changing conditions of instruction. Academics especially will make the case that, just as colleges and universities have had no call on scholars' earnings from books and articles (a tradition that may come to haunt the institutions), so these institutions should have no right to share the income scholars may gain from teaching outside institutional walls. But schools and colleges are likely to respond that their interests in their members' extramural Internet instruction are analogous to the claims they long have had on patents secured by academics by virtue of their research on campus – or claims that corporations have on the work of their employees. Courts will no doubt be called on to settle the issue.

Further stress may also be felt on the employment of historians due to the emergence of the World Wide Web. Because more students will inevitably be attracted to Web-based degrees to avoid the high costs of college, some small independent colleges and schools may be forced to close their doors. Yet if some positions for historians are thereby lost, the more entrepreneurial among them will no doubt find broadened opportunities to offer instruction on the Web, which for some may make the professoriate more attractive. It is not clear whether or how schoolteachers and, say, museum curators will be able to take advantage of technology to teach for greater income. Threatened by all of this will be individuals' loyalty to the institutions that employ them – loyalty already at a discount.

Surely we have yet to see or understand the full implications of this transformation in the means of teaching.

Just as one is not a historian unless one teaches, so one is not a historian unless one writes – whether monographs for other scholars to advance knowledge, books and articles for a general readership to diffuse knowledge, book reviews, texts of some sort for teaching colleagues, or plans and reports for professional colleagues designed to apply knowledge. We too often forget that it is not just with evidence and ideas that one creates historical knowledge, but also with words. Yet while this may seem a commonplace and while the distinctiveness of historical writing may pose somewhat fewer questions than does the distinctiveness of history teaching, the matter of history writing is not without heavy weight for historians in an era of changing professional conditions and expectations.

History writing, of course, takes many forms and is confined to no single style. But historians' prose can be said to fall into two general modes – academic and popular. Both may be good and both quite bad. Criticism of academic prose comes cheap, and cheaply it is often produced; those who make fun of academic writing are rarely held to account for their claims and their ignorance of what academics seek to achieve. Yet there can be little dispute that gradually over the past century the literary qualities of history have surrendered place to prose that no longer aspires to art.[25] The resulting gains in precision and depth have been offset by losses in readability and appeal; one often summons great respect for works of history without taking much pleasure in reading them. The invention and use of academic language, much of it, while undoubtedly useful to specialists, in mimicry of the terminology of the physical, biological, and social sciences, has injured historians' past reputation for having a certain way with words. Too many historians seem ignorant or uncaring about how

---

[25] A brief and incisive exposition of this complaint, which blames the decline in the quality of history writing principally on graduate instruction, is Louis Masur, "What It Will Take to Turn Historians into Writers," *Chronicle of Higher Education*, July 6, 2001, B10. It must, however, be added that serious commentary and criticism about historical writing, as contrasted to grumbling complaint, are nonexistent. Aside from passing and unillustrated comments about the quality of writing in particular books, reviews ignore style. When have we read, as we do in literary and art criticism, of the *literary* influences on a historian, of the other historians from whom a scholar seems to take inspiration for argument, evidence, and style in addition to ideology and research approach, of the shaping of traditions of historical writing and form rather than of method or subject? Historical knowledge is impoverished to the degree that that question must be answered with silence.

unnecessary, intimidating, and foolish their academic expression appears to a public thirsty for comprehensible historical knowledge; too few try to rid their work of formulaic, denatured prose. And this is all the sadder in some of the younger subfields of historical research, such as gender, ethnic, and cultural studies, which otherwise might have built up a greater public following had their practitioners written with greater felicity and good sense. In fact, more than a few historians, either scornful of their fellow citizens' pleas that they write fluently or fearful of being unable to write winning, intelligible prose for them, never try. Not that the public's complaints about academic prose and some historians' efforts to satisfy its desire for readable history are new: after all, Allen Nevins and other historians founded the Society of American Historians in 1939 precisely to reclaim an audience that seemed to be fleeing history because of the growing obscurity of its presentation. That obscurity has only worsened since then.

But if historians are often foolishly heedless of the cost of their unwillingness to write clearly, it is also the case that the discipline's critics are frequently bent on grinding ideological axes and seem themselves willfully uncomprehending of the nature of scholarly work. Some of them apparently believe that where their often political attacks on historians for pursuing "trendy" subjects, such as gender, sexuality, race, and ethnicity, fall short of getting a hearing, they can broaden the audience for their accusations by assailing historians for ignoring the general reader and thus being "elitist." In this aim, unfortunately, they have been partly successful. Yet whatever the critics' ideological purposes, it must be said in their defense that most of them write with a clarity, if often without the very balance whose absence they decry in the targets of their attacks, that ought to be emulated by everyone who writes history.

Nevertheless, many of the critics' charges specifically against scholarly writing have little basis in fact. Examples of history written by academics that finds wide appeal among the general public – historical prose that avoids scholarly jargon and aspires to reveal the past rather than simply to analyze and argue – remain numerous. Yet, as in all disciplines, historical knowledge advances in part through the exchange of recondite knowledge among specialists and the refinement of research methods and concepts that probably need not concern a general readership. What counts is what these specialists freshly discover and freshly understand – before, presumably in clearer terms, they or others present it to larger audiences.

Specialized research and abstruse, sometimes technical, written scholarship – indeed, the sharp ideological bent and often bitter ideological disputation that result – have become a common precondition to progress in knowledge and understanding in many fields of history. Some of the most significant advances in the content and method of historical research have resulted from technical, argumentative, specialized journal articles written only for other historians, not for general readers. And even if the accumulation of such works often defies, sometimes defeats, the aims of general knowledge and the creation of new syntheses and fuller narratives, its publication cannot and ought not to be curtailed in the interest of public comprehension, for too much fresh knowledge would risk being lost as a consequence. After all, does one expect astrophysical knowledge to progress through exchanges among physicists published in the pages of popular magazines? If so, one should expect of historians' critics their similar condemnation of the contents of the *Physical Review* and the *Journal of the American Mathematical Society* for not being written in a style suitable for *Parade Magazine*. Critics' conventional retort that physics and mathematics are justified in their use of technical language because they are sciences is, of course, tautological. It is more to the point that critics object to historians' use of academic language because they correctly believe that history is a discipline of the humanities rather than of the sciences and as such ought generally to be presented in colloquial prose that the general populace can comprehend. They understand, perhaps better than many historians, that history emerged out of people's need to define and understand their existence as nations, peoples, communities, and kin groups and that practicing historians have some responsibility to respect their civic responsibilities, to speak to their fellow citizens in language they can make out, and to give history the weight of a moral art.

When aimed to awaken historians to their ancient role, critics' accusations are legitimate. But must every historian be both specialized scholar and popular writer? Here is a question that critics of academic history fail to address. Surely there is a place both for specialized academic discourse and for more general historical prose – for both "scientific" and artful writing – and the two kinds of expression can be employed by a single historian who, over an entire career, will enjoy, and ought to seek, opportunities to write for many kinds of audiences. Surely, too, it is not possible to build an edifice of historical knowledge that is both aesthetically pleasing and able to withstand critical scrutiny without its being firmly grounded in scholarship that is sometimes arcane. That does not, however, mean that all scholarly writing in history ought to read as if it were extracted from *Historical Methods* or *History and Theory*.

In their professional lifetimes, historians have opportunities to write both specialized and popular history. Fortunately, many seize those opportunities. The problem is that, when learning their professional crafts, they are not, as they might be, offered instruction and practice in doing so and are thus in effect discouraged from learning to write for many kinds of audiences or to see prose style as a function of intent.[26] As remains the case with learning the practices of public history, learning to write all history well, whether it be for academic specialists or nonacademic informed readers, is at best a residual category of professional instruction in graduate school. In fact, learning to become a skilled writer of even academic history prose is left more or less to chance; students are expected to gain an ability to write scholarship on their own, with occasional assistance from fellow students and mentors who provide only modest corrections, if those, to research paper and dissertation prose. Historians must therefore prepare to make themselves writers, not to be taught to be so.

In undergoing that preparation, however, they must bear in mind the meaning and requirements of craftsmanship. No one becomes a great glassblower by tossing off a few vessels or a great cabinetmaker by taking a few turns at the saw and lathe. Craft inheres in constant practice and refinement, in fastidiousness, in care and attention to detail, in the dedication of time and effort toward perfection, and in experience – the very honed skills that make up fine writing. It has been possible to hear it said in circles of historians in my lifetime that "he does good history even though he writes poorly" or that "she can't write well but turns to a good editor to make her seem to." The first statement is self-contradictory in its assumption that thinking and scholarship can be separated from the language in which both are presented. The historian in the second fails by conceding to another a task that is central to historical reasoning and writing – the perfection of argument and statement. Those who present themselves as historians without having attended to the art of writing, without having learned the grammar and syntax of their language – without in short having paid their dues to the craft of writing history – are defenseless when criticized for not writing well.

Yet the qualities of good historical prose – clarity, ease, and precision of expression for general audiences and command of the more technical,

---

[26] Here and there, students can benefit from graduate-level courses in writing, like that of Stephen J. Pyne at Arizona State University on "Literary Non-Fiction." But often these courses are offered by universities, not by history departments, and sometimes by those who have not committed themselves to writing nonfiction for large and diverse audiences.

specialized prose of each genre of history for scholar-colleagues – do not exhaust the qualities of writing that ought to be every historian's goal. The possession of a distinctive voice or angle of vision – be it like that of Edward Gibbon or Henry Adams, W. E. B. Du Bois or C. Vann Woodward, Natalie Zemon Davis or Bernard Bailyn – should be another. Such a voice, of course, originates in a distinctive cast of mind; it cannot be created, and it is not a matter of style. All historians have the potential to summon and perfect a manner of writing that arises from within and reflects themselves, a manner of writing that is more than the flat, denatured language so characteristic of specialized scholarship. To do so, however, requires close attention to the resources, nuances, and extraordinary versatility and range of English, its power to give expression to a distinctive voice and to mirror a particular cast of mind. Learning to write well also requires long and hard work, the results of which typically lead to less reward among professional colleagues than is desirable.[27]

Yet the burden of proof of the argument that attention to writing can be left to writers and not historians, that craft and finesse should go into thinking, not writing – baseless distinctions if there ever were any – and that historians are safe in leaving the mechanical matters of their prose to their peer reviewers and editors falls on those who maintain it. For is it not the case that other professionals – athletes, actors, and surgeons, for instance – endlessly practice and repeat their efforts in order to perfect their skills? Rare is the pen, as rare as the finger on the keyboard or the backhand on the tennis court, that has a genius of its own which the mind knows not. Historians ought to expect to hone their writing skills just as pitchers must try endlessly to perfect their throws and ballet dancers their *grands jetés*.[28]

---

[27] According to a perhaps apocryphal but credible story, the great prose stylist and critic Lionel Trilling, when once asked what could imaginably be easier for him than writing, answered, "Breaking rocks." He is also reputed to have responded to someone who asked him what he did for a living, "I edit other people's prose." Since that is the necessary lot of historians, too, it behooves them all the more to try to become the writer that Trilling was.

[28] I know of no historian who has formally studied writing in an MFA program that teaches nonfiction writing, as programs like the Iowa Writers' Workshop prepare writers of fiction. But there appears to be a growing number of nonfiction writing workshops, none of them however yet designed specifically for historians or academics. The New York University School of Journalism offers an M.A. in cultural reporting and criticism. Analogous programs exist at the New School and the University of Chicago, and writing is the core of the Professional Development Program at the University of Texas at Austin. Historians would serve themselves well by taking advice from Stephen J. Pyne, *Voice and Vision: A Guide to Writing History and Other Serious Nonfiction* (Cambridge, MA:

Unfortunately, they receive little help in doing so. By this I do not mean that their teachers and colleagues fail to read their work attentively. Usually they do. But the entire focus of such reading is likely to be on substance; and to make matters worse, historians have at their disposal neither a tradition nor a body of criticism of historical prose. They are not immersed, as are writers of fiction, in reflective evaluation of their prose craft. Aside from an occasional complaint about a historian's writing, one rarely comes upon an analysis of the qualities of a particular historian's prose, of what gives it its characteristic style or of what errors or traits make it hard going. Most historians know too little of the grammar and syntax of their language, and few are those who have actively studied others' writings for what tricks of the writing trade they can learn from them. No wonder that historical writing, especially academic historical writing, so often fails to carry its readers along and to rise above a declarative, unvaried, bone-dry style.[29]

The same considerations apply to the other nonwritten forms and media in which historical knowledge is increasingly presented – films and television, radio, and dramatic productions. Because these forms are almost exclusively popular, their art must be expressed in decently popular terms. But the very nature of these media make less likely the adoption of academic language, for by their very nature they possess and utilize many of the qualities – drama, emotion, variety, inflection, pacing – that are difficult, although surely not impossible, to capture in

Harvard University Press, 2009), a work by a master of history nonfiction whose writings have broken through to large, general audiences. A zesty forum on the subject of its title is "How to Teach the Writing of History: A Roundtable," *Historically Speaking* 11 (January 2010): 15–21. Also useful remain Peter Elbow's influential works, especially *Writing without Teachers* (New York: Oxford University Press, 1973), *Writing with Power: Techniques for Mastering the Writing Process* (New York: Oxford University Press, 1981), and, helpful for assisting others to write well, *Everyone Can Write: Essays toward a Hopeful Theory of Writing and Teaching Writing* (New York: Oxford University Press, 2000). Guides to scholarly publishing also exist. Among the best are William P. Germano, *Getting It Published: A Guide for Scholars and Anyone Else Serious about Books*, 2nd ed. (Chicago: University of Chicago Press, 2008); Germano, *From Dissertation to Book* (Chicago: University of Chicago Press, 2005); Beth Luey, *Handbook for Academic Authors*, 4th ed. (Cambridge: Cambridge University Press, 2002); and Robin M. Derricourt, *An Author's Guide to Scholarly Publishing* (Princeton: Princeton University Press, 1996).

[29] It might be said of the introduction of theory-laden terms into history what Edmund Wilson wrote of Jules Laforge's bringing German philosophy's vocabulary into his verse – that he was "contributing thereby to Symbolism perhaps the one element of obscurity it had lacked." *Axel's Castle: A Study in the Imaginative Literature of 1870–1930* (New York: Scribner's 1931), 96.

nonfiction prose (and are certainly not natural to academic discourse). In any event, the embodiment of historical knowledge in sound and visual image renders many of the rules of written presentation irrelevant, and those who aspire to present history in nonwritten form must master the "languages" of their respective media with the same practice and determination that they must bring to their writing.

Because aural and visual media are younger than the written word, they are likely for years to remain in a period of inventiveness, innovation, and change. That is not, however, the case with historical prose. Once complaints about the decline of fluent historical writing and the increased use of scholarly jargon are acknowledged, it remains the case that, overall, styles and forms of historical prose have shown remarkable stability over more than two centuries. Neither has been affected by changes in other arts, such as dance, music, painting, and sculpture, as well as poetry and fiction. No doubt, many of the kinds of changes that have swept these other forms of expression would be inapplicable to history and contrary to its aims. Yet historians have proved largely impervious to experiments with new forms of written presentation, to the constant innovation that has characterized all other forms of expression in the modern era.

This deeply held resistance to change is, however, showing its first signs of disintegration. The advent of hypertext and the World Wide Web has begun to make newly accessible some forms of documentation, particularly aural and visual sources, that before could not previously be easily or inexpensively printed in books and journals; and their availability is already expanding the kinds of illustrative and substantiating sources that can be incorporated into historians' work and the links that can be established among them.

Among the most venturesome recent such publishing endeavor was the History E-Book Project (distinct from the Gutenberg-e Project that I have taken up elsewhere) under the auspices of the American Council of Learned Societies, five history-related learned societies, and seven university presses. While one of the project's chief aims is "to assure the continued viability of the history monograph in today's publishing environment," its principal consequence will no doubt be the alteration, through the use of the Internet, of the way knowledge is presented. E-books (which for this project include both existing scholarly, not popular, books retrospectively supplemented with new material and new books, like Gutenberg-e works) allow photographic, film, video, cartographic, and other images, sounds, and text to be conveyed as illustrative and substantiating inclusions. In addition, E-books are searchable and allow indefinite links between and within texts, collections, and libraries. It will, of course, take some time to develop agreed-on standards for presenting and peer-reviewing such books. What is most attractive about the project is that it seeks to use technology to serve, rather than to drive, publication and thus research scholarship. It is likely also to deepen the authority of written texts by providing greater access to the resources on which they are based. It remains to be seen, however, whether the results will simply be clever additions to existing formats of presentation or a deeper transformation in the conveyance of knowledge. Nor is it yet clear to what extent, if any, such "books" will affect the traditional publication and distribution of conventionally published – that is, printed – works of history.[30]

More influential in the long run are likely to be vastly larger and more comprehensive projects like Google Books (thrown into question at the time of my writing by the 2011 collapse of a tangled legal settlement regarding the scheme) and such less controversial and equally promising digital collections like the Open Book Alliance, the Digital Public Library of America, and Hathi that will make hundreds of thousands of out-of-copyright works available electronically.[31] Such endeavors are likely to prove a boon to historians, especially to those without recourse to great libraries. In addition, e-readers, like the Kindle, iPad, and other tablets, will eventually make available to historians at modest cost many books, especially new ones, useful to their teaching and research. As with all such developments, new approaches are announced, fresh products appear, and their refinements occur with dizzying speed – all driven by commercial interests. Historians will be hard put to keep up while finding it increasingly essential to do so.

History journals are also gradually making their appearance online, a development that is likely to speed the emergence of innovations in the presentation of historical knowledge. Already the availability of history journals has proceeded far with the digitization, among other publications, of the *American Historical Review* and the *Journal of American History* by their publishers and by JSTOR – the electronic journal storage system now widely available through libraries and other institutions.[32]

---

[30] The Web site of the History E-Book Project is www.HistoryEBook.org.

[31] The best guide to the complexities and problems with Google Books is the series of articles, starting in 2008, by Robert Darnton in the *New York Review of Books*. Darnton has long been a critic of the original settlement terms as well as a champion of a publicly established national digital library.

[32] Its URL is www.jstor.org. Some journals are also available directly online.

Before long, the availability of history journals online (either through libraries or individually) will permit the retrospective addition of images, sounds, text, and citations to previously published journal articles as well as the publication in digital form of "articles" in new and expanded formats analogous to those envisaged by thee History E-Book Project.[33]

But because all of these varieties of on-screen presentation, often required of Web-based publishing, have their own deficiencies of comfort and ease, digital publication and display are likely, at least for a time, to supplement, not to supplant, printed books and articles. What will change will be the addition of documentation and illustrative material, creating perhaps larger, and surely somewhat different, audiences for history. A greater range of expressiveness, not only through sounds and visual images but through instant colloquies, question-and-answer formats, the enlargement of images, and the breaking up of images and sounds, will make possible putting different kinds of evidence together in one place, so that the depth of evidence and argument will more easily be seen. Archives themselves, by becoming more accessible, will also become more important and subject to rapid supplementation. Consequently, different "editions" of electronic publications will be able to incorporate authors' revisions without limit on their frequency or extent.[34] Such possibilities are likely to alter, if not upend, such venerable conventions of print presentation as sequence, substantiation, and citation. And finally, as is already becoming clear, Web-based publication will require the development of new critical standards that govern peer review and critical review.[35]

Digital publication does not of course exhaust the possibilities for novel presentation of historical knowledge. Other evidence of historians'

---

[33] The retrospective addition of text and other materials to already published works, addition made possible by electronic digitization, is making rapid progress and is likely to be a large element in the presentation of knowledge in the future. For instance, almost as soon as Oxford University Press had published the twenty-four-volume *American National Biography* in 1999, it began accepting for addition to its electronic version of the volumes such materials as the portraits of subjects, additional citations to published sketches, and, most significantly, entirely new biographies of figures not included in the published volumes. There is no reason why the *ANB* could not eventually link each sketch with the electronic version of every citation that has been digitized, thus providing an almost endless web of pathways into the past through a single publication.

[34] Which will require that, for archival and citation purposes, each revision be clearly noted and dated.

[35] A beginning is already being made. See "Suggested Guidelines for Evaluating Digital Media Activities in Tenure, Review, and Promotion – an AAHC Document," *Perspectives* 39 (October 2001): 32–34. AAHC is the American Association for History and Computing.

willingness to venture new forms of presentation can be seen in conventionally published work. Some historians are simply endeavoring to bring some of the techniques of novelistic art to the presentation of historical knowledge.[36] Others, their work appearing principally in Robert Rosenstone's journal *Rethinking History* (founded in 1990), are experimenting more radically with form. Largely a response to postmodernist theories and trends in other arts, the journal's contents exhibit and debate these developments as they pertain to history. While its writers experiment with form and content – they offer, for example, "miniatures," or brief essays on limited events – they nevertheless continue to employ linear prose, still remain well within the conventions of nonfiction prose, and still value content over form. One does not find, even in this journal dedicated to new ways of conveying historical knowledge, many of the devices of good literature like satire, wit, and playfulness. Revealing how difficult it seems for historians to escape the venerable conventions of their discipline, much of the journal's content is about history and theory rather than exemplifications of the presentational forms history might assume. Even the most venturesome historians appear to be more comfortable discussing what might be done rather than doing it.

Anyone entering upon a career in history today will have to adjust in some measure to these new realities. They constitute what can justifiably be called a crisis in scholarly publishing, a crisis of economics, medium, form, and style whose resolution (or resolutions) remains in the future and thus demanding of every historian's keen attention. Just as all historians have long been well advised to become acquainted with every form of historical pursuit – public as well as academic history – and as many subfields as they can, as well as with new methods such as statistical calculation, if only to keep generally informed and to be of assistance to their students and colleagues, so now all historians will be under obligation to know something of and adjust to the rapidly developing new species of teaching and presentation. Just as it took centuries for the codex to develop into its current book form, so it is likely to be decades – possibly no less than the entire professional careers of those just now becoming historians – before teaching and writing with new media become stable.

---

[36] See, for example, Richard Wightman Fox, *Trials of Intimacy: Love and Loss in the Beecher-Tilton Scandal* (Chicago: University of Chicago Press, 1999), in which the author opens the book at the end of the story and then proceeds to narrate and explain how that outcome was reached. Another example of experimentation in the presentation of historical knowledge is Richard Price, *Alabi's World* (Baltimore: Johns Hopkins University Press, 1990).

For the foreseeable future, conventions of both will undergo change, some of it deep. It is too soon to tell whether the pressures of change will force more historians than is now the case to confront directly the challenges, both old and new, that face them as they become teachers and writers of history. It is certain, however, that they will be better historians for doing so.

A Note on Popular History

Just as not every historian will, or should feel obliged to, make an exclusive choice between becoming an academic or public historian, neither should every historian feel obliged to choose between becoming a writer either of academic or of more popular prose. To pose the matter as one of mutually exclusive choices makes no sense if only because, just as many historians long have moved between academic and public history, many can and do move back and forth as writers between different roles at different times for distinct purposes.[37]

Some of today's criticisms about academic history arise from many academics' inattention to the differences between these two kinds of writing. No good sense attaches to a historian's ignoring the mature conventions of scholarly presentation when writing a monograph or journal article or even when writing a larger study intended signally to advance knowledge of a particular subject. The audiences in mind for these kinds of works are small groups of specialist colleagues, occasionally somewhat larger audiences of dedicated students (or "buffs") of a large subject, rarely nonhistorians however well informed. But to approach a general public audience with the scholarly prose of a graduate seminar paper or the heavily footnoted look of a monograph is neither to endear history to that audience nor to move readers to see the past in fresh terms. A different approach, one that meets those who seek historical knowledge as much on their own terms as possible, is required.

The purpose of popular history is to convey knowledge of the past to readers who neither are academics and intellectuals nor are likely to seek knowledge unless their mental journey into the past is pleasurable. Popular history wants to bring to life the past's often inert remains, much

---

[37] A case in point is the History News Service, a syndicate of historians, most of them dyed-in-the-wool academics, who write op-ed articles that contextualize current events in historical terms for newspaper readers – that is, for popular audiences. See www.historynewsservice.org.

as artists create our images of extinct dinosaurs from the desiccated bones
that paleontologists dig from the earth, but it wants to bring them to life
for generally informed, knowledge-seeking readers. This is not to say that
these readers are less serious or less demanding as readers than academics,
although they may be so; rather, it is to say that they look for qualities in
what they read that academics usually do not supply and in fact sometimes
do not even themselves want. They are readers who put more store in
the basic ingredients of all art – story, drama, voice, gesture, color, form,
pace, description – than do most academics. It is through the means of
art that their attention is captured and held. They are quick to sniff out
and turn away from any elitist and uncourageous academic prose that
hides, rather than reveals, meaning. Even if the qualities of historical
prose they seek are the qualities principally of narrative history, it would
be a serious mistake to conclude that the popular audience for history will
consume only anecdotes about the past.[38] That audience wants analysis,
explanation, and meaning as much as any other audience; but it does
not want them in the architectonic, often heavy-handed form of much
academic writing. While these readers may not consciously recognize
subtlety and nuance, rhetoric and color, variety and pace, and the creation
of meaning as some of the specific aesthetic qualities that make them wish
to read on, it is by such characteristics of writing that they are held to any
work of history. Historians who wish to write for the general populace
must therefore employ the kinds of means that will hold its members'
discerning attention.

That is not to say that popular history, even when written by skilled
historians, can pass muster as history simply because it ingratiates itself
with its readers. Too much popular history written by professional writers and journalists, in fact, underestimates its audience's discernment.
Some is short, very short, on ideas. Its authors often succeed in holding their readers' attention while travestying the basic requirements of
historical thought and presentation. The worst are those, like Edmund
Morris, who simply make up characters.[39] The least capable are those

---

[38] Although this is often the assumption of popular writers of history. See, for example,
Edmund Morris, *Theodore Rex* (New York: Random House, 2001), and the damning
review of it by Christine Stansell, "Details, Details," *New Republic*, December 10, 2001,
28–32. It is a not unhealthy development that academic historians sensitive to the value
of good popular history are challenging popular writers of history to do a better job,
both at history and writing, than they do.

[39] *Dutch: A Memoir of Ronald Reagan* (New York: Random House, 1999). Notice the
characterization of the work, which has the intent of biography, as a memoir – that of

who, seeming to believe that if something is written down it is true, cling to sources without verifying or evaluating them or offer citations so spare that one cannot confirm the precise sources of facts and quotations.[40] But there are subtler defects, caused by subtle lures, that mar many quite fine popular histories and their always popular near cousins, biographies. One is celebration without balance or analysis, a characteristic of David G. McCullough's otherwise appealing and accurate biographies of Harry Truman and John Adams and of Stephen E. Ambrose's less artful renderings of the Lewis and Clark expedition and the building of the transcontinental railroad.[41] Another is sentimentalism, a quality that often mars ideologically slanted popular work that looks toward the past as a golden

Morris's fictional character. Attempting to clear himself of the controversy that *Dutch* aroused, on the publication of his succeeding work, *Theodore Rex* (New York: Random House, 2002), the second volume in his three-volume biography of Theodore Roosevelt, Morris beguilingly claimed, "I do not think of myself as a historian. I've always thought of myself only as a writer." Quoted in Bill Goldstein, "No Fiction in Roosevelt's Story," *New York Times*, January 2, 2002, B1, B5. Morris, like everyone else, is free to think of himself as he wishes. But when sales of his work have receded into past time and any celebrity that now attaches to it has faded, his work will be judged as much as history as art. Therefore, to the standards of historical writing and substantiation it, like all such writing, must aspire, and it must meet those standards. Nothing that Morris avers will save him from other historians' stern assessment. A withering critique of the shortcomings of one venture into popular biography is Sean Wilentz's review, "American Made Easy," of David McCullough's *John Adams* in the *New Republic*, July 2, 2001, 35–40.

40 The *locus classicus* of this genre is Carl Bernstein and Bob Woodward, *All the President's Men* (New York: Simon & Schuster, 1974), in which the infamous "Deep Throat" plays a leading role. Woodward has become the particular master of the form. See, for example among many others, *Veil: The Secret Wars of the CIA, 1981–1987* (New York: Simon & Schuster, 1987), in which there is no way to verify claims made about interviews Woodward conducted. In extenuation of the author, it ought to be said that he holds himself out as a journalist, not a historian. But this raises the nice issue as to whether journalists writing history ought to be held to the same standards as historians. Only their belief that they are exempt from these standards would seem to explain their occasional laziness and arrogance. Would they have us take as authentic the Donation of Constantine or the Protocols of the Elders of Zion just because their authors at one time vouched for their origins and claimed their validity? For one example of fine history written by a journalist, see Taylor Branch's three-volume work *America in the King Years, 1954–1968*, 3 vols. (New York: Simon & Schuster, 1988–2007).

41 David G. McCullough, *Truman* (New York: Simon & Schuster, 1992) and *John Adams* (New York: Simon & Schuster, 2001); Stephen E. Ambrose, *Undaunted Courage: Meriwether Lewis, Thomas Jefferson, and the Opening of the American West* (New York: Simon & Schuster, 1996) and *Nothing Like It in the World: The Men Who Built the Transcontinental Railroad* (New York: Simon & Schuster, 2000). These are some, but not all, of the works of each of the authors that exhibit the qualities I indicate. Many, suffering from a kind of gigantism, are brought out by the same publisher.

age. Some popular history, such as the film presentations of Ken Burns and Oliver Stone, hold fast to outdated or conspiracy interpretations of the past when more recent, and usually more complicated, ones would prove equally appealing while being more accurate. Alternatively, much popular history indulges itself in sensationalism in order to advance a dubious argument.[42]

The best popular histories, like those of Catherine Drinker Bowen, Bernard DeVoto, and Shelby Foote earlier and Joseph J. Ellis, Kevin Starr, and Garry Wills more recently, both relate and analyze.[43] While not openly challenging other histories or arguing against other interpretations, the works of these authors have a critical edge; their angle of vision is frequently skeptical or ironic; standing free of piety, they seek to shake their readers loose from previous conceptions of the subject, from the myths and tales that surround it. It is history, not story, that they write; interpretation, not anecdote, that they offer. They call on their readers to be actively engaged in the author's quest for truth, not simply entertained by heart-warming epics and well-told tales.

None of this is to say that writing popular history is easy, even when one has mastered its art. In fact, every historian wishing to write for the general public will want to appreciate its perils, especially in the charged ideological atmosphere of American culture today. No well-intended act is likely to go unpunished when calls for more accessible history so frequently arise from the same conservative sources that attack the academy for its liberalism and scholars for their supposed obscurantism.[44]

---

[42] See Robert Brent Toplin (ed.), *Ken Burns's The Civil War: Historians Respond* (New York: Oxford University Press, 1996), and Toplin (ed.), *Oliver Stone's USA: Film, History, and Controversy* (Lawrence: University Press of Kansas, 2000). For an extended view of the ways in which some films have accurately and sensitively portrayed the past, see Toplin, *Reel History: In Defense of Hollywood* (Lawrence: University Press of Kansas, 2002).

[43] I have in mind here Catherine Drinker Bowen, *Miracle at Philadelphia: The Story of the Constitutional Convention, May to September, 1787* (Boston: Little Brown, 1966); Bernard A. DeVoto, *The Year of Decision, 1846* (Boston: Houghton Mifflin, 1950); Shelby Foote, *The Civil War, a Narrative*, 3 vols. (New York: Random House, 1958–1974); Joseph J. Ellis, *Founding Brothers: The Revolutionary Generation* (New York: Alfred A. Knopf, 2000); the many works of Garry Wills; and the volumes in Kevin Starr's history of California, *Americans and the California Dream*, 8 vols. (New York: Oxford University Press, 1973–2009).

[44] An example of this sad fact is the columnist George F. Will's "review" of David M. Kennedy's Pulitzer Prize–winning *Freedom from Fear: The American People in Depression and War, 1919–1945* (New York: Oxford University Press, 1999). Kennedy's work is a volume in an in-progress multivolume Oxford History of the United States, a series designed to bring the most current scholarship about the volumes' respective subjects

The very act of putting scholarship before nonacademic audiences – even if that scholarship is presented in appealing narrative form, crafted as art, carefully constructed to reveal the full range of a subject's interpretive possibilities, and devoid of heavy-handed ideological arguments – now runs the risk of offending someone and gaining the scorn and attack of someone else. Historians who try to convey serious scholarship to non-scholars in readable terms must be possessed of firm convictions and a broad appreciation of the human comedy to venture what remains so necessary for intellectuals: writing for their fellow citizens.

Therefore, historians who wish to write widely read histories need to become students of writing as well as of history. They would be well served to develop a conscious regard for the riches of English – for the extraordinary size and variety of its vocabulary, for its structure, grammar, and syntax, and above all for its wonderful flexibility – and not expect editors or others to render thought into word. But most of all, as with so many other dimensions of history, they must take their discipline to be a moral one, a means of persuading readers, through presenting aspects of the past, that the past has meaning for each reader's own life. To consider popular history a lesser form of history because it aspires to moral significance as well as intellectual weight is to lose sight of history's ancient roots as a branch of humane enlightenment.

before the public in pleasing and readable form. In an act of what can only be called willful deceitfulness, Will transmogrified Kennedy's effort to portray the memories of war that Americans "might" have recalled after 1945 were they not so concerned to forget or suppress memory of how awful and destructive World War II was into an effort to say what Americans "should" have recalled. In advice to his readers that needs no evaluation either for its weight or for the evidence it provides of its author's vaunted learning, "Kennedy's volume can be skipped," Will wrote. "A Stinker of a Pulitzer," *National Review Online*, April 11, 2000. Richard Hofstadter was right in pointing out that anti-intellectualism lurks in all corners of American culture, even among those who hold themselves out as the paladins of sound thinking and high intellectual standards. *Anti-Intellectualism in American Life* (New York: Alfred A. Knopf, 1963). A recent work along the same lines as Hofstadter's is Susan Jacoby, *The Age of American Unreason* (New York: Pantheon, 2008).

7

Professional Principles, Responsibilities, Rights

Historians are typically not diffident in expressing their views about the conduct, beliefs, and ethics of others, whether of their fellow historians or of those in other disciplines and professions. Yet they have a tendency to run for the exits when the phrase "professional ethics" is uttered or when they are asked to evaluate, against established standards of rights and responsibilities, the professional behavior of other historians. Because it is difficult to rid discussions of historians' professional behavior of moralism, self-righteousness, and "oughts" and because few like to stand in open judgment of their peers, uneasiness infuses all attempts to come to terms with ethical issues. And because all historians believe that they adhere to professional principles (as most do), they often resist suggestions that the topic could bear some clarification – except when egregious cases of unethical behavior break into the news. They also tend to want emphasis in any discussion of ethics to fall principally upon the protection of historians' rights.

Accordingly, save for moments of crisis (like the era of McCarthyism) or in response to major instances of, say, plagiarism, historians rarely debate the problematic nature of professional rights and duties. Moreover, there exists little sustained professional literature on the subject, an absence hard to justify any longer, given that more than thirty years have elapsed since professional associations of historians began to develop codes of practices for their members and created some at least elementary disciplinary mechanisms and enforcement procedures to accompany those codes. The canons of professional conduct can now be examined in their own right. They rarely are. The reflections that follow are meant more to focus attention and elicit discussion about some subjects that rarely receive formal attention than to propose any particular lines of action. I suspect that even raising them will arouse dissent and the argument that, in the absence of any immediate crisis, little worry about professional principles is warranted. Even if so, no reason exists not to subject these matters to debate during the preparation and careers of all historians.[1]

Even though general professional canons are supposed to guide historians' behavior, few historians are acquainted with them in any detail. To my knowledge, no graduate program exposes its students to formal consideration of them, and few courses in the ethics of professional history or of the humanities seem to exist.[2] Because graduate study is already exacting enough of the time and resources of aspiring historians, to propose that space be made in the curriculum for the study of professional responsibilities and that each graduate student be required formally to examine the topic is likely to be resisted, and students are unlikely to enter into consideration of it without incentives or requirements to do so. While other newly prepared professionals, like doctors, attorneys, and even now students in some business programs, are asked to pledge themselves to canons of conduct early in their careers, historians (and, for that matter, practitioners in other disciplines of the arts and

---

[1] Most of the existing literature about historians' ethics is narrative and critical, not analytical. A tough-minded review of cases of historians' misconduct is Jon Wiener, *Historians in Trouble: Plagiarism, Fraud, and Politics in the Ivory Tower* (New York: New Press, 2004). It examines the uneven conduct of historical and educational institutions when faced with ethical lapses, the power exerted by outside forces, the role of the press and special interest groups, and the failure of the discipline to police steadfastly its own practitioners. A similar work is Peter Charles Hoffer, *Past Imperfect: Facts, Fictions, Fraud – American History from Bancroft and Parkman to Bellesisles, Ellis, and Goodwin* (New York: Public Affairs, 2004), which bears down on the claims of those charged with dishonesty and the mordant effect on standards of postmodern relativism. The "Roundtable" on ethics in the March 2004 issue of the *Journal of American History* 90, 1325–1356, is also useful. On academic ethical offenses more specifically, see Ron Robin, *Scandals and Scoundrels: Seven Cases that Shook the Academy* (Berkeley: University of California Press, 2004). Robin argues that the older, traditional system of intradisciplinary investigation and discipline has broken down because of the inability of former gatekeepers to restrict coverage of each breakdown in professional ethics to the disciplines themselves. Robin also sees the public's involvement in these scandals not as evidence of the absence of standards but rather as occurring when "the conventional means for controlling doctrinal discourse malfunction."

[2] There do appear to be courses on academic and professional ethics in the Professional Development Program at the University of Texas at Austin and at the Graduate Center of the City University of New York. On the latter, see David Glenn, "Course Reminds Budding Ph.D.'s of the Damage They Can Do," *Chronicle of Higher Education*, October 30, 2009, A10–A11, a mistitled report of Steven M. Cahn's rare course on academic ethics. There may be others of similar sort.

social sciences) have never developed such pledges, nor have history departments required that historians swear to honor professional canons of conduct before receiving their doctorates. While such pledges would not prevent fraud or other unprofessional acts, they would at least help to strengthen agreed-on canons of expected conduct and make easier the application of sanctions against those who broke their pledges.[3]

Historians' professional associations have also recoiled from stepping in where departments fear to tread. In 2003, after years of involving itself in cases of alleged professional misconduct, the American Historical Association (AHA) withdrew from investigating, reporting on, and adjudicating charges of unethical conduct brought before it because of the burdensomeness of investigating them, the lack of adequate AHA resources, and the meager results of its reports.[4] In deciding to conclude its short history of looking into instances of misconduct, the organization did not urge on its members or on historians generally any steps to substitute for its foregone efforts. Nor has the AHA proposed any mandates, such as those instituted in the late 1980s by the National Institutes of Health, that require fellowship holders and public agency grantees to have been trained in responsible research. Historians have therefore been left to be, as they are in so many other ways, self-taught and on their own.[5]

---

[3] On the spread of voluntary ethical oaths among graduating M.B.A. students at such universities as Columbia and Harvard, see "A Promise to Be Ethical in an Era of Temptation," *New York Times* (National Edition), May 30, 2009, B1ff. For evidence that the merits of ethics education are debated in business schools, see Julian Friedland, "Where Business Meets Philosophy: The Matter of Ethics," and Daniel Baer, "By the Numbers, Business Schools Barely Care about Right and Wrong," *Chronicle of Higher Education*, November 13, 2009, A26–A27.

[4] An explanation of the AHA's decision is contained in William J. Cronon, "The Professional Division," in *Annual Report, 2004* (Washington, DC: American Historical Association, 2005), 8–9. Out of that decision came a new *Statement on Standards of Professional Conduct* (http://www.historians.org/PUBS/Free/ProfessionalStandards.cfm).

[5] Two thoughtful introductions to matters of academic ethics, but to those alone, are Edward Shils, *The Academic Ethic* (Chicago: University of Chicago Press, 1984), especially "The Academic Obligations of University Teachers," 41–72, and Donald Kennedy, *Academic Duty* (Cambridge, MA: Harvard University Press, 1997). Two standard works on professional ethics generally are Michael D. Bayles, *Professional Ethics* (Belmont: Wadsworth, 1982), and Albert Flores (ed.), *Professional Ideals* (Belmont: Wadsworth, 1988). See also Robin Levin Penslar (ed.), *Research Ethics: Cases and Materials* (Bloomington: Indiana University Press, 1995). On scientific misconduct, see John M. Braxton (ed.), *Perspectives on Scholarly Misconduct in the Sciences* (Columbus: Ohio State University Press, 1999), and *Professional Ethics Report*, a quarterly issued by the American Association for the Advancement of Science. Relevant also is John M. Braxton and Alan E. Bayer, *Faculty Misconduct in Collegiate Teaching* (Baltimore: Johns Hopkins

To make matters more complex in an era of expanded professional opportunities, historians still adhere to assumptions about their ethics and freedoms that derive from a time when historians were overwhelmingly academics.[6] Educated in academic settings by academic historians, historians early learn to associate their rights with academic rights. Thus they reflexively adopt the term "academic freedom" to denominate the privileges they assume are theirs as historians when in fact the issues that now challenge historians should more properly be thought of as general professional issues and discipline-wide principles, ones that spread beyond academic boundaries and affect historians in a wide range of occupations. Rather than monopolizing the terrain of freedoms, "academic freedom" has instead in effect become just one of a number of subcategories of professional freedom, "academic responsibility" a segment of professional responsibility. Yet little formal thought has turned to the rights and responsibilities of historians in an inclusive world of institution and activity, nor have issues as diverse as the ethics of collegiality, court testimony, historic site presentation, film editing, and serving the public generally been brought within the compass of ethical and professional consideration and subject to discussion and assessment consonant with the broadened scope of historians' positions and work.[7]

The earliest of the codes of professional behavior that applied specifically to historians came into being in the early 1970s. Not surprisingly, they

University Press, 1999). A unique collection of articles specifically about the ethics of historians – but, note, about a particular group of historians only – is Theodore J. Karamanski (ed.), *Ethics and Public History: An Anthology* (Malabar, FL: R. E. Krieger, 1990). No one seems to have proposed that the National Endowment for the Humanities follow the lead of the National Institutes of Health and institute requirements for the ethical training of NEH grantees.

6 Not surprisingly, too, most works about ethics are works about academic ethics. See, for example, Steven M. Cahn (ed.), *Morality, Responsibility, and the University: Studies in Academic Ethics* (Philadelphia: Temple University Press, 1990).

7 Yet there is one notable exception to this general rule: from the beginning of its recent history, the discussion of ethics has been front and center to the development of public history. One reason is the number of ethical issues, especially of objectivity and professional independence, raised by work that sometimes lacks adequate peer review and is compensated by those who hope for particular outcomes from historical research and presentation (such as expert testimony). Another is public history's felt need to justify itself against the supposedly superior status of academic history. While the AHA's structure includes a professional division of its governing council whose time was, in the past, often consumed by ethical issues brought before it, neither the *American Historical Review* nor the *Journal of American History* – nor, for that matter, the newsletters of either the AHA or the OAH – gives over any of its pages, as sometimes does the *Public Historian*, to serious and sustained reflections on professional ethics.

reached primarily to the conduct of academics. Engendered in large part by the civil and women's rights movements of the 1960s, those standards represented an effort to reduce the conventional, discriminatory behavior of the then largely white and male professoriate toward new kinds of entrants – African Americans and women in particular – and to protect against prejudice those students' progress through graduate school and toward further professional advancement. In addition, the standards sought to give teeth to efforts to diversify the various professions of history. The writing, adoption, and promulgation of these early standards were also propelled by a sharp rise in the unemployment of doctoral recipients generally and attendant anxieties about the future professional employment of graduate students who sought to protect, at least against capricious actions and racial and gender bias, their declining, mostly academic career prospects. In addition, the creation under the new AHA constitution of 1974 of a tripartite structure for the AHA's governance, a structure that included a professional division with its own elected vice-president, created an institutional mechanism by which the senior membership organization of historians in the United States could develop, refine, and apply professional standards. Soon after, the Organization of American Historians (OAH) followed suit in developing its own set of largely consonant professional norms. Finally, the organizations representing newly emerging historical professions, such as oral history and public history, sought to enhance their authority by establishing codes of conduct that indicated their seriousness of purpose and adherence to generally accepted canons of professional conduct – codes that gave as much emphasis to professional responsibilities as to professional rights.

The AHA was the first historical association to prepare standards that sought to establish the rights and responsibilities of historians as distinguished from professionals in other disciplines.[8] The earliest of these were the guidelines issued in 1974 by a temporary committee of the AHA, the Ad Hoc Committee on the Rights of Historians. The very title of that committee indicated the focus of its concerns, which were characteristic of most guidelines issued by similar institutions at the time: the protection of historians against prospective threats to their professional pursuits during the Vietnam War and the presidency of Richard M. Nixon.

---

[8] The principal all-discipline guidelines were those of the American Association of University Professors, whose 1940 *Statement of Principles on Academic Freedom and Tenure* set forth the protections expected to cover college and university faculty members. See below.

The guidelines did not enunciate historians' obligations toward the institutions in which they worked, the students and clients they served, the subjects of their research, or the audiences they might address; and the guidelines' concerns were overwhelmingly those of academic historians about academic issues. Despite these limitations, the guidelines represented a major advance in the definition of historians' professional situations, for no such guidelines had existed before, nor had any means been available to evaluate complaints of misconduct, by either historians or their employers.

These initial guidelines were followed in 1987 by a revised version issued under a significantly amended title, "Statement on Standards of Professional Conduct." These standards, revised again subsequently, continue to be those against which the professional behavior of historians is supposed to be evaluated (although by whom is left unsaid). They, as well as related AHA guidelines concerning such issues as plagiarism, historical documentation, discrimination, harassment, and conflict of interest, are periodically published, with revisions, in the AHA pamphlet *Statement on Standards of Professional Conduct.*[9]

The standards declare, on behalf of the membership of the nation's senior and largest professional historical association, what has come to constitute (and by implication what is excluded from) professionally acceptable behavior and bearing. They assert their applicability to all historians, who "should be guided by the same principles of conduct." And they offer an appropriately capacious and contemporary definition of the institutions (historical societies, government agencies, and corporations as well as colleges and universities), activities (film making and exhibition design as well as monograph writing), and audiences (students and members of the public as well as other scholars) with which historians are involved.

Yet while the AHA's statement is a respectable declaration of basic principles, much about it is unsatisfactory in content, weight, and expression. While the claimed applicability of these standards to the "historical profession" betrays the typical confusion between the larger discipline and its constitutive elements, the standards are also noticeably reticent about stating specifically, emphatically, and even imperatively what historians must and must not do, which thus renders uncertain their applicability. Historians, the statement for example declares,

---

[9] See http://www.historians.org/pubs/Free/ProfessionalStandards.cfm. Additional AHA statements appear from time to time in *Perspectives on History*.

"must protect research collections and other historical resources and make those under their control available to other scholars as soon as possible." Worthy goals indeed. But by what standards are the protection or endangering of research collections to be determined and who is to determine them? Because the preservation and accessibility of sources is stated to be the responsibility of historians (as certainly they ought to be), how is this responsibility to be integrated with that of archivists and curators, who are the professional custodians of most historical resources? Who has a right to bring charges of neglect of resources? What specifically should historians do to protect and provide access to resources? The very abstractness of the statements that engender such questions detracts from their potential authority and applicability.[10]

Since the issuance of the initial AHA statement in 1974, organizations affiliated with the AHA – the National Council on Public History (NCPH), the Oral History Association, the American Association for State and Local History, and the Society for History in the Federal Government (SHFG) – have issued their own standards of professional conduct. They do not make for easy reading. Couched in carefully abstract terms and often embarrassingly written, they, like the AHA standards, avoid the specificity that might strengthen their applicability and discomfit too many historians. As a result, these codes of professional conduct create as many difficulties as the ones they address.

For instance, the proliferation of these codes would make it difficult for individual historians to determine by which set or sets of professional standards they are governed should anyone be charged with some infraction under one of them or forced to claim protection under another. In consequence of the recent decades' burst of professional conduct codes, practicing historians can now find themselves under the "jurisdiction" of three sets of professional canons. One set, like those issued by the AHA and OAH, claims to encompass, even if not govern, the general rights and responsibilities of all historians. The second is made up of those standards issued by the professional associations that represent the kinds of institutions at which historians work – standards adopted, for example, by the American Association of University Professors (AAUP), which apply to all

---

[10] These are precisely the problematics and matters that any consideration of ethics for historians would take up. I note them here only as examples of the kinds of issues that a more comprehensive statement of principles might encompass. I have made no attempt to put the entirety of the AHA's or any other organization's principles to thorough analysis. Such an analysis would be welcome.

faculty members of colleges and universities, and by the American Association of Museums regarding people employed in museums. The third set of guidelines is composed of those issued by associations that represent the various kinds of history that historians practice – the standards, for instance, of the National Council for Public History, which affect those who pursue public history; of the Oral History Association, for those who employ the direct interviewing of living subjects as a means of historical research; and of the American Association for State and Local History, for those involved in state and community historical work.

If it is unclear which ones of these codes might govern a historian's conduct at any particular time (especially since most historians are unacquainted with the codes and since the AHA and other organizations lack enforcement authority), it remains no more certain under which ones individual historians must or should seek redress of grievances or clarification of their responsibilities in particular circumstances (if redress or clarification is even forthcoming from any particular organization). Nor is it any clearer where to seek appeal after some judgment has been rendered, whether disciplinary action under one set of standards precludes further action under standards issued by other organizations, whether a rule of comity ought to govern these matters so that a ruling by one body is accepted by others, and, of great importance, whether historians are governed by these canons when not members of the associations that have issued them. The issuance and application of so many professional standards for historians has thus diluted the force they might have gained had a single body or consortium of organizations issued a single code of conduct.[11]

It is nevertheless worth noting that all of these standards have at least originated from within the community of historians, principally from its senior organizations. Increasingly, however, and further to complicate

---

[11] To my knowledge, no institution or department has ever formally adopted any of these guidelines, nor has the American Council of Learned Societies, as the most all-encompassing general organization of organizations in the humanities and social sciences, made any effort to examine the standards of all its constituent members and recommend how they might be adjusted, made general, and implemented. Even if a scholarly or professional organization were to claim that its standards governed non-members, it is difficult to imagine how the standards would be applied and with what consequences. How, for instance, might plagiarizing, nonacademic, popular historian-writers be brought to account by any particular organization? Public obloquy has so far proved to be the only available response in such instances, and its utility has not been significant in affecting those widely believed to be guilty of plagiarizing or of being unprofessionally sloppy in their methods.

historians' work, regulation of their behavior is coming from outside the precincts of history. For example, all of those engaging in oral interview research must now look over their shoulders at legally enforceable regulations issued by the federal government. While, after much tense negotiating that involved the AHA, AAUP, and other organizations, oral historians formally escaped the threat that their interviews would be placed under the same federal restrictions as scientists undertaking human subjects research and would have to be approved by the review boards of the institutions at which they work, those institutions have apparently disregarded oral history's exclusion from federal guidelines. No one can justifiably question the delicate ethical nature of oral interviews, which are no more and no less sensitive than the rest of historians' fiduciary responsibilities to the past, the truth, and their audiences. At issue instead is historians' freedom to conduct interviews in consonance with guidelines adopted by the Oral History Association and actively supported by the AHA. Despite the best efforts of these organizations, oral historians find themselves hindered by institutional procedures more restrictive than warranted by regulation and law. And even if no immediate threat of further federal and institutional intrusion into historians' work is on the horizon, all historians have reason to worry that what was once their freedom of action governed only by professional guidelines will in the future be constrained by external interests. All the more reason, then, that their own practices meet the highest ethical standards and that ways be found within the discipline itself to make those standards a matter of discussion during historians' professional preparation and throughout their careers.[12]

---

[12] A convenient text of the federal guidelines can be found in *Perspectives* 41 (December 2003): 13 and further clarification in 42 (March 2004): 9. The *AHA Statement on IRBs and Oral History Research* (2008) can be accessed at http://www.historians.org/perspectives/issues/2008/0802/0802aha1.cfm. On the complexities of the issue, the history of its relevance to historians, and the continuing difficulty in freeing historians from restrictions that should not apply to them, see Jeffrey Brainard, "Federal Agency Says Oral-History Research Is Not Covered by Human-Subject Rules," *Chronicle of Higher Education*, October 31, 2003, A25; Robert B. Townsend and Meriam Belli, "Oral History and IRBs: Caution Urged as Rule Interpretations Vary Widely," *Perspectives* 42 (December 2004): 11–12; Robert B. Townsend et al., "Oral History and Review Boards: Little Gain and More Pain," ibid., 44 (February 2006): 7–9; Linda Shopes, "Negotiating Institutional Review Boards," ibid., 45 (March 2007): 36–40; E. Taylor Atkins, "Oral History and IRBs: An Update from the 2006 HRPP Conference," ibid., 41–43; Zachary M. Schrag, "Ethical Training for Oral Historians," ibid., 44–46; and Schrag, "How Talking Became Human Subjects Research: The Federal Regulation of the Social Sciences, 1965–1991," *Journal of Policy History* 21 (2009): 3–37. Schrag has also written

The right gained in recent decades by faculty members and more recently by graduate student teaching assistants to organize into collective bargaining units on the campuses of both private and public universities raises similarly sensitive issues. Once again, external pressures – in this case the terms of union contracts – on the professional standards heretofore considered to govern historians' professional bearing and acts are the principal threat. Here the matter is complicated by the insertion of labor unions between universities and their students.[13]

The successful attempts by teaching assistants to unionize may be taken as a proxy for the larger issue. As early as 1969 at the University of Wisconsin, teaching assistants gained the right to unionize, but not until early in the new century were teaching assistant unions at private universities given legal warrant to organize, when a 2002 decision of the National Labor Relations Board (NLRB) gave the United Auto Workers a victory in competition with the American Federation of Teachers to represent doctoral candidates at New York University. At NYU, where graduate students gained more generous stipends and full health insurance coverage, the UAW agreed to distinguish economic from academic issues and to leave the latter to the determination of the university alone. It yet remains to be seen whether the distinction can be maintained, as it long has been on the Madison campus, where strikes have been avoided, possibly because that university is governed by state, not federal, law.[14]

---

a comprehensive and sharply critical study of the intrusion of IRBs into historical and related scholarship in *Ethical Imperialism: Institutional Review Boards and the Social Sciences, 1965–2009* (Baltimore: Johns Hopkins University Press, 2010). A thorough canvassing of many of the issues involved in the subject of its title is the work of historian and judge John A. Neuenschwander, *A Guide to Oral History and the Law* (New York: Oxford University Press, 2009).

[13] Union organizing at public universities is governed by state law, at private universities by regulations and decisions of the National Labor Relations Board. Because the NLRB did not act favorably regarding unionization at private institutions until 2000, graduate students at public universities in New York, Michigan, Wisconsin, and California organized under state law earlier. Those at Cornell voted in 2002 against doing so.

[14] Kate Masur, "Unionizing at the University," *Perspectives* 39 (January 2001): 7–1; Scott Smallwood, "NYU and Its TA Union Reach Pact on Contract," *Chronicle of Higher Education*, February 15, 2002, A18. Lost in debates about this issue is a consideration of particular relevance to historians. Many of those who are teaching assistants today may remain part-time instructors tomorrow, well beyond receipt of their doctorates. Even more pertinent is that many aspiring historians, both by necessity and choice, will not become academic historians, and teaching assistantships may not respond to their needs or interests to begin with. But as so often is the case, one solution rather than many is being sought for and applied to a problem that is many-dimensioned.

The efforts of teaching assistants to unionize themselves on various campuses, efforts that have had such weighty support as that of the AAUP, arose out of the conviction that the conditions of teaching assistants' "employment" (the very term in dispute) had been unsatisfactory. Citing evidence that they were underpaid, received fewer personnel benefits than faculty and staff members, and lacked access to the professional facilities enjoyed by full-time faculty members, many teaching assistants believed themselves to be unjustifiably underprivileged and undercompensated. While behind these students' frustrations often lay coincident, conflicting claims to faculty and worker status (a pattern of dual claims that was established by faculty unionization under the auspices of the National Education Association, the American Federation of Teachers, and the AAUP as early as the 1970s), there can be little doubt that many universities have often failed to devote adequate attention to the many concerns that necessarily weigh heavily on people who, during their years of study, occupy a dependent, apprenticeship status and are long uncertain about the chances of their future employment.[15]

Had universities been more attentive to these concerns (and to the changing demography, employment prospects, and economic situations of their graduate students), the continuing recent conflicts might have been avoided. But probably not, for those conflicts (which have found their way onto court dockets and into federal agency deliberations) center on disagreement over the very status of teaching by graduate students in all disciplines: whether, because they are serving as teachers, teaching assistants are workers, students, or proto–faculty members – or perhaps all three. Thus arises the question as to which standards – those that govern workplace functions or the professional ethics and behavior of students and academics – are to govern teaching assistants' work. It is an issue that begs for resolution, although, even after its partial regulation by the NLRB's 2000 decision, it is not likely to gain resolution soon.[16]

---

[15] On the AAUP's support of graduate student unionization, see Courtney Leatherman, "AAUP Reaches Out and Takes Sides," *Chronicle of Higher Education*, June 23, 2000, A16–A19. A history of the AAUP's involvement with unionization is Philo A. Hutcheson, *A Professional Professoriate: Unionization, Bureaucratization, and the AAUP* (Nashville: Vanderbilt University Press, 2000).

[16] In its 2000 ruling, the NLRB ruled unanimously that because graduate student teaching assistants perform paid services under the control of their university "employers," the students' relationship with the university "is thus indistinguishable from a traditional master-servant relationship." *New York Times*, November 2, 2000, A1, A29. An opinion concurring with the NLRB majority noted pointedly that graduate students cannot be considered students since they are required to become instructors in order to secure

Teaching assistants – graduate students employed by their departments to teach undergraduates as part of their professional preparation and in partial offset of the financial aid extended to them – are in an anomalous position. They must serve in the status, first, of teachers to students to whom they are bound by conventional ethical standards; second, of students – themselves – who receive financial aid; and, third, of employees – again, themselves – who are paid. Admitted to graduate study on the basis of their academic records and intellectual promise, not on grounds of their prospective or proven abilities as instructors of undergraduates, they become responsible as teaching assistants for the welfare of their own students, usually (although not uniformly) without prior assessment of their abilities to teach.[17] In those cases in which they are prepared for their teaching responsibilities, they are often prepared by other graduate students who are themselves serving as teaching assistants and who, while somewhat more experienced in teaching, are only slightly senior to those they train. Moreover, the time spent in graduate study has lengthened while, in general, the relationships between faculty members and their graduate students have over the years become attenuated. In addition, while all of these teaching assistants are compensated in some form (usually with pay but also through waivers of their tuition and other fees), they are compensated at a lower rate than full-time faculty members and often lack the latter's many benefits. Universities argue that teaching assistants' compensation comes in the form of the student aid (tuition and fee waivers) they receive, while the students believe that they are being, and should be better, compensated for the teaching they undertake. It is the students, therefore, who, feeling ignored, taken advantage of, and undercompensated, have seized the initiative in a matter, however resolved legally, that contains ethical and professional tangles that cannot

---

their degrees. It cannot yet be said whether repealing this requirement for graduate students would affect their right to organize. *Wall Street Journal*, November 2, 2000, B22. The NLRB also ruled that despite the fact that assistants were students benefiting from instruction, they were also employees falling under the protections of the National Labor Relations Act. Also, as this statement asserted, students are usually not required to teach as a condition of their enrollment since they are allowed to support themselves in other ways if they can, teaching not being a condition of their education. *Chronicle of Higher Education*, November 10, 2000, A14. It remains to be seen whether, as some fear, the decision will affect academic freedom.

[17] In this regard, teaching assistants are very much like the academic faculty members that many of them hope to become: they are compensated for the discharge of responsibilities for which they are not trained and seek recognition – in their case, graduate degrees, after demonstrating their research and scholarship – for which they are not compensated.

be overlooked.[18] Here again is one dimension among many others that might be cited of the ethical conundrums of history today – conundrums rarely taken up in graduate preparation or wider professional circles.

Even were the many organizations of historians to address these complexities, the authority in law of any particular set of standards remains uncertain. In the modern world, all learned professions require specified training for their practice. That training must take place in institutions that have gained or by law have been given authority – usually through a license to perform accredited functions – to testify formally to trainees' preparation for professional work. In learned professions like the law, medicine, and architecture, such preparatory training takes place in professional schools specifically dedicated to educating students in those disciplines. As part of that preparation, fledgling attorneys, medical doctors, and architects are required to take courses in ethics. In addition, training in those professions must be followed by licensing and certification after the successful passage of bar and medical board exams, which include segments about professional ethics. Many, if not most, professional fields now require their members to secure continuing education in their subjects, and the retention of licenses to practice depends in part on the provision of evidence that such professional education, including a review of ethical practice, has been sought and gained. Moreover, once one is licensed to practice law or medicine, one is bound by oath to abide by the ethical canons of the professions. Failure to do so can result in disciplinary hearings and actions, including loss of license; and disbarment prohibits someone from practicing in the jurisdiction from which licensure was originally gained.

That is not the case in the various professions in which historians serve. The discipline of history possesses no legally defined qualifications for entrance or practice. No historians – indeed, no recipients of any doctoral degree, to my knowledge – take an oath on receiving their degrees, such as that taken by medical school graduates, "to keep this Oath and this covenant." Without certification and without enforcement mechanisms, the professions of history – to say nothing of the professions in the other fields of the liberal arts – cannot bring effective, concerted,

---

[18] For evidence that, contrary to university fears and assertions, graduate student unionization does not seem to disrupt the relationships between faculty members and their students, see "Graduate Student Unions Don't Hurt Professor-Advisee Relations, Survey Finds," *Chronicle of Higher Education*, November 5, 1999, A18.

and discipline-wide penalties to bear on their erring members. Thus, historians judged to have committed some infraction of standards promulgated by one organization – say, the AHA – may nevertheless remain in good standing on their faculties (because their institutions have not called them to account) and as practitioners in their profession (say, oral history) because they are not judged to have committed breaches of the standards of that particular profession. As a result, the history professions always harbor a few people – fortunately, very few – who have broken professional rules at one place but who have gone on to uninterrupted careers elsewhere, where news of their behavior has not preceded them.[19]

The discipline of history also differs from law and medicine and from many occupations like paralegal work in that those who emerge from graduate school with doctoral degrees can enter full pursuit of their professions without passing any further qualifying or licensing examinations. No public body or professional, certifying, or accrediting association requires aspiring historians, subsequent to the completion of their graduate training, to demonstrate their ability to create, disseminate, and evaluate history according to standards of accuracy, veracity, objectivity, judiciousness, and balance. Evaluating their fitness in these regards is left to the institutions that hire and advance them and to reviews of their work in the worldwide forum of ideas.[20]

In addition, historians are not required to demonstrate, maintain, or upgrade their qualifications through continuing or in-service education as are many other professional practitioners – one thinks here for example of schoolteachers and clinical social workers – in order to retain their licenses to practice their work.[21] Historians assume about themselves

[19] In the academic world, for instance, there are a number of people who have been eased out of professorships or positions of administrative leadership at one institution because of sexual harassment or substance abuse but have secured positions elsewhere because no one at the first institution alerted colleagues at the new one as to the problem. Others, having been adjudged guilty of plagiarism, have remained academics in good standing because of the protection of patrons or superiors.

[20] As Victoria Harden has pointed out to me, professional licensing (in addition to the Ph.D. degree), by which historians demonstrate to others what specific skills and knowledge they possess, may be the only way that historians will be able to gain a mandate that a doctorate is required to hold particular positions, especially for those historians outside the academy. The failure to secure these mandates has been particularly injurious to historians seeking history work in government, where those without demanding, formal historical preparation often vie for and secure positions that should go to trained historians. Librarians and archivists, to mention two related groups of professionals, have succeeded in having a senior degree required for federal employment where historians have not.

[21] Not that the quality of such in-service education does not vary greatly from profession to profession, for surely it does. The quality of in-service instruction for teachers, for

as well as about their colleagues that proximity to other historians, the challenges of instruction, and the frequent critical evaluation of their own and others' scholarship keep them fit as scholars, teachers, curators, editors, and the like. Yet much evidence suggests otherwise. Not only are the historians who have not updated their lectures since their early years as assistant professors or not kept up with the literature in a field since their first books well known in fact as well as in caricature. Authoritative surveys repeatedly indicate that only a small proportion of all historians publish even a single book review in any given year.[22]

Nor, in contrast to those in other professions and occupations, are historians required to demonstrate their conversance with professional ethics. I know of no college, university, or professional organization that requires its members to do so. And even if a particular university made instruction in professional ethics a required part of its graduate curriculum, no professional advantage (say, in a claim to new intellectual expertise or in recognition or pay) would be gained by those who received that instruction. In addition, apparently concluding that they have no direct stake in the accreditation of professionals in the arts and sciences, individual states have not seen fit to mandate that the universities at which aspiring professionals in history and other disciplines receive training offer further examinations before one can become a member of a university faculty or a museum curatorial staff or put oneself forth as a historical consultant. The difference is made vivid by the fact that while one cannot legally hang out a shingle saying "doctor of dentistry" or "attorney at law" without licensure, one can hang out a shingle as "consultant in history" or "professional historian" without let or hindrance, save for the discipline of the marketplace and the evaluation of one's professional peers.[23]

---

instance, is notoriously poor and of no exemplary use for historians; that for psychotherapists is quite high.

[22] For some related recent figures on the publishing records of academic historians, see Robert B. Townsend, "A Profile of the History Profession," *Perspectives on History* 48 (October 2010): 36–39.

[23] It can, of course, be argued that receipt of the doctorate and of tenure constitute licensing; and there can be no dispute that they do so within the community of coprofessionals, who thereby testify to a historian's fitness to practice the kinds of history that are thought to require deep and extensive study and learning. But formal licensure entails the state's granting an institution or accepting within its own powers the specifically granted authority to license practitioners. No such license is anywhere issued to historians by any state agencies or anywhere required in order to practice history; nor does the absence of either a doctorate or tenure legally disqualify someone from teaching or writing history or pursuing the many other occupations of historian. It is relevant here, also, that, in addition to those occupations that require their practitioners to remain conversant

One example of the complexities involved in drawing up a code of conduct for historians of any kind is illustrated by the struggle in the 1990s to draft a set of standards to govern the rights and responsibilities of museum historian-curators and historians who work in such institutions as the National Park Service.[24] For some time before this code-writing effort began, concerns about the intellectual and professional freedoms of museum-based historians had been increasing – concerns, it should be emphasized, arising from generally positive developments in the museum world – and calls for a curator's "bill of rights" had increasingly been heard. Because of a decline in the number of academic positions in the 1970s, more graduates of history doctoral programs, accustomed to the conventions of academic freedom, had sought and gained museum employment. By 1990, museums themselves had become more professionalized than they had been before; their nonhistorian staff members were better trained, their financing and their cultural and intellectual functions were more complex; and they were laying claims to a larger role in intellectual culture than they had earlier played. Partly in consequence of museums' increased stature and their growing social and economic impact on their communities, their programming had become more venturesome as well as more responsive to changes in both academic intellectual inquiry and social expectations – much of those arising out of the increasingly acknowledged diversity of American society. Gradually but unmistakably, as museums' own exposure to public scrutiny and criticism was growing, museum historians' tasks were becoming more important, sensitive, and vexed. The need to clarify museum historians'

---

with ethical principles pertaining to each line of work, the federal government requires periodic attendance at ethics workshops of its employees. A rare reflection on this issue is Adam Hochschild, "Do You Need a License to Practice History?" *Historically Speaking* 9 (March–April 2008): 2–6, and the discussion following.

24 The fullest account of this effort is Victoria A. Harden, "Museum Exhibit Standards: Do Historians Really Want Them?" *Public Historian* 21 (Summer 1999): 91–109. Harden's citations lead to additional discussions of the subject. It should be noted that the call, originating from the OAH, for such a statement of principles envisaged the prospective statement as protecting museums from outside interference, while in the end historians on the task force formed to draw up such a statement found themselves protesting against museums' refusal to acknowledge curators' rights and authority within museums. That is, from the start there existed a misunderstanding about the task force's purpose, a misunderstanding that helped doom the effort. A penetrating, and it seems to me incontestable, case for the symbiosis of historical scholarship and museum exhibiting, both joined to the mission of teaching history to all citizens, is made by Barbara Clark Smith, "Claiming the Museum Floor," *OAH Newsletter* 28 (February 2000): 5, 12.

rights and responsibilities would no doubt have manifested itself eventually. But it was the divisive public tumult that resulted in the cancellation of the original plan for the *Enola Gay* exhibit at the National Air and Space Museum of the Smithsonian Institution in 1994 that precipitated the first concerted effort, originating within the OAH, to throw some protections over the work of museum historians.[25]

Those spearheading that effort hoped that it would result in a statement of standards functionally equivalent to the AAUP's 1940 *Statement of Principles on Academic Freedom and Tenure* – a statement that would help protect curator-historians against unwarranted intrusions on their professional work (and, as surely it would do, provide museums with a measure of institutional cover in defending themselves against attacks on the contents of their exhibits and the interpretations offered by their historian-employees). Those drafting the statement also hoped to erect some kind of protection for historian-curators against their employing institutions, much as academics, almost a century earlier, had had to do. That the interorganizational task force formed to seek consensus on such a statement could not agree on a set of principles provides instructive evidence of the dangers involved in assuming that the norms that govern the museum-based creation and diffusion of historical knowledge must closely resemble those applying to academic history. The effort's failure also reveals the divisions, themselves the product of the spread of professional historical work into so many professions, among people responsible for disseminating history through museums.

The endeavors of the task force, composed of representatives of a number of historical and museum organizations, foundered in the whirling currents caused by the very museum controversies its members sought to address. Those controversies had gradually forced into conflict two imposing "goods" that, under better circumstances, might be kin: the

---

[25] See especially Alfred F. Young, "A Modest Proposal: A Bill of Rights for American Museums," *Public Historian* 14 (Summer 1992): 67–73, and Young, "SOS: Storm Warning for American Museums," *OAH Newsletter* 22 (November 1994): 1, 6–8. On the *Enola Gay* exhibit, see the *Journal of American History* 82 (December 1995): 1029–1144, and Edward T. Linenthal and Tom Engelhardt (eds.), *History Wars: The Enola Gay and Other Battles for the American Past* (New York: Metropolitan Books, 1996). Widely reported public controversies over other exhibits – especially the notorious, canceled exhibit of the photographs of Robert Mapplethorpe by the Corcoran Gallery of Art in Washington, D.C., in 1989 and *The West as America* at the National Museum of American Art in 1991 – might have aroused historians and curators to action, but those uproars concerned art, and their assailants were less well organized than those who attacked plans for the *Enola Gay* exhibit.

independence and authority of curatorial experts and museum historians – their rights – and the public service and cultural functions of museums – their responsibilities. Academic institutions had learned in the twentieth century to deflect such conflicts through their commitment to AAUP principles; colleges and universities found that they could defend themselves against attacks for harboring faculty members who uttered words or took actions deemed unacceptable to members of the public by saying that, under long-standing principles as well as First Amendment law, faculty members were protected against penalties for what others might find offensive, contrary to the public interest, or ridiculous. But museums had not yet come up with an equivalent, functionally useful set of principles to cite against critics; and because their staff members also could not summon in their own defense any standards analogous to AAUP principles of academic freedom and tenure against museum administrators and trustees desirous of penalizing them, both institutions and curators were comparatively defenseless against attacks on their integrity. Curators had no conventionally agreed-on rights, and museums had not accepted any widely shared notions of responsibilities. Therefore, if any situation would seem to have called for the development of curatorial standards that members of all humanistic and scientific disciplines as well as all museums could accept – there being, after all, museum collections devoted to almost every conceivable human and natural subject – this one seemed to be it. Nevertheless, circumstances decreed that historians, rather than members of other disciplines, would venture the first step toward creating a set of curatorial principles.[26]

Their effort was not successful. On one side of the group were museum administrators – whether they faithfully represented the views of their museum colleagues was not clear – who believed that museums must reflect their communities' views before anything else. One of these administrators, rejecting the museums' role as an institution that might follow the course of scholarly research and understanding and present knowledgeable perspectives on the past, argued that "historical organizations exist to provide a sense of continuity, historical context and perspective on ... enduring issues and a forum for their discussion." Museums'

---

[26] The challenges facing museums and their professional curatorial staff members would seem to argue for an all-points effort under the joint aegis of the American Association of Museums, the American Council of Learned Societies, and the National Academy of Sciences to develop some protective standards analogous to those of the AAUP. As is regrettably so often the case, the ACLS, the sole all-discipline institution of the humanities and social sciences, shows no sign of taking up the challenge.

utilitarian "community-oriented mission," he asserted, requires them to present a community's "core values" and help construct a community's identity through recording and commemorating its self-image. Museums and their communities should be "indistinguishable," with curators and historians kept from controlling exhibits through their application of scholarly knowledge and scholarly standards and with administrators firmly ruling the roost.

On the other side were historians who argued that museums had larger and weightier responsibilities than simply commemorating and reflecting communities' beliefs about themselves and their imagined pasts. In the words of a commendably muscular set of draft standards submitted for consideration to the task force by the SHFG, museum exhibits ought to "encourage the informed discussion of their content and the broader issues of historical significance they raise." To this end, as public forums for the discussion of issues, not solutions to them, museums must not attempt "to suppress exhibits or to impose an uncritical point of view, however widely shared." To do so in the name of community or any other particular interests is "inimical to open and rational discussion" of exhibits' subjects.[27] Furthermore, as Victoria Harden, the endeavor's historian who played a major role in drafting the society's standards, pointedly has asked, "If historians and curators have no authority in interpreting the past and should always yield to community desires, what is the point of [museums'] hiring professional historians to work on exhibits?"[28]

Because the reconciliation of these competing conceptions of historical museums' functions proved impossible, the attempt to draft a set of curatorial standards acceptable to the group ended in an impasse. After all, one group represented the view that knowledge has a critical, enlivening role in an open society and that museums serve posterity itself, the other that knowledge is finite and relatively inert, existing to strengthen and confirm, rather than to deepen and throw fresh light on, conventional understandings of human affairs. The museum professionals

---

[27] The society's proposed standards can be found in full in Harden, "Museum Exhibit Standards," 109. It is worth noting that it was federal historians, those who are too easily considered to be captive of the policies and ideological interests of the agencies that employ them, who put forth and championed the adoption of these resolute curatorial principles. For insight into efforts to design and mount an exhibit responsibly in the absence of a statement of curatorial principles, see Harry B. Rubenstein, "Good History Is Not Enough," *Perspectives* 38 (May 2000): 39–41.

[28] Personal communication with the author, May 15, 2011.

failed to make a compelling case as to why museums, instead of families, genealogical societies, patriotic organizations, or churches, must be expected to bear the burden of providing identity for individuals, communities, or groups. Nor could they justify their defense of what might be called institutional official history – a particular interpretation of the past, which their museums would sanction and actively promote, even if to the detriment of the stories and accurate histories of marginal groups, which would have difficulty making the case for their being "stakeholders" in museums' communities. But the historians also failed to convince their museum colleagues that curatorial should be likened to monographic, and museum to academic, historical work – that curators (who, like faculty members, are employees of their institutions) ought to be permitted to design and explain exhibits as expressions of their scholarly knowledge and understanding with relatively few fetters on their freedom to do so. In fact, the position of the museum historians on the task force seemed ambivalent. On the one hand, they resolutely stood up for the creation of protective standards, yet on the other they argued, in Harden's words, for recognition of the "inherent difference in the terms of employment for scholars in academia and those in government"[29] – especially that historians in the former are covered by academic freedom, those in the latter not. An authoritative statement of that difference has yet to be set forth.

A strong case can be made that, like college and university provosts and deans, museum administrators must learn to accept as a given the professional autonomy of the scholars who serve on their professional staffs. But more is at stake for the future of historical museums than the curatorial standards that might govern the work of, or at least offer some protection to, museum scholars. To accept administrators' arguments that museums should serve their community by mirroring its self-image is to accept the erroneous notion that communities are uniform, homogeneous, and inherently coherent – that biography, identity, belief, ideology, and hope perfectly correspond and overlap. That is the case only with the smallest communities, rarely in a larger, contemporary, diverse society like that of the United States.

The question therefore remains as to which part of any community individual museums are supposed to represent, the identities of which part they must choose to create or protect, and, consequently, which part

[29] Victoria A. Harden, "Museum Exhibit Standards: Do Historians Really Want Them?" *Public Historian* 21 (Summer 1999): 91–109, quotation at p. 97.

of their communities they must exclude. In a multicultural society, different groups will interpret the same events, the same texts, artifacts, and displays, in widely different ways. Why must museums choose among them? If the museums' position were to gain full primacy, the ability and authority of various "communities" to shut down, as well as design, exhibits not to their liking, much as the Air Force Association forced the Smithsonian to buckle under its assault on the proposed *Enola Gay* exhibit, would be unchallengeable. In addition, to ask museums to determine what is representative of any community is to force an abstract and essentially impossible obligation on them, one that is certain to weaken, rather than to strengthen, their roles and authority. Such a view is also inherently patronizing: museums that adopted it would in effect be saying that informed citizens are incapable of determining for themselves what they seek to know and believe and that, consequently, museums must take upon themselves the duty of telling citizens what their views ought to be. To adopt a mission to mirror particular communities would also in effect put museums in a position of simply ignoring the inevitable discontinuities, divisions, and tensions of life itself; happy memory and unnatural continuity – that is, fantasy – would replace reality in museum display cases.

Given these considerations, one can see how invocation of "the public trust" in the SHFG's draft standards would be read with concern by museum representatives. Yet it is precisely this issue that warrants the most critical attention on the part of the scholars and administrators who serve history museums. For as it turns out, agreement as to what constitutes historical museums' public trust has not yet been reached. Moreover, the central issue of the nature and methods of the peer review of museum exhibits has not yet been adequately addressed. As with the peer review of written scholarship, that of history exhibits would serve the same functions. It would identify errors, strengthen interpretation, alert curators to additional, perhaps conflicting, evidence, and throw a mantle of general professional support over the resulting work. But who has legitimate claim to preparing exhibits and determining their contents? Perhaps historian-curators' positions are more sensitive than those of their comparatively more autonomous academic colleagues; perhaps, as Harden writes, scholars are "accountable only to themselves for their published arguments" rather than to larger circles of the public. Perhaps "scholars who practiced their historical skills as employees of the federal government, and those working in state and local governments as well, could never assert a claim to academic freedom identical with that of their colleagues in universities." As with all government historians, those working in government museums have to gain clearance for their work, submit to the perhaps unavoidable influences of politics and the pressures to convey "official" versions of the past, and thus bend to the gods of utility and community. But both the nature and limitations of museum curators' academic freedom, suitably affected by peer review, remain to be defined.

As the ranks of historian-curators grow in size and authority, the issues raised by this initial attempt to adopt some standards of curatorial rights and responsibilities will increasingly require attention. It is difficult to believe that some standards, analogous to those adopted by the AHA, OAH, SHFG, and NCPH, will not eventually be embraced by curators and museums for their own mutual benefit. In the meantime, however, having to carry on their work without the professional safeguards enjoyed by their academic colleagues, museum historians and all other historians with their welfare in mind would be well served to try again to develop of set of curatorial principles for themselves. How might they proceed? Since, in the initial attempt to develop such standards, an approach using a coalition of organization representatives failed, the responsibility for adopting and promulgating standards could reasonably fall to the SHFG, which earlier put forth to the coalition the only set of draft principles presented to it – principles that remain admirable. Those principles could then be accepted by other organizations like the AHA and OAH and, like the AAUP's standards of academic freedom and tenure earlier, gradually come to be accepted as the norm. In addition, the SHFG could, again like the AAUP, establish its own mechanism, like the AAUP's Committee A, to hear and act on complaints brought under the standards. Another approach would be to solicit some major figures in history and the museum worlds to call for the development of standards and to write them. The continued lack of such standards and the means to enforce them leave this sector of historians' work as well as historians practicing within it battered by the uncalmed crosscurrents that affect all history work exposed to wide public scrutiny.

The standards that have traditionally governed the particular pursuits of academic historians present their own problems in a changing professional world. The fact is that the freedom of academics, by contrast with those of other historians, remains satisfactorily, if by no means perfectly, protected. Since its gradual formulation after the Civil War, coincident with the maturation of American research universities and the professionalization of academic faculties, academic freedom has been taken to be the bedrock principle of intellectual life – and thus of professional life in the intellectual disciplines whose principal location is academic. This has been justifiable only as long as one assumes that both the term "academic freedom" and the reach of the protections encompassed under it are and must be static; that the freedoms protected by "academic freedom" only are and must be academic freedoms; and that academic freedoms exhaust the freedoms by which intellectual work should be governed – the very issues that roiled the world of museum historians in the 1990s. But those assumptions are themselves problematic and perhaps never more so than today. The difficulty is that the reach of what we conventionally think of as academic freedoms does not automatically extend more broadly into what ought now to be termed "professional freedoms." If and how they might do so is a major, troubling issue confronting historians.

The resistance to broadening the definition of freedoms associated with doing history and of acculturating historians to think in wider terms about their professional rights and responsibilities stems from the long association of academic freedom with academic tenure. The marriage of the two was cemented by the issuance, in 1940, of the influential *Statement on Academic Freedom and Tenure* of the American Association of University Professors, an institutional artifact of the era in which academic disciplines and the academic profession came to maturity. The 1914–1915 creation principally of Arthur O. Lovejoy and Edwin R. A. Seligman, the AAUP broke onto the academic scene with its 1915 *Report on Academic Freedom and Tenure* which laid the groundwork for its related *Statement* of twenty-five years later. That 1915 document and those that succeeded it originated out of a concern to establish the obligations and responsibilities, as well as the rights and interests, of academic scholars and teachers, although it is the latter – each academic institution's responsibilities toward its faculty members – that have since predominated in debates about academic freedom.[30]

One gets a glimpse of how strong the pull of the academic monopoly of the discussion of academic intellectuals' freedoms has become in the assertion by Joan W. Scott, in a larger discussion of academic freedom and tenure, that "disciplinary communities consist of people who agree

---

[30] The standard history of academic freedom in the United States is Richard Hofstadter and Walter P. Metzger, *The Development of Academic Freedom in the United States* (New York: Columbia University Press, 1955). On the AAUP specifically, see pp. 407–412 and chap. 10. This classic account, now over fifty years old, is greatly in need of updating. For an apposite case, omitted from Hofstadter and Metzger's coverage, see W. B. Carnochan, "The Case of Julius Goebel: Stanford, 1905," *American Scholar* 72 (Summer 2003): 95–108.

to follow a certain set of rules in order to be trained." As unassailable as this statement is, it neglects the fact that the behaviors required of graduate students are assumed to carry forward into professional careers that expand far beyond the boundaries of the academic departments in which students are necessarily prepared and into professional work often quite unlike the activities – principally teaching and research – covered under the canons of the AAUP. It is also the case that the rules that historians are required to follow "in order to be trained" include most of those that they are expected (at least by implication) to follow throughout their careers with no compensating grants of freedoms from those institutions in the more freewheeling professional world in which a mounting proportion of historians work without tenure. Yet even when students agree to the rules governing academic work as they must during their preparation, they often find these rules not recognized or applicable where tenure has no hold. Nor, of course, do those canons apply necessarily or with due penalties to those people, writers especially, who serve effectively as historians without having been trained in doctoral programs.[31]

Not only do the traditional standards governing academic history not reach to the nonacademic employment of historians. The classic

---

[31] Joan W. Scott, "Academic Freedom as an Ethical Practice," in Louis Menand (ed.), *The Future of Academic Freedom* (Chicago: University of Chicago Press, 1996), 163–180. The quotation is from p. 174. This collection of essays is the most searching and penetrating of recent discussions of its subject and advances the argument, with which I am not in full agreement, that academic freedom, and by extension all intellectual freedom, can be justified and enforced only through self-regulation in each intellectual discipline, each a self-governing community. It is in this respect – in its failure to accommodate its canons of conduct to current realities, its ethos of responsibility to the larger culture, and its preparation of historians in ethics consonant to the new professional world in which historians practice – that I believe history increasingly risks its authority and opens itself to attack from those who have lost confidence in the authority of historians' knowledge, indeed of academic knowledge generally. An egregious example of this kind of disrespect, arising largely from opposition to tenure, is the ignorant attack on tenure by James F. Carlin, "Restoring Sanity to an Academic World Gone Mad," *Chronicle of Higher Education*, November 5, 1999. Carlin, a businessman and then a trustee of the University of Massachusetts and chairman of the Massachusetts Board of Higher Education, argues that tenure borders on being "immoral" and of course doesn't comport with business practices, which he believes as a businessman should be applied to academic matters. Unfortunately, corporate norms are already infecting the academy, even if not yet through the abolition of tenure. A fair trade, no doubt beyond Carlin's ken, would be for academic norms to invade business. Those would include collegial, nonhierarchical governance; a sense of civic responsibility; products and services based on ethical standards and knowledge free of conflicts of interest; a prohibition on funds being applied to election campaigns; and more gracious behavior than that held up as exemplary by vulgar, if widely admired, businesspeople – all fully functional norms within colleges and universities.

protections of academic freedom, such as freedom of expression and professional independence, no longer cover all historians employed by colleges and universities. Some institutions, like Bennington College, have defied the AAUP by abolishing tenure outright. But an even graver incursion on academic freedom is the increased employment of historians occupying adjunct, part-time faculty berths. Lacking contracts and not considered "line" faculty members, these historians, postdoctorate scholar-teachers and graduate students alike, lack the protections of academic free speech and can be dismissed without much concern about the penalties or censure that might be imposed by such organizations as the AAUP.

Because of these discouraging recent developments, historians, no more than others, cannot afford to retire from the larger field of battle of academic and professional freedom. Reducing institutions' reliance on part-time faculty members, an effort now broadly under way, is an appropriate and needed aim, and historians have to continue to work through the AHA, OAH, and AAUP to throw the protections of academic freedom over adjunct faculty members and secure for them the benefits of line appointments enjoyed by all regular faculty members. Yet historians are unlikely to gain more protections for themselves in the years immediately ahead without confronting some defects within their own discipline.

The chief of those, stemming from the lamentable, continuing separation of academic from public history, is the absence of a set of standards applying equally to historians in all occupations, at least in general terms. Each of the discipline's principal membership organizations – the AHA, the OAH, and the NCPH – has promulgated standards of conduct. The AHA's standards, adopted by the OAH, are by far the most authoritative, searching, and encompassing and imply their applicability to all people, nonmembers as well as AHA members, who practice history.[32]

The National Council's code of conduct covers members only, even though an increasing number of historians not members of the council practice various forms of public history in their professional lives.

[32] See the AHA's *Statement on Standards of Professional Conduct*, http://www.historians .org/pubs/Free/ProfessionalStandards.cfm; the *OAH Statement on Honesty and Integrity*, http://www.oah.org/pubs/nl/2003may/integrity.htm; and the National Council on Public History's *OAH Statement on Honesty and Integrity*, http://www.ncph. org/AbouttheCouncil/BylawsandEthics/tabid/291/Default.aspx. Although what I write in this chapter makes clear that the chances of getting an agreement on such a set of standards is presently slim, that goal should be kept in view. Efforts to agree on general principles might first be undertaken, then attempts to narrow remaining differences essayed over time.

And most notably, while the AHA's standards take up public history, the very fact of the National Council's not having adopted those standards reveals the continuing division within historians' ranks as well as the failure of graduate departments to prepare all historians equally for work in academic and public history. However, the council's code has an advantage over the AAUP's canonical 1940 *Statement of Principles on Academic Freedom and Tenure* in that it presumptively applies, ethically if not legally and effectively, to historians serving as teachers, museum curators, archivists, filmmakers, and other professionals.

Another defect in historians' standards of conduct is their failure to formally acknowledge the responsibilities they owe to the society that yields to them the freedom to recruit and police their fellow professionals. After all, even if historians are bound by no Hippocratic oath, they do possess a general professional ethos. Collegiality, for instance, brings with it a strong expectation that, on request, historians will read others' manuscripts prior to formal peer review, will serve on search committees of departments and offices, will join meeting panels as commentators, and will encourage fledgling historians along their paths. They will review books, exhibits, films, and collections. They will accept peer-review assignments from journal and book publishers, from government agencies, and in their own workplaces. Yet historians, especially academic historians, are less inclined, because less expected, to shoulder professional responsibilities beyond the borders of their immediate institutions and responsibilities. Not all historians feel themselves obligated, as part of their professional activities, to work with local schoolteachers, support their professional associations, and stay informed about laws and regulations that may affect their work and join in efforts to lobby their public officials. They do not see themselves as occupying an office, of holding a position of trust and responsibility to others charged with a wide array of duties and functions. That they do not do so arises in part from the independent, often solitary, nature of so much history work, especially that involving archival research and scholarly writing and, as always, the lack of adequate incentive and recognition, locally and nationally, for extramural historical activity.

Yet as is so often the case, much of the weakness in historians' professional ethos originates in their graduate training – which is to say, in this instance, in what is missing from that training. Preparation for the ethical dimensions of a career in history is assumed to occur through osmotic acculturation rather than from direct training. Such a deficiency in historians' preparation exposes the discipline to criticism that it does not fully meet its responsibility to society and places on ground weaker than desirable those historians who would criticize others for their ethical failings. None of this is to say that the discipline has fallen egregiously short of its professional and ethical responsibilities. On the whole, historians are probably less deficient in their stance toward others than many other professionals. Yet to leave the current situation of ethical preparation and discussion as it now is is to risk danger to all historians, to say nothing of exposing the discipline to attack. It would be far better to make provision for programs, training, and debate about the ethical and civic responsibilities of historians than to move from one intradiscipline crisis to another without addressing the ethical situations of all historians. This is another challenge facing the discipline in its evolving, new, public-oriented era. The discipline would be well served to take it up.

8

Being Oneself as Historian

> Oh, Hell! To choose love by another's eyes.
>> A Midsummer Night's Dream

One purpose of this book has been to emphasize the great variety of pursuits now undertaken professionally in history's name, as well as the responsibilities that fall on the shoulders of those who take any of them up. I have also tried to make clear my conviction that, barring widespread changes in university-based graduate instruction, historians must now prepare themselves on their own more consciously and intently than they have in the past both for the many, broadened kinds of professional historical work on which they can embark and for the obligations that work entails. Because probably never before have so many contributions to historical understanding originated from so many quarters, in so many forms, and for so many uses, so probably never before have the burdens of determining the courses of their professions and careers in history fallen so heavily and directly on those who practice any of the historical arts. Surely never before have the choices, decisions, and responsibilities facing aspiring and experienced historians at all points in their working lives been so great.

It should thus occasion no surprise that the recent, great half-century transformation in the discipline of history has not arrived free of problems or been met with full embrace by all historians and all the institutions that prepare and support them and link them together as professionals. Many historians – sometimes complacently, more often ruefully, sometimes bitterly – have concluded that all is not well in the house of history. Some years ago, in a penetrating, wise, and balanced book that warrants reading by everyone concerned with history in American life, Theodore S. Hamerow cheerlessly concluded that the organized profession of history (as he termed it) was in the midst of a "grave crisis," one of almost Copernican proportions. Despite a generally beneficial "revolution in historical scholarship," the study and practice of history, he concluded, was "in retreat," not just in the United States but throughout the world. The symptoms of its retreat he espied in such conditions as the fragmentation of previously broad fields of scholarship; the professional insecurity, sometimes affecting their sense of professional self-worth, of so many historians; a full-blown sense of history's inutility; the decline, if not the marginalization, of historical study in school and college curricula; and the prospects, often the actuality, of unemployment for those being trained up to practice Clio's art.[1] Hamerow's sense of crisis was then widely shared and often continues to mark the attitude of those who prepare young people for work as historians as well as those who face the graver and more exacting challenges of finding that work – aspiring historians studying at research universities and seeking employment after completing their studies.

While, as I have tried to indicate throughout this book, the troubles that continue to afflict the discipline are many and in great need of remedy, history's condition twenty-five years after Hamerow wrote looks much more promising and altogether more robust than it then did. While many historians no doubt continue to share his sense of crisis, others look on recent transformations in the conditions of historical work as the necessary cost and confusions entailed by the arrival of long-overdue and welcome changes in historical thinking and practice. It is a grave mistake to believe that the discipline of history that we know today has ever been stable or that its governing norms, intellectual foundations, and institutional arrangements have ever been free of contest and assault. To be sure, there have been brief periods, perhaps a decade or two, in which relative stability in professional prospects or intellectual perspective has existed; and individual historians have sometimes enjoyed secure careers relatively unmolested by external forces. But such periods have been rare, and such historians have set the ideal but not been the norm. No more than in any arena of human existence, as historians should be the first to remind themselves, has a golden age of historical practice and thought existed.

---

[1] Theodore S. Hamerow, *Reflections on History and Historians* (Madison: University of Wisconsin Press, 1987).

So although we may be frustrated that many of the assumptions, practices, and institutional structures that are products of an earlier day have not yet adequately changed to fit history's current conditions, the lag between altered personal desires and altered professional realities should not surprise us either. Some decades more will be required to bring historians' hopes, preparation, outlooks, and institutions once again into the kind of general equilibrium that characterized them in the 1950s – if that equilibrium can in fact ever be reestablished. And then, of course, the conditions facing historians may again have changed to such a degree that someone writing another book like this will voice fresh concerns about the preparation and understanding of their colleagues.

But to acknowledge the great variety of professional pursuits now open to historians is not the same thing as to grasp fully the implications of this altered reality for individual historians, whether just commencing their careers or well launched into them. For the culture of aspirations left over from previous eras still exerts a powerful, frequently decisive influence over those who practice history today, its pull often keeping them from fully understanding that the abundance of professional occupations in history now allows those who choose careers in history to do so in ways, scarcely imaginable forty years ago, freely consonant with their own aspirations, abilities, and inclinations. The irony is that this new freedom to make choices and decisions in harmony with their personal dispositions, a freedom paralleled in so many other dimensions of modern life, has also become one of historians' most perplexing circumstances. It therefore remains for me in concluding this book to reflect on how personal vision, individual temperament, and professional endeavor might be brought into greater congruence and how all historians might experience their discipline in its many forms.[2]

The context of the existing incongruities in the discipline of history is one that I have taken up more extensively earlier in this book and that

---

[2] A book that begins in a critical spirit to address the inherently personal nature of an academic career is Donald E. Hall, *The Academic Self: An Owner's Manual* (Columbus: Ohio State University Press, 2002). It wisely points to the difficulties of defining and maintaining an academic persona, urges upon academics the never-ending reexamination of their goals, desires, comforts, and dispositions, and warns them against being pulled and hauled by others' expectations. But while Hall's wisdom can be generalized, he writes as a scholar of literature, his illustrations drawn from that discipline. Moreover, his book, as should be clear from its title, is relevant principally to academic careers and not to careers in the world of learning more broadly considered.

invites only brief review here. Until well into the twentieth century, the discipline of history was firmly organized and tightly governed around an academic core. Most of those who entered upon historical work and sought to make history their vocation – the overwhelming majority of them Protestant white men – anticipated joining the faculties of colleges and universities on completing their advanced training. Consequently, they modeled themselves on the ideal of college or university professor. Catholics, women, and Jews who were bold enough to seek professional legitimacy through doctoral training were, until the second half of the century, often shunted into less prestigious and auxiliary positions when they were not discouraged or prevented outright from practicing their chosen occupation. African Americans were by and large simply barred from professional historical work. And those who by inclination chose to pursue a professional career outside the academy had to struggle to justify their decisions against the overpowering force of the ideal of historian-as-professor.

Discriminatory this situation surely was. But to see it only as discriminatory is to miss its other costs. In its heyday, the academic ideal distilled the professional aspirations and lives of all historians, of those experienced as well as in training, of female as well as male, of those of African and Asian as well as of European descent, into a kind of clear, pure form. Most aspiring historians could become only what they were expected and acculturated by others to become: academic historians – academic historians, that is, if they were allowed to become historians in the first place. People of widely differing dispositions, hopes, and abilities were fashioned into the single mold of historian-professor and prepared only for lives of academic scholarship and teaching. Many who more successfully and happily, as well as equally proudly, might have pursued other kinds of history work were compelled by the deeply rooted patterns of graduate education and professional status and rewards to prepare themselves to join college and university faculties. In effect, these particular historians could not easily remain true to themselves and be historians at the same time.

One need be neither sociologist nor psychologist to suspect that this forced choice made itself felt somewhere, somehow, in injuries of some sort. Bitterness – over low pay and slow promotion, poor students, inescapable appointments at isolated and less than desirable colleges and universities, and imposed measures of advancement and prestige in many academic berths – was often one result. Boredom in the repetitious work of instruction or a lack of professional fulfillment in a life of continuous

library research was another. Abilities that might better have made themselves felt in other kinds of history occupations were expected, and often
forced, to be applied to one pursuit alone. Surely one of the most notice-
able consequences of the power of the academic ideal was its effect on
the quality of history produced outside the academy. Careers in public
history, usually then considered second-rate occupations, did not, with
some notable exceptions, attract the finest minds and the most aspiring
professionals. As a result, history museum curating, history film production, government history, and other forms of what we know now as
public history remained weaker and more amateurish than they should
have been. The discipline of history, as well as individual historians and
the general public, paid a price.

That day of uniformity has in considerable measure passed, but it is
by no means wholly gone. It lingers in the form of expectations, aspirations, self-images, attitudes, incentives, and rewards that are no longer
at one with present realities. More important, while that uniformity has
lessened, its weakening has placed only more complex choices upon historians, especially upon younger ones who can no longer expect, and in
other cases choose not, to move automatically from graduate schools into
professorships or from their instructorships through academic ranks to
retirement with emeritus benefits. So with their choices no longer being
made for them, historians are more responsible than they once were for
their own careers. Younger historians are no longer relieved of major decisions early in their working lives as they were when they followed their
teachers into the academy and perhaps at worst faced a choice between
competing academic offers. No longer can they blame some abstraction,
like "the system," for any problems they may face. They now have the
opportunities to form themselves into the historians they wish to be; in
fact, with that freedom comes the responsibility to do so. In order to be
satisfied as professionals, they now have the chance to be faithful to their
individual selves.

That is no easy task. The snares set in a historian's path appear
immediately on matriculation in graduate school, if they have not been
encountered earlier. There, the dominating presence and authority of
scholar-professors – people delegated the authority to grant or withhold
doctoral degrees in history – quickly inaugurate (if college faculty members have not already done so) the process of acculturation to academic values and professorial aspirations. Other fledgling and senior
graduate students who surround the initiate lend added force to a kind
of natural assimilation into academic culture and into the hopes and

expectations of a permanent academic future for everyone. Many, perhaps most, faculty members themselves have little acquaintance with history work beyond academic walls and often shrink from offering encouragement and patronage to those who show signs of not following in their footsteps. And thus, almost without a student's knowing it, the absorbing, sometimes monopolizing academic ideal takes hold.

While few historians will deny that the academic ideal is a worthy model to which an intellectual can aspire, it is not the only one to which a professional compass can be set, nor, as I have been at pains to emphasize throughout this book, is it any longer consonant with the full range of professional needs and opportunities to which historians can direct their knowledge and skills. Therefore, it is not against the ideal itself but rather against its monopolization of aspirations and self-image during graduate study that aspiring historians must guard. Just as understanding of the past enables humans to free themselves in some measure from the past's thralldom, so understanding and awareness of the process of academic acculturation ought better to enable historians-in-training to make more reasoned and freer choices among professional careers, subjects, and activities available to them in their chosen discipline. Along the way, such greater freedom, borne of more conscious understanding, ought to protect every historian from the possible hurt and bitterness that can arise from disappointed, because unrealistic or inappropriate, expectations.

Among all the forces bearing in on graduate students and fashioning the academic ideal is students' relationships with their dissertation advisers. The influence of one's mentor is the gravitational academic force most resistant to change. The nature and extent of a young student's dependence on the person who serves as intellectual and professional counselor through graduate school can determine one's entire outlook on professional work. Over the past few decades, it has become fashionable to speak of these guides as "mentors" and their guidance as "mentoring." The assumption embedded in discussions of this kind of tutelage is that becoming a historian requires that those aspiring to master Clio's arts put themselves under the protective wings of senior professors – experienced, wise, and caring adults – who will not only educate them in the details of intellectual discourse and professional conduct but will also guide them, parent-like, in professional (that is usually to say, academic) ways.

Talk about mentoring has been concentrated among, although not confined to, women and nonwhite graduate students. Younger women and people of non-European backgrounds have particularly sought out, and often particularly needed, the advice and guidance of experienced, older historians like themselves as succeeding generations have sought to escape the difficulties that these historians faced in their earlier and well-known struggles for acceptance and recognition among men (many of the women and African Americans, of course, having enjoyed the backing of senior, white, male professors). Encased in discussions of mentoring lies the assumption that all male historians had previously derived much of their own achievements and preferment from the tutelage of advisers who had also been mentors – men who looked after their young charges, placed them in desirable positions, and thereafter provided professional shelter and personal advice and succor to these younger colleagues. It also came to be assumed that only men could wisely mentor men, women mentor women, and so forth. The monopolization by men of historians' positions, mostly in the academy, could be in large part explained, so it was argued, by the professional guardianship of other, older men.

Yet, while no study of the extent of past mentoring has to my knowledge been published, one should doubt the validity of these assumptions. For one thing, because for roughly the entire century from 1870 to 1970 older men almost without exception taught younger men, any mentors by definition had to be men. To avoid the tautological problems embedded in claims about the extent of male mentoring, the proportion of earlier male graduate students who enjoyed the active guidance of their senior professors, a proportion not yet calculated (if it could be), would have to be known. For another thing, in the professional lives of many earlier male historians, students' relationships with their advisers have often turned out to be troubled and fraught with difficulty. Weaker students, however defined, or those who found no fit with a senior adviser could not expect mentoring care. Resulting resentments were sometimes long lasting. Many, perhaps most, aspiring historians did not need or seek mentors and instead made their way through their early career more or less on their own. What is more, early women historians and African American historians who received any guidance had perforce to receive it from white men, and the first full cohort of women and African American historians – those receiving their graduate education after 1950 – similarly had no option but to be helped on their way by white male historians. Nor should it be overlooked that most mentoring took the form of advice given toward academic employment almost exclusively, even when in individual cases such counsel was inappropriate.

Perhaps more to the point, despite the widespread view that male historians always enjoyed the patronage of their (male) teachers, many aspiring male historians have had dissertation advisers who were in no sense mentors, instead merely guides to research scholarship and dissertation writing who then sponsored their students for initial faculty appointments but in no sense extensively helped them. Many faculty members were indisposed, as many remain, to offer any thoughtful professional guidance or care to their students at all.[3] The presence of a high proportion of negative and neutral, as well as positive, mentoring relationships should thus alert us to the dangers inherent in associations that ideally ought to prove beneficial to students and advisers alike. It should also suggest as well that the strong emphasis that some commentators have placed upon the supposed benefits of mentoring may have been misplaced and that graduate students must always assume major responsibility for their own professional growth and welfare.[4]

Of course, for the thoughtful advice and support of older and more experienced professionals, both academic and others, there is no substitute. Yet to fall too much under the wing of a senior professor – to begin to write like her, aspire to his particular goals, take on her research agenda, adopt his ideology – risks the surrender of one's self, to say nothing of one's self-regard, to another's expectations. The risks of overdependence on an adviser or a too close identification with the adviser's work are greatly increased today by the speed with which scholarly perspectives and approaches change. What may be a lively field of inquiry at the start of a student's preparation may soon become exhausted and its practitioner ignored by hiring committees only a few years later, to say nothing of the subject's status at one's midcareer. Therefore, someone entering upon a career as historian is on safest ground in seeking to be as broad-gauged in research interests as possible and to be a professor's student, not disciple; a professor's peer in chosen achievement, not in the same research subject or professional line of work; a professor's teacher and colleague, not follower. As Jorge Luis Borges somewhere wrote, one has to discover one's own precursors. To be able freely to choose what pursuit of history to practice rather than to live up to a mentor's idea, whether imposed or internalized, of what one should become ought to be one of

---

[3] Some hints of the absence of (and thus students' resulting dissatisfaction with), as well as the presence of (and thus students' gratitude for), mentoring in male historians' early academic lives appear in Michael Kammen, "Personal Identity and the Historian's Vocation," in Kammen (ed.), *In the Past Lane: Historical Perspectives on American Culture* (New York: Oxford University Press, 1997), 5–71.

[4] The diversity of relationships between fledgling historians and their senior advisers is apparent in the memoirs of the historians included in James M. Banner, Jr., and John R. Gillis (eds.), *Becoming Historians* (Chicago: University of Chicago Press, 2009).

the most satisfying outcomes of the long and arduous journey of historical learning. Similarly, to gain the practiced ability not only to change
fields of inquiry as history's discipline changes but also to develop the
firmness of spirit to resist, if one wishes, these disciplinary changes and
follow one's own intellectual compass are among the most demanding
challenges of one's preparation and growth as a historian.[5]

Another obstacle to a free and independent choice of professional work
in history is the existing structure of rewards and recognition within the
discipline. Just as becoming a university professor is thought to constitute
the apogee of professional achievement in history, so the allocation of the
discipline's principal elective offices, of the oldest and most prestigious
awards of history's scholarly and professional societies, and of such honors as invitations to deliver the discipline's great endowed lectureships
seem to fall almost naturally to members of that same group. Whether
the best historical minds in fact find their way into university professorships or whether professional recognition finds its way only to university
professors has yet to be demonstrated conclusively. But one is warranted
in harboring a certain suspicion that more than raw talent is at work in
the winnowing process by which the same relatively few historians gather
to themselves similar honors.

In recent decades, much progress has in fact been made in recognizing the achievements of talented historians who occupy less prestigious
academic berths, who practice their discipline outside the academy, and
who pursue research and writing in historically unconventional fields
and subjects like gender and film history or the history of technology
and medicine. Ever-increasing numbers of subject-specific scholarly and
professional societies whose members devote themselves to the history
of specialized topics now offer their own honors and prizes. Positions
for history professionals who pursue nonacademic work, such as public
history, and who work in, say, community colleges have been set aside on
the councils of some of the major historical organizations, like the OAH.

---

[5] I recall in this regard a conversation with a senior and justly celebrated historian, one of
whose favorite graduate students, while remaining an academic, had turned to writing,
teaching, and consulting, always to high praise, on issues of public history rather than on
the presumably more toplofty and highly intellectual work of his former mentor. "Why
did he do that?" his bewildered teacher asked me. The answer to such a question is probably always overdetermined and highly individual. One portal to insights as to why young
scholars leave the academic world for other kinds of work is Beyond Academe, found at
http://www.beyondacademe.com. I am grateful to John R. Dichtl for an introduction to
this site.

Yet segregating such recognition serves to protect many of the highest honors – association presidencies, for instance, or awards for contributions to the discipline – for those who have long monopolized them: academic historians. Until such honors fall in decent proportion to nonacademics because of their own particular achievements, the thralldom of the academic ideal will not diminish.[6] In fact, for the discipline as a whole, a systematic review of its structure of recognition and honor is long overdue.

Related to the discipline's structure of recognition and rewards are the expectations, born in graduate preparation, by which historians are measured and by which, consequently, they come to measure their own progress and achievements. The tales we like to tell of tenure committees counting the number of candidates' published books and articles or weighing the relative merits and prestige of the journals in which they have published their articles may be apocryphal, but those tales suggest a sociological truth: once academic standards become internalized and faculty members acculturate their students to academic norms, these norms create enduring self-measures of professional worth. For academic work, such norms are serviceable (although there has never been, and never will be, a firm, perhaps not even a strong, link between the number and the quality of individuals' publications). Academics, and surely most of those at research universities, are employed to create, as well as to transmit, new knowledge. That they are expected to expand understanding of the past makes justifiable and appropriate the conventional measures of their success in doing so, such as the quality and influence of their scholarly work. But like so many other dimensions of history today, while worthy in themselves these expectations are functional principally to a segment, not to the whole, of the discipline. Surely the work of even many academic historians, such as those at teaching institutions like liberal arts and community colleges, is assessed at their own institutions by the quality of their instruction rather than of their scholarship. Those historians who write film scripts, put up museum exhibits, acquire and manage manuscript collections, or direct historic sites in their turn have responsibilities and purposes even further from academic ones. The challenge for every historian is thus to learn, often to steel oneself, to adopt expectations fitting for particular professional employment.

---

[6] The first nonacademic historian in memory to be president of the OAH, Pete Daniel, served in 2008–2009. It can, however, be argued that Daniel gained this honor in large part because of his many contributions to scholarly written history.

The academic ideal exerts unrecognized forces of another kind as well. Because training in historical research, methods, and writing makes up such a large proportion of historians' preparation and because the overwhelming percentage of resulting dissertations are monographs that students hope will display their skills in research, argument, citation, and style, to say nothing of a fresh contribution to knowledge, monographs become the model for the great proportion of historians' subsequent work. No one can dispute the essential role of monographic research in introducing aspiring historians to scholarship and to the advance of knowledge and in expanding knowledge itself. Since the nineteenth century, the monograph, proven in its value, has been at the center of progress in historical understanding. It remains the case, however, that not all historians take well to monographic research and writing, that not all skills and temperaments are gathered around monographic scholarship. Neither are all contributions to historical knowledge found in monographic form, nor do all professional historical pursuits today call for the preparation of monographic papers and books. Graduate school preparation that fails to introduce students to additional means of creating and presenting historical knowledge – interviews, films, museum exhibits, and Web presentations being uppermost among them – therefore falls short of introducing students to the many other skills they may need, if only to help prepare their own students, to enter fully upon the many kinds of work that their professional world now offers. For those students not enrolled in public history programs, the call on their own initiative in seeking preparation for extra-academic contributions to history remains weighty.

Not that all academic historians adhere slavishly to the monograph once they have the chance to spread their intellectual and professional wings. Historians have always demonstrated a wide variety of distinct mentalities and produced works of history in many different forms. To secure the point, one need only name a few major academic historians of the past fifty years whose contributions to history reveal an expansive range of approaches, intentions, and intellectual dispositions – William H. McNeill, Marshall G. S. Hodgson, E. P. Thompson, Bernard Lewis, C. Vann Woodward, Peter Gay, Fritz Stern, Gerda Lerner, John Hope Franklin, Richard Hofstadter, Lawrence Stone, Natalie Zemon Davis, and James M. McPherson, to list only Anglophone historians. In the works of these historians are encompassed, respectively, extraordinary syntheses of world history (McNeill), multivolume analytical narratives of an entire civilization (Hodgson), sharply ideological reconstructions of the history of social groups (Thompson), historical knowledge put to the service of contemporary issues (Lewis, Stern, and Woodward), the effective creation of entirely new subjects that transformed historiography (Lerner and Franklin), interpretation through engaged irony (Hofstadter), sweeping surveys of vast, complicated subjects (Gay), the application of social scientific methods to historical problems (Stone), the recovery of the past through the reconstruction of long-buried individual stories (Davis), and basic storytelling informed by broad research and learning (McPherson). Each of these historians made a distinctive contribution to historical knowledge in his and her individual way.[7]

Indicating the wide variety of historical minds that inhabit the academy should alert us that the substantial contributions to history made outside the academy are also deeply affected by personality, interest, ability, and bent of mind. In fact, the comparative youth of organized public history and the wide range of activities encompassed under that term offer a wider range of professional options for differing aspirations and dispositions than within the academy. In addition, no venerable hierarchy of institutions, established conventions of awards, or set notions about professional precedence has yet taken root in public history to inhibit individuals from being professionally venturesome and from being professionally themselves. Here again, one need only name as examples of different kinds of public historical achievements that have made their mark the work of such historians as Herbert Feis, the diplomatic historian with a long career in the State and War Departments; Richard A.

---

[7] Among the many works of each author that I might name, I have in mind in this instance William H. McNeill, *The Rise of the West: A History of the Human Community* (Chicago: University of Chicago Press, 1963); Marshall G. S. Hodgson, *The Venture of Islam*, 3 vols. (Chicago: University of Chicago Press, 1974); E. P. Thompson, *The Making of the English Working Class* (New York: Pantheon, 1964); Bernard Lewis, *Islam and the West* (New York: Oxford University Press, 1993); C. Vann Woodward, *The Strange Career of Jim Crow* (New York: Oxford University Press, 1955); Peter Gay, *The Bourgeois Experience*, 5 vols. (New York: Oxford University Press, 1984–1998); Fritz Stern, *Five Germanys I Have Known* (New York: Farrar, Straus and Giroux, 2006); Gerda Lerner, *The Creation of Feminist Consciousness: From the Middle Ages to the Eighteen-Seventies* (New York: Oxford University Press, 1993); John Hope Franklin, *From Slavery to Freedom: A History of American Negroes* (New York: Alfred A. Knopf, 1947); Richard Hofstadter, *The American Political Tradition and the Men Who Made It* (New York: Alfred A. Knopf, 1948); Lawrence Stone, *The Crisis of the Aristocracy, 1558–1641* (Oxford: Clarendon Press, 1965); Natalie Zemon Davis, *The Return of Martin Guerre* (Cambridge, MA: Harvard University Press, 1983); and James M. McPherson, *Battle Cry of Freedom: The Civil War Era* (New York: Oxford University Press, 1988). Of course, many other historians, and not just those practicing in the United States, and many other works could easily be cited.

Baker and Raymond W. Smock, the founding historians, respectively, of the historical offices of the U.S. Senate and House of Representatives; Philip L. Cantelon, founder and principal historian of History Associates, Inc., probably the most successful (surely the earliest most successful) for-profit history consulting firm in the nation; and Kevin Starr, the state librarian of California.[8]

There is of course no purpose in hiding the fact that to follow one's own course as a professional historian, whether it be in a particular professional pursuit, a line of research, a style of teaching, or some sort of institutional or creative innovation, incurs risks. Failure is one. The perplexity or criticism of colleagues, many of them bound to older norms of professional expectation and reward that permeate academic history, is another. Professional work in the intellectual disciplines, especially within the academy, seems to breed a particularly intense kind of criticism, and setting one's professional itinerary in a direction of one's own choosing does not lessen the risk of disapproval and censure, to say nothing of puzzlement. When people cannot understand another's choice of action, they easily fall to criticizing, rather than trying to comprehend, it. Thus historians determined on a distinctive course of their own must prepare themselves to withstand the winds of disparagement that may blow upon them.

All of this is to say that, because of the diversity of prospective historical careers within the many professions in which history is pursued, historians, whether within or outside the academy, should no longer be expected to prove themselves against the single standard of academic achievement as they used to and in some quarters still must. Academic expectations may serve for academic historians, but they do not and cannot for those like film-making historians or the curators of history museums, whose professional compasses are differently set. Rewards – of recognition, income, and the plain satisfaction of doing what one wishes to do – have greatly broadened. Opportunities to make lasting contributions to historical understanding have enormously increased in kind and number. It is all the more important, therefore, for aspiring historians to

---

[8] Because of the nature of their work, many of the scholarly and professional achievements of public historians take forms other than books. That is surely the case with Baker, Smock, and Cantelon. Nevertheless, many public historians manage to produce important works of published scholarship. See, for example, Herbert Feis, *Between War and Peace: The Potsdam Conference* (Princeton: Princeton University Press, 1960), and Kevin Starr's eight-volume work under the collective title *America and the California Dream* (New York: Oxford University Press, 1973–2009).

be firm in charting their own courses as aspiring and experienced professionals. With many fewer constraints on them than before, historians are freer than they have ever been to be themselves while being historians.

But what might being oneself as historian mean? If it means anything, it must mean to follow one's considered instincts, whatever they may be, about the historical subjects of one's greatest interest and to pursue a kind of work that fits with one's curiosities, temperament, and abilities. Following one's interests ought to include a certain wariness about historiographical, ideological, and epistemological trends and even to lively lines of inquiry that, as experience has often proved, may soon wear themselves out and, giving way to new ones, leave historians who have hitched their careers to them professionally high and dry.[9]

No one can dispute the fact that in every era, different historiographical challenges demand and gain the most attention and, often conforming to surrounding cultural circumstances, come to be understood to be the most promising avenues of research. In our own time, social, cultural, ethnic, and gender history have attracted some of the greatest talents and surely the greatest number of adherents; in those subfields of historical inquiry the greatest progress in understanding has been made. One cost of such progress, however, has been the difficulties faced by historians interested in other and more traditional subjects, such as political and diplomatic history, by those skeptical of the staying power of recently influential theories, like deconstruction and postmodernism, and by those not clearly part of the ideological Left. Many of them have had to proceed without the support of graduate school advisers and in the face of declining employment prospects and, worse, ideological antagonism. But since risks always accompany particular choices – whether they be the pursuit of personal interests or of currently, but perhaps temporarily, important fields of inquiry – to consider and assess these risks deliberately is far better than to ignore them.

---

[9] Peter Novick, *That Noble Dream: The "Objectivity Question" and the American Historical Profession* (Cambridge: Cambridge University Press, 1988), chap. 1, reveals how naïve now seem those historians a century ago who misread Ranke, Bacon, and Darwin and joined the company of radical empiricists, only to have the philosophical foundations of their proudly held assumptions soon destroyed. Fashion comes in many forms. For the past quarter century, the runway of new historical styles has been populated by Continental and postmodernist theories. But these, too, have begun to pass, leaving evidence of their existence in other waves of designer historiography, which in their turn will give way to new fashions or older ones rehabilitated with new names and new decoration.

Following one's interests also requires an independence of existing expectations, such as those that seem to induce male historians disproportionately to write about politics and institutions, women about women, African Americans about the history of their own people.[10] While one of the classic ends of historical study is somehow to get inside the people and events of the past, so it has long been an equally meritorious, if often conflicting, end to gain as much objectivity on past reality as possible by remaining intellectually somehow outside it. Projecting one's identity, or one's group or national interest, onto the past always endangers the integrity of the past itself and can transmogrify it into some reflection of the present. One cannot be unmindful that those who make little attempt to limit the intrusion of present concerns into their historical research are often the very people who assail other historians' failure to step outside other fields of view, such as those of nation or ideology, which the critics happen not to share. But of all the costs of projection, the greatest is that it prevents historians from achieving another great end of historical study – freedom from the past. While unshackling oneself from the bonds of the past is a never-completed task, the struggle to achieve it nevertheless remains one of the most demanding and exhilarating undertakings of a life spent in history's service.

One of the surest ways to work clear of the past is to keep free of too many external influences and to look inward for inspiration. There must be some emotional link between what one pursues as a historian and what one studies, teaches, curates, films, collects, writes about, and does. Historians best serve themselves in striving to ground their professional pursuits upon their own, not others', engagement with a subject or activity. A particular hunger to pursue some subject, for some line of work, or for the achievement of some particular goal can make a professional life in history endlessly more rewarding than its routine practice along paths blazed by others. The historic struggle to gain detachment from the subject one pursues in order to gain some degree of objectivity,

---

[10] Most historical literature is in fact the result of living historians' efforts to understand times in which they did not live, events they did not experience, societies and cultures that were not theirs, and people whom they did not know – and thus requiring energetic stretches of vision, empathy, and imagination to recapture. Nevertheless, historians probably need to be reminded of particular examples that reveal their colleagues reaching as far beyond themselves as possible. Surely one of the most riveting examples is Arthur Golden's powerful novel, *Memoirs of a Geisha* (New York: Alfred A. Knopf, 1997). The historian-novelist Golden – a late twentieth-century American, Jewish, white male – writes the "memoirs" of an early twentieth-century Japanese woman.

a struggle whose worth and realization is much in dispute these days, must be balanced against the need to engage one's spirit in the very work that calls for unremittingly hard effort to achieve accuracy and to be faithful to evidence. Historians no less than others must call on what Lionel Trilling termed "the moral imagination"[11] – for historians a resistance to ideological indignation or parti pris attachments in favor of extending understanding and, where warranted, empathy to all historical subjects and times while not suspending critical intelligence. The moral imagination does not ask for or permit easy positions. Historians must often study, portray, and write of subjects (like famine or massacres) that sear their emotions or of detestable people (like Hitler and Stalin) whom they revile, for otherwise the history of terrible events and irredeemably grotesque figures would never be known. Yet it is often under such circumstances that historians find themselves yielding to a deeper understanding of, even if not sympathy for, those very subjects. It is also under such circumstances that a book, film, or exhibit alters forever the way in which a particular subject is understood, so that no one can ever again think of it in the same way.

Yet if following one's own way may be risky, so can be accepting the expectations cast by others. Having to make a choice between betraying one's most deeply felt interests (say, becoming an independent filmmaker of history) and accepting the lure of an otherwise highly desirable post (say, as an academic) can be the most fateful decision facing any historian. Fortunately, the recent expansion of the discipline of history to accommodate more occupations and a wider range of temperaments has significantly reduced what earlier could be a hard tension between historians and their almost uniformly academic futures. Nevertheless, navigating the shoals that lie between self and career will continue to call for exquisitely acute instincts and skills.

Being oneself as historian also calls for freely determining, through reasoned consideration, how best to contribute to historical understanding.[12]

---

[11] From "Manners, Morals, and the Novel" and "Huckleberry Finn," both in *The Liberal Imagination: Essays on Literature and Society* (New York: Viking Press, 1950).

[12] L. P. Curtis, Jr., *The Historian's Workshop: Original Essays by Sixteen Historians* (New York: Alfred A. Knopf, 1970), contains some academic historians' reflections about the autobiographical origins of their work while unfortunately revealing little about the authors themselves. See also the autobiographical sketches of a wider range of scholars in Douglas Greenberg and Stanley N. Katz (eds.), *The Life of Learning* (New York: Oxford University Press, 1994). A wonderful, brief, and more revealing autobiographical account of the formative role of temperament and personality, as well as of experience and education, in influencing a historian's scholarly endeavors,

Because no one is altogether clear-eyed in self-evaluation, determining a career path in history may require the honest evaluations of others – instructors, friends, and colleagues – about what might best combine one's individual abilities with the many kinds of history work and subjects that can be pursued. Getting such candid assessments of one's strengths and weaknesses is, however, notoriously difficult, more so, it seems, than in the world of commercial work. Advisers understandably wish to protect from hurt those students whom they may think not suited for university professorships; and most students, like most humans, would prefer not to learn unpalatable truths. The results of such avoidance are found in oblique discouragement or lukewarm (and thus damning) letters of recommendation. Furthermore, research professors accustomed to their particular professional lives may be incapable of providing wise advice about a broad range of professional options and of assessing the nonacademic historical gifts and promise of younger historians not intent on following academic careers. At the start of a career, nothing is more useful to historians than frank evaluations of their potential for various kinds of history work, and students of history should hope for and expect nothing less from those they ask.

Being oneself as historian also may mean yielding to changing interests and concerns. Some, perhaps even most, historians maintain their early interests throughout their careers. But others do not. Major shifts in historical interests or kind of work probably always can be explained by personal factors – a growing fatigue with what one has done, encounters with new knowledge, the felt need to pursue some new line of inquiry or work, an experience in life. But such changes and their explanations often puzzle others and cause perplexity in those responsible for setting teaching assignments, maintaining a range of faculty specialties, or relying on particular skills. How is a department to assess the promise of a colleague who was once a scholar of early modern Europe but who now wishes to study more recent intellectual currents? And what if that colleague, advanced in order to maintain the department's strengths in European history, now wishes to specialize not in late Renaissance France but in the emergence of pragmatism? The navigation of such changes, for both the individual historian and the department, is fraught with complexity,

as well as cautionary reflections on "glib moralizing," is Leo P. Ribuffo, "Confessions of an Accidental (or Perhaps Overdetermined) Historian," in Elizabeth Fox-Genovese and Elisabeth Lasch-Quinn (eds.), *Reconstructing History: The Emergence of a New Historical Society* (London: Routledge, 1999), 143–163. See also Banner and Gillis, *Becoming Historians.*

sometimes with misunderstanding and resentment. Yet to ask or expect such historians to defer pursuing their interests is to ask them to deny themselves.

It is also the case that one can be a different kind of historian at different times, serving at one moment as academic scholar and teacher, at another as public historian. Just because historians occupy academic posts does not bar, and has never barred, them from involvement in nonacademic pursuits. The careers of countless skilled academics testify to the permeability of academic walls. So, too, the ability of nonacademic historians to produce superb works of written history is now widely acknowledged. Bringing one's particular sensibilities and interests into a setting in which they are distinctive enlarges the course that a career can travel and lends to that course what it may otherwise lack.

Associated with sensibilities and interests is voice, often known as style and a too-often neglected characteristic of practicing historians. Yes, we describe good history as having style and hope that all historians will write in ways pleasing to their readers. But voice is an emanation of self, not a manner that can be gained through practice, not mere adornment. Like so many other qualities in historians, it must be recognized, nurtured, and accepted. Voice, like disposition and sensibility, is inherent; voice, we might say, is the man or woman. It is voice that lends personality to one's writing, speaking, and bearing, that makes one distinctive as a historian. It is, as Helen Vendler has said of style, "the actual material body of inner being,"[13] one way of being true to one's nature. And so like artists and composers, historians differ (although within perhaps narrower compass) in the words they use, the gestures of their teaching, and the allusions of their films just as their minds and sensibilities differ.[14] Too seldom do we acknowledge and give ourselves over to our own particular consciousness and allow our own voice to be heard. In often having to abnegate, or at

---

[13] "A Life of Learning," *ACLS Occasional Paper* 50 (2001): 2. An extended and classic work on style is Peter Gay, *Style in History* (New York: Basic Books, 1974).

[14] Which raises a nice question: Why do we have so little whimsy, anger, and wit – to name but a few qualities – in written history (much less than we have in the teaching of history) when historians are no less whimsical, angry, or witty than other humans? Why is the range of historical writing, when compared to that of the arts – one thinks, for example, of the difference between the music of Bach and that of Berg or the art of Rubens and Picasso – comparatively so small? No doubt, the narrower perimeters of historical expression owe much to history's empirical foundations and the historian's need to construct arguments and convince readers, students, and viewers. But much owes also to convention and to the discipline's inhospitability to a wide variety of styles and voices.

least confine, our selves in deference to evidence, historians should also, in keeping with our own era's growing acceptance that each of us constructs the past as well as preserves and interprets it in distinctive ways, surrender themselves to being impressionists offering their own evocations of the past and learn to awake and sing in their own manner.

Similarly, historians would serve themselves well by giving themselves over to producing what they find most congenial to their temperaments and in ways they find most effective. While books are the coinage of the scholarly realm, some historians excel in the essay form and feel most at home writing short texts. Others seem to be able to work only in tandem with someone else. Some are at their best in monographs, others in sweeping syntheses. Some, usually unknown for their skills, are masters of the consultant's report, others (usually also working behind the scenes) are the moving forces behind museum exhibits that appear and then dissolve.[15] Each of these historians is contributing to public enlightenment, to public affairs, and to the satisfactions of others in ways consonant with their own abilities and bents. The discipline is richer for that.

When all is said and done, there is no single way to practice history or to be a historian. Nor should there be in an era that has proved to be the most fertile age of historical endeavor and achievement yet known – fertile in the expansion of subjects, interpretive approaches, and scope; in the invention of practices and institutions; in the penetration of history into public consciousness and public affairs; and in the public popularity of history.[16] Within the discipline itself, considered in the widest way, little now exists to prevent all historians from following their own ways and seeking the satisfactions and achievements consonant with their own natures.

Yet to gain those satisfactions and enjoy those achievements requires unremitting care and self-scrutiny as well as, often, hard choices. Historians become the professionals they are through the choices they make and never without practice, experiment, and experience and often through

---

[15] One historian who is principally an essayist is David A. Hollinger. See his "Church People and Others," in Banner and Gillis, *Becoming Historians*. A celebrated example of historians, close friends from graduate school, who, their first books written independently, often wrote as coauthors are Stanley Elkins and Eric L. McKitrick.

[16] Margaret MacMillan terms history's popularity "the history craze." See MacMillan, *Dangerous Games: The Uses and Abuses of History* (New York: Modern Library, 2008), chap. 1.

risk. David Riesman has written of the "nerve of failure," of what he calls "the courage to face aloneness and the possibility of defeat in one's personal life or one's work without being morally destroyed."[17] Historians ought not to shrink from the risk of failure (against which academic tenure is one of the great protections), and their colleagues would do well to honor them for the risks they take – intellectually, professionally, personally. In the early twenty-first century, historians have the good fortune to have a broader field for risk, because of a larger field for recovery, that few before them possessed – the fortune to become, in the fullest sense imaginable, the historians they choose to be. That is because most older molds of pursuit and practice have broken. While preparation to be a historian takes place in a single kind of institution, the choices that lie before aspiring historians are numerous and diverse and more so in each case than they have ever been. Much more than previously, historians are free to embrace all of the many options that the worldwide freemasonry of history now holds out to each of them. The sway of opinion and convention over them has yielded to a looser bundle of options and opportunities that permit freer choices to be made with clear eyes, full information, and fidelity to self. That being so however, each historian has to take responsibility for creating coherence out of the myriad of now-possible approaches to work. Each has to have a vision of what he or she wishes to achieve; only then can each try to live one's vision as well as to study what one wishes to study, to endeavor what one wishes to carry out.[18]

In the end, all historians have to define for themselves what it means to be a historian. In the end, only each historian, and no one else, has the right to do so. There is comfort to be gained from the classic, austere conviction that all knowledge is coequal, that all knowledge, in Ranke's phrase, is "unmittelbar zu Gott" – immediate to God. If in the decades ahead that ideal is to be preserved, it will have to be accompanied by the conviction that most activities undertaken, as well as all research

---

[17] David Riesman, *Individualism Reconsidered and Other Essays* (Garden City, NY: Doubleday, 1955), 70.

[18] Three historians, chosen from among many others, who have lived their visions – combining deep and expansive learning with a purpose that their learning fulfilled – are Fritz Stern, Gerda Lerner, and George L. Mosse. Many others who lived their visions through writing them also could be named. Mosse recounts his life and how learning gave it meaning in *Confronting History: A Memoir* (Madison: University of Wisconsin Press, 2000). Lerner has set forth her life's vision in her memoir *Fireweed: A Political Autobiography* (Philadelphia: Temple University Press, 2002). Stern's life and career are brought vividly to life in his *Five Germanys I Have Known.*

subjects investigated, in history's name are equally meritorious, that no single approach, theory, subject, or activity is of any greater value than another. And yet nothing is more exhilarating than to have one's heart as well as mind captured by the search for historical understanding, to find in that endeavor what Natalie Zemon Davis has called "a constant joy, a privileged realm of intellectual eros."[19]

Throughout this book, I have signaled my conviction that those who inhabit that realm today are the fortunate beneficiaries of changes in their discipline unprecedented in their scope and unimaginable fifty years ago. In that earlier era, the office of historian was defined narrowly. Its occupants were men – almost always men – of high intelligence but relatively circumscribed view, of wide ability but often limited felt responsibility for the entire discipline, of great achievement in written works but of less accomplishment in other endeavors. Historians as professional citizens were academics alone. Safe and typically serene in their academic fastnesses, they often failed to grapple in their professional lives with the realities of the larger world and the situations of all their fellow citizens. That is no longer the case and no longer can be. By virtue of the example of historians carrying on their professional work as they choose, the discipline has vastly expended itself, made new contributions to American and international life and culture, increasingly become part of the warp and woof of public debates, and strengthened its engagement with public and civic affairs. In fact, evidence from the past half century suggests strongly that it is the changed behavior, aspirations, and attitudes of historians, rather than any abstract alteration in professional expectations, which have broadened the notion of what is acceptable within the boundaries of professional history.

Most of us look forward to the time when the complexities of our discipline will be reduced, when its troubles will have abated, when the differences between historians will have softened, and when we can foresee at the start of our careers how we will inhabit the house of history throughout our lives. That is, we look ahead, as have many of our predecessors, to a kind of disciplinary order – a placid utopian moment when each professional decision will be rewarded, each hope satisfied, each choice confirmed. Yet as historians above all people should know, a world without surprise and wonder, unintended consequence, setbacks, and chance occurrences has never existed and – so our practiced knowledge tells us – never will. Stability, whether of subject or career, has

---

[19] "A Life of Learning," *ACLS Occasional Paper* 39 (1997): 23.

not been historians' lot. And it is not likely to be their lot in the years ahead.

Thus the person who takes up history as a vocation today assumes an office of unprecedented promise, opportunity, and flexibility but also of constant change and choice. It is a vocation, at its best, of fellowship and community as well as intellectual pursuit, of moral witnessing as well as the advancement of knowledge. In whatever ways pursued, history retains its moral weight, engaged as much in troubling existing complacencies as in confirming them. While much of what historians face today is not unlike the crisis of authority of the late nineteenth century, any fresh search for disciplinary order must now embody an acceptance of the greatly expanded orbit of history's practices and contributions over more than a century's time and of the greatly expanded opportunities for the application of historical knowledge to the world's affairs. Whether we wish to respect and embrace or to arraign and escape the past, that past is what we inherit from others. By contrast, the future is ours to make.

Index

academic careers, 63–68

academic freedom. *See* professional freedoms

academic history, emergence of, 10ff.

academic ideal, 17, 39–40, 63–65, 241–243, 247, 250

academic profession, sociology of, 39–40, 63–65, 242, 247

academic publishing, choice of, for career, 68–69

Adams, George Burton, 45

Adams, Henry, 99, 200

Adams, Herbert Baxter, 15, 17

Adams, James Truslow, 27

adjunct faculty members. *See* teaching assistants

Advanced Placement tests, 58

Alcohol and Drugs History Society, 46

Amazon.com, 82, 83n21

Ambrose, Stephen E., 208

American Antiquarian Society, 35

American Association for State and Local History, 50, 135, 217–218

American Association for the Advancement of the Humanities, 53n21

American Association of Museums, 135, 228n26

American Association of University Professors, 217ff., 232ff.; *Statement of Principles on Academic Freedom and Tenure*, 227, 233

American Commission to Negotiate Peace, 27

American Council of Learned Societies, 52–54, 52n19, 53n20, 128, 218n11, 228n26; e-book support, 84n22

American Federation of Teachers, 221

American Historical Association, 5, 15ff., 27, 41, 59, 60n31, 87, 88n25, 91, 152, 156, 183n12, 235; affiliates of, 45–46, 48; Committee of Seven, 18; Committee on Teaching, 27; and graduate education, 41–42; Gutenberg-e project, 83–84; history of, 42ff., 48–50; Pacific Coast Branch, 48; and professional ethics, 213, 214n7; Review Board of, 44n10; and schools, 43; Service Center for Teachers of History, 25

American Historical Review, 16, 19, 44–45, 46, 128, 203, 214n7

American Pageant, 25

American Social Science Association, 14, 15, 35, 42

Annals of American Sport, 25

Appleby, Joyce, 87, 90, 94n30

applied academic history, 130–132

Aptheker, Herbert, 23n22

Made in the USA
Middletown, DE
11 August 2017